ALSO BY MAC McCLELLAND

For Us Surrender Is Out of the Question:
A Story from Burma's Never-Ending War

IRRITABLE HEARTS

A PTSD LOVE STORY

MAC McCLELLAND

FLATIRON
BOOKS
NEW YORK

Some names in this book have been changed or omitted.

Some of the content, reporting, and scenes in this book originally appeared in *GOOD* and *Mother Jones* magazines.

www.flatironbooks.com

Designed by Steven Seighman

Library of Congress Cataloging-in-Publication Data

McClelland, Mac.
    Irritable Hearts : a PTSD love story / Mac McClelland.—First edition.
        pages cm
    ISBN 978-1-250-05289-6 (hardcover)
    ISBN 978-1-250-05349-7 (e-book)
    1. McClelland, Mac—Mental Health.   2. Post-traumatic stress disorder—
Patients—United States—Biography.   3. Journalists—United States—Biography.
4. Earthquakes—Psychological aspects.   5. Man-woman relationships.   I. Title.
    RC552.P67M33 2015
    616.85'210092—dc23

                                                            2014034163

Flatiron books may be purchased for educational, business, or promotional use. For information on bulk purchases, please contact the Macmillan Corporate and Premium Sales Department at 1-800-221-7945, extension 5442, or write to specialmarkets@macmillan.com.

First Edition: February 2015

10   9   8   7   6   5   4   3   2   1

For Nico

and for Chris

IRRITABLE HEARTS

PROLOGUE

He was on his knees when he did it, but I wasn't doing what I was supposed to be doing at all. Or rather, I was doing what people are supposed to do, which is cry, but not like that, because I'd *been* crying, for hours already, before he slid off the couch where were we sitting, dropped down in front of me, and proposed. Actually I'd been crying, choking—sobbing, really—on and off for three days straight in our rented room in a winter-abandoned wine village. Or actually, since almost the moment I'd arrived in France. Or, in fact, since I'd been diagnosed seventeen months earlier, when these kinds of episodes became part of my personality, when it became not at all unusual to break down like this. Just that now, something electric bloomed in my gut and shot through my torso, constricting my throat. So I turned my face away from him and cried some more.

Nico did not say "Will you marry me?" That is not what the French say. A few months before, he had seen the English version of *Jerry Maguire* for the first time and learned that Tom Cruise had not asked Renée Zellweger if she *wanted to* marry him as he had in the dubbed French translation—*Veux-tu m'epouser*—but if she *would*. "Do Americans really say that?" he'd demanded. "It's so . . . *aggressive*." So he'd inquired after my desire instead.

"This is as bad as it gets," he said about my crying. "But I still want to make my life with you." He said, "Even though you tell me this is what you're really like."

I'd been telling him that since shortly after we met, a year and a half ago, while he was peacekeeping and I was reporting a story in Haiti—where I'd experienced something that had shaken me such that I'd never managed to properly put myself back together. Where two days later I'd escaped an isolated room where a stranger stripped down to his undershirt had backed me into a corner and promised me that my father should be worried. I'd told Nico that I had nightmares, flashbacks, that I dissociated—an interruption of normal psychological functioning in which my consciousness was suddenly and completely unable to integrate with reality. But he hadn't really seen what that looked like yet.

"You tell me this is what you're really like," he said. "And I tell you I'm still here."

Empirically speaking, he could be forgiven for thinking that I was good wife material. I had a job, and a savings account. Straight A's all through school, master's degree, summa cum laude. Culinarily and sexually outgoing. Tall. Healthy hair. Relentlessly on time. I'd kept my shit relatively together during a year and a half of brief reunions with him in Dutch hotel rooms, Belgian B&Bs, a borrowed Parisian apartment, rented Riviera or French Caribbean abodes, in cities on the way to one of my assignments or to which he'd been deployed. And the few scenes I'd caused could be mistaken for jet lag or disoriented fatigue or even a penchant for high relationship drama instead of what they really were: symptoms of post-traumatic stress disorder.

But then the other morning, I'd been stepping into our chalet bathtub when I glimpsed myself in the mirror, and paused.

No, I thought. *Oh, no.*

Changes in self-perception and hallucinations—those are some of my other symptoms.

Historically, I was on good terms with mirrors, which generally told me that I was lucky for having been born with the long, athletic shape that happened to be popular at the time. But now, the two big mirrors hanging on the walls to the front and side of the bathtub were saying something else.

All I could see was a boy. A flat, weak, castrated, insubstantial fragment of a boy. The curve of my hips seemed medically wrong. Awful. *I shouldn't be showing any of this to Nico*, I thought urgently. *I shouldn't be letting him see this disgusting thing.*

I ducked down into the tub, out of sight of the reflection, and pressed my hands into my face.

You are fucking insane, I told myself. *You know it's not true. Look again.*

I hesitated, remaining crouched, nude.

Look at it again.

I popped my head and chest up.

No. Not better. I could see breasts this time, but they were misshapen, meaningless lumps.

I went about turning the water on and washing myself, careful to keep the mirrors out of my line of vision, but by the time I emerged from the bathroom, I was nearly hyperventilating, partly because I was the grossest thing I'd ever seen, but mostly because I couldn't convince myself that it wasn't true, even though I knew for a fact that it wasn't. I couldn't trust myself. I'd lost all credibility with, of all people, myself. And I'd been in rough shape already; the day before, I'd woken up incapable of believing in possibility. *Can you make a coffee cake?* I asked myself on days when I suspected I wasn't mentally well, and when everything in my being responded, *No*, though everyone knows my blueberry coffee cake is delicious, I knew I wasn't stable, and shouldn't listen to anything else I said.

After the bath, I turned shameful and cold. When I walked into our bedroom, Nico told me I was gorgeous, and I yelled that he was a liar. Started screaming when he tried to touch me, pulling clothes on spastically, strangled by tears. Hurled myself around the kitchen, fuming that we'd let a baguette go stale.

I knew that one thing that would help alleviate the grief and fury suddenly charging through my veins was opening up my mouth and throat and screaming and screaming. But I wasn't going to do that in front of another person. As usual, I considered how effective it would be to do myself harm, open my skin up or shatter a bone, perhaps, get a *real* crisis on my hands, the kind of crisis people I met the world round were uniformly impressed I took in such stride. But even when I was alone, I acknowledged that that was a line I wasn't supposed to cross—doctor's orders—and if I did it in Nico's presence, he might have me committed. Half a liter of Johnnie Walker would have done the trick, too, but I didn't consider that, because I didn't have any, and because it was 9 A.M., so Nico would be alarmed.

Compared with these, crying was the best option. I let it overtake me and flush out, and after I sobbed for hours, I sat an exhausted Nico down. "I know I've been telling you this the whole time we've been together," I said. "But now you can see what I mean. Sometimes I can't experience emotion, when I go into self-defensive shutdown. And when I can, it often looks like this." I told him how unpredictable and nonsensical the PTSD triggers could be, how a month ago on a subway platform I'd become engulfed by a rage so strong I couldn't take it standing still, honestly fearing that if I hadn't started running up and down the platform my arms would take hold of my left leg and rip it out of my pelvic bone as the first step of my body's tearing itself to pieces. Just because I missed a train. Even though the next train was coming in seventeen minutes. I told him how when I was in Congo I interviewed people who swore to me that if I didn't help them they would be murdered, and my translator was shaky and breathless, as any normal person would be, and I . . . wasn't. I told Nico that I had days like this all the time, when I could not stop crying, even if I was only watching TV, much less trying to have an intense romantic relationship. Especially once I had already failed the coffee cake test. Then everything flooded in worse, and it wasn't better until it just was, no matter how hard I tried to make it otherwise.

Now here we were again. Another night, another breakdown, because of the tone of something he'd said. Because of my sudden conviction that I was a monster. Because I'd awakened from a nightmare that morning with all-day pain and fear quaking my limbs.

And he still wanted to marry me.

Could I be forgiven for consenting, when, empirically speaking, I knew the things that I knew? Like how many people with PTSD never recover? How many spouses contract PTSD from their partners, the symptoms of one traumatized person absorbed into another through psychotic osmosis? How long and sob-strewn the path to "normal" sex is for trauma survivors?

Over the past couple of days, I'd already made Nico cry. Two days in a row. And hard, hard enough to shake his sturdy frame one of the times, then hard enough to put him in a bed, temporarily immobilized, during the other. An otherwise healthy twenty-six-year-old soldier, he wasn't much of a crier. But he'd been blitzed by my sickness. When, finally defeated by my paranoia, panic, and despair, he couldn't stop his own tears from coming, he looked more than sad. He looked surprised.

"Just think about it," he said now, repeatedly, after proposing. "Don't answer me now. I just want you to know that I'm ready."

Well. I certainly wasn't. Since my diagnosis, I'd written about PTSD, researched PTSD, was taking more assignments about PTSD while still trying aggressively to treat my own PTSD. There was no way I was permanently attaching Nico to me until I knew more, did more and better work toward recovery, even if he was the best thing about being alive, one of the only good things left that I recognized, the most magnificent miracle of a being. Not until I was sure people who were "severely impaired," as I'd been deemed in a state-certified psychiatric evaluation, could get better, and how much better I could get, and what impact I would have on my loved ones in the meantime. I hadn't even got to the point where I thought I had the right to *be* traumatized and impaired—acceptance being one of the earliest getting-better steps.

That night, I woke to moonlit silence and trained my eyes on the strong, smooth back muscles under Nico's skin. He spent 230 days a year in barracks and was accustomed to being disturbed in the middle of the night, but never by something as pleasant as a naked lady. So he was never mad to be awoken by a kiss to his shoulder or hand on his chest, no matter how tired he was or what he had to do the next day. But this time, for the first time since we'd met, I stayed alone, restless, watching him.

Yes, I had too much more work to do. This was hardly sustainable, staring hard through the dark at his form, preferring to weather my distress and insomnia by myself, even for hours, rather than touch him. *You are poison*, I chanted silently to myself to keep from reaching out. *And your poison is contagious.*

PART ONE

If your heart turned away at this, it would turn away at something greater, then more and more until your heart stayed averted, immobile, your imagination redistributed away from the world and back only toward the bad maps of yourself, the sour pools of your own pulse, your own tiny, mean, and pointless wants.

—Lorrie Moore

1.

Later, I would go back over every detail. Like it was a crime scene. Like a detective. But when I arrived in Port-au-Prince on a mid-September morning in 2010, everything seemed—everything was—perfectly ordinary.

As ordinary as could be expected in Haiti's capital then, anyway. Nine months earlier, a 7.0 earthquake had shaken the country into a shambles, dropping or damaging 290,000 buildings, killing or maiming at least as many. You wouldn't know it just to step off a plane. I smiled at the band that greeted us, several guys singing and playing upbeat twoubadou on guitars and maracas. They were cheerful in the blasting heat. But inside the airport, I waited at customs in a long line of other after-disaster interlopers: aid workers, religious workers, groups in matching T-shirts—a youth mission, old ladies spreading the wisdom of naturopathy. Guys I suspected were journalists, like me, and guys I knew were journalists, with the aloofness and cameras and occasional opening up and rearranging of black trunks full of equipment. I stripped down to a tank top, and forgot to fill out some form. Got waved through anyway, and grabbed one of the drivers crowding around outside baggage claim. Hopped in a nice white van, and made the acquaintance of post-earthquake, mid-recovery, pre-reconstruction Haiti. Three and a half million people had been affected. Fewer than 10 million people lived there.

"It's intense," a program officer for a nonprofit had told me at home in San Francisco two days before. She'd admitted that as much as her organization dealt deep in countries' worst problems, forced disappearances and femicide and hate crimes, she hadn't quite been prepared for the shape Port-au-Prince was in. But she couldn't quite say why.

My editors wanted a narrative postcard from Haiti, a description of a disaster that people knew but couldn't meaningfully imagine. I was going to be in town for two weeks, and I was supposed to write shorter stories for the magazine's Web site daily, then a feature-length cover story for print when I got home. How was the aid delivery and rebuilding going. How was morale. Based on my prearrival interviews, the story would probably include the epidemic of sexual violence against women. One of the activists to whom I'd spoken before I left had encouraged me to investigate "coerced transactional sex" for food-aid cards. Two had mentioned "rape gangs."

Beyond the gates of Toussaint L'Ouverture International, the first thing you saw was the camps. "Tents" was the word everyone used to describe what constituted them, but the shelters were barely deserving of that designation, the makeshift tarp boxes erected with sticks and held together with ropes and strings. They undulated along and away from the road in seas of various sizes, camps all the way to the hotel, tucked into every spare space, plastic sheets in gray and white and blue, plastic from USAID, plastic from any place that it could be had. More than a million Haitians, they said, lived displaced like that, crammed into more than a thousand camps. As the months wore on, and the interminable summer, they'd become mires of starvation and increasing hopelessness.

The driver of my hired van was a slim twentysomething named Henri. He was eager to share his expansive knowledge of American rap, and proudly dialed up an iPod playlist with his lanky fingers while I surveyed the scenes of my new assignment. Standard no-infrastructure traffic chaos. Diesel fumes and hot urban dust. The shops were crowded next to each other, as were the people who walked in front of them along the side of the road. There were peacekeepers all over the place, one of the largest United Nations forces on the planet, on foot and in trucks, Koreans and Nepalese and Italians in uniform, the Brazilians in particular decked out for war with assault rifles and helmets and flak jackets. Everywhere there were half-shaken buildings that looked bombed out, gaping holes in their cement facades, or buildings that had been reduced to piles of debris. Nineteen million cubic meters of rubble—enough, people liked to say, that if you put it all in shipping containers, the line of them would stretch from London to Beirut.

Henri gave me the audio tour to this exhibition of his country: It looks different, he said, with people and cars skirting rubble—one of the debris piles a car wash he'd used just hours before it crashed down—but there was also a lot that had not changed. It didn't help now that most of the national government buildings had been damaged, but politicians had always been corrupt, he said. There were always people who were too poor to know what they were going to eat the next day. Henri was from a middle-class family, but said he was going to become upper class someday.

We drove for forty-five minutes. Though the van was air-conditioned, we sweated. Everybody honked, whether to say *Thank you* or *Fuck you* or *I'm turning!* Another car hit us, but nobody really cared. As Henri explained why this was the most opportune time for a businessman to invest in Haiti, I registered my surroundings—the tent citizens wet and nearly naked next to the car, taking baths out of buckets in the street along the edge—a bit mechanically. *Like*, I remember thinking, *a person who's too used to registering surroundings*. I and Henri both, maybe. He said his heart was breaking when two tiny kids pressed themselves against my window to beg for money at a traffic stop. But when we inevitably passed another displacement camp fifteen seconds later, and I asked him if that wasn't heartbreaking, too, he shrugged.

I was tired. I'd spent nearly four straight months in New Orleans covering a disaster of the manmade kind, the Deepwater Horizon oil spill, and I'd been on a beach vacation for a week and back home in San Francisco for just two days before hopping a plane to Miami, spending the night at the shabby airport hotel, then rising early to clear security again and catch the plane to Port-au-Prince. I was relieved when Henri pulled up to the Hotel Oloffson, a storied Gothic gingerbread mansion at the top of a steep driveway. The rest of the street was all bustle, and across it was a displacement camp, but on this side of the road it was high gates tended by men in uniform and, behind them, the hotel's pretty white face rising from among palm and pine trees. I walked up the outdoor stairs and across a huge porch to the reception desk. I took my key straight to my room, a freestanding concrete cottage with a thin wood door, down some stairs to the right of the porch. It was just behind the small pool. My movements were automated as I prepared myself for bed and climbed into it.

Exhausted though I was, I was restless once I lay down, the way one is in a new place. There were new smells of food and fumes and humidity. Despite how the twoubadou guys had made everyone feel for an instant at the airport, I wasn't on holiday. But it was always stimulating to be on the brink of getting to know a place.

*   *   *

After a long time, I finally napped. After that, I got up, met with one contact, talked to some locals at the hotel bar so I'd have a story for the Web site the next day, and went straight back to bed.

The Hotel Oloffson's front porch, high up two sets of stairs, was vast and beset with tables, an open-air restaurant populated with foreign and elite Haitian drinkers and diners. Journalists held court there, the only place in the hotel with Internet, meeting with politicians and each other. The next day, I set up an impromptu office there as well, filing the story, making phone calls, arranging interviews.

I worked reluctantly, in my fatigue. The breeze off an intermittent rain was pleasant, and as I watched a slow trickle of patrons come and go through the day, I had moments when I wished I could hang around drinking tea, too. Outside, there was always a lot to take in, and given the hard-running, news-breaking, petro-tragedy I'd just worked in Louisiana, I'd resisted this assignment's timing. But I was on a publication deadline. By the end of the afternoon that first day, I wouldn't say I was ready to go out reporting, but I was pleased with my progress toward getting ready to do it. I'd resolved to make myself game. As the early evening came, I continued to e-mail and lay groundwork, stopping only to look around, or to scowl now and then at a large, loud group partying at a long table to my right.

Eventually, a prospective driver and translator—a "fixer," in journalism parlance—that I'd called joined me at my table. His name was Marc. We made introductions and haggled over fees, and after we'd agreed to work together, I told him more about my assignment. When I told him that I wanted to cover the rape survivors and activists trying to help new victims, he told me that, coincidentally, he worked with these groups and could make introductions. Sometimes he drove rape victims to the hospital—women who'd been gang-raped, mutilated. He helped orchestrate their care and took them money and medicine—when money and medicine were to be had—or moved them to secret locations when their rapists threatened to revictimize or kill them—again, if funds allowed. Actually, he said, he was doing work like that tomorrow.

Marc retreated to a quieter section of the grounds to phone an American lawyer who had founded a charity that paid for some of the assistance he'd be providing the next day, to see if everyone involved was willing to share their story. While he was gone, I observed my fellow patrons in the low-lit ambience. I got a better look at the obnoxious partiers, who were, I realized eventually, belting out songs in French. They were abnormally attractive, every one of them too fit and lithe; probably soldiers like the military-cut guys I'd seen outside my room window earlier. Those guys had been making an all-out waterpark of the old, largely unused pool, diving and cannonballing and synchronized-backflipping into the water in their Speedos. Indeed these were likely the same assholes, unless there were multiple packs of underwear-model-grade Frenchmen roving the grounds. Which, given the flood of post-quake foreigners, also seemed entirely possible.

Marc returned to the table, then went home, with an arrangement to pick me up at this same spot early the next morning if all the sources were still comfortable with my presence. I would be ready to go just in case. I wrapped up my work, and headed toward my room. I'd resolved to go swimming before going to bed, to try to settle, try to wrest some of the tiredness and tension from my muscles, try to exercise myself into a hard and healthy sleep. When I got to my room to change, I cursed the Frenchmen. I could see they'd overrun the pool again.

I forced my plan forward. I made eye contact with several of them in the darkness as I approached the pool, entering the water without a word. I swam around them, sticking to the narrow edges. As irritated as I was, I couldn't help watching one through the dim light at the side of the pool as he leaped over another who had bent at the waist, somersaulting through the air into the water.

What must it be like, I had to marvel, to have so much trust in one's center of gravity?

"Excuse me," he said. He swam over slowly, but purposefully, as if we had something to discuss. I saw when he was close that it was the one with the shining green eyes who'd caught my gaze every time I'd glared at them on the balcony. In fact, he was swimming over now because he'd told his platoon mates at the table that I kept looking at him as if I wanted him, and they'd told him that now was his chance to prove it.

"Do you speak French?"

I didn't. He and his best friend, Jimmy, turned out not to speak English, though we'd taken each other's languages in school.

We tried words in our own languages, slowly, until one sounded familiar enough in the other's to get the gist, or used the few French or English words in our vocabularies. I was a pro, one of the best I knew, at deciphering heavy accents—and thank God, as neither of them had exercised their pronunciation since high school. Mine wasn't any better. But pretty efficiently, we were able to clear up that I was American, not British. After that, I confirmed my suspicions about them.

"Are you military?" I asked.

"Yes," they said. "Police."

"You're military? Or police?"

". . . We are . . . military. And . . . we are police."

They knew the words "United Nations," so I understood that the French government had lent them to Haiti's international peacekeeping force. They asked me what I did, with as few words as possible ("You?"); we all said where we lived. Though they repeated it six times, I didn't recognize the name of their city—or know if it even was a city or a region—but they had heard of San Francisco.

We talked, occasionally swimming. After a while, the one with the eyes, who introduced himself as Nico, tried pantomiming something to me for several minutes to explain where their lieutenant was. He touched his forefingers and thumbs together to make a little circle with his hands. He made sort of a V in the air, with a circle maybe on top of it. He said some words I didn't know, but then "*gateau*" and "*glace*," and threw his hands up exasperatedly when I said "Dessert?" because he hadn't tried that word. And it was the same word in both languages.

So as their lieutenant had dessert—on the balcony, I gathered from the pointing—we chatted. The rest of the guys had disappeared, and the three of us treaded the quiet black water together. Nico and Jimmy spoke among themselves often, in French, sometimes to try to come up with an English word. When Nico turned his back to me, I wondered what he would do if I wrapped myself around him, pressing my chest into his shoulders.

It startled me a little.

I wasn't given to wrapping myself around strangers. As they continued talking, I interrogated myself. Was I lonely? That didn't seem right; I'd been away from home for four months, but in New Orleans, I'd connected with an old love interest, and loved, been loved while I was there. I figured I was probably disoriented, but I couldn't see why I'd try to orient myself around some random French guy.

Eventually, he hopped out of the pool and put pants on. When he came back, we sat next to each other at the edge of the water. We pointed to each other's tattoos and talked about them by giving key words about their histories, our faces close. "I cannot make tattoo," Jimmy said, from where he was hanging in the deep end near us, shaking his head. "About ze needles . . . I am. . . ." He mimicked cringing, a kind of prissiness, while searching for any English word in his vocabulary that might convey it. "I am . . . *gay*." When I left to go shower for bed, both of them urged me to instead shower and meet them back on the hotel porch.

There, Haiti's most famous *mizik rasin* ("roots music") band, fronted by the hotel's proprietor, was gearing up to play the regular Thursday-night gig that drew huge mixed crowds from across Port-au-Prince. I made an appearance, as I'd promised the boys, but only briefly. The hotel was suddenly packed. It was hot and loud. Nico reached in his pocket and shook car keys at me when I mimed that he wasn't drinking like everyone else, and I wasn't, either. I told them I couldn't stay, that I had to get up early to maybe go with Marc as he helped rape survivors, and they shook their heads and pooled their English to say it was like that all the time in the camps, the violence and rape—a *lot* of rape, they repeated. Soon, the rest of their unit crowded around us, thrilled to meet a U.S. citizen; they were provincial French, not Parisian-mean. They spoke even less English than Nico and Jimmy did but were drunkenly determined to try, enthusiastically shouting one word at a time in my face, any word, as it came to them.

"Hello!"

"New York!"

I said good night. I kissed everyone, the men, their female lieutenant, on both cheeks when they leaned in the way the French do. "Too many French people," I said as I kissed Nico's second. I paced the floor when I got back to my room, brushing my teeth and debating going back to get him. Tired, conscious of my work and wary of the crowd, I reluctantly decided against it.

When he knocked on my door five minutes later, he could tell, he would say later, what the answer was the moment he saw my face, but he asked me the question he'd been standing outside practicing the whole time anyway. "Excuse me. But, just to know please if I can to kiss you."

Minutes later, he was gone. Within those minutes, I became desperate to remain in his presence, which, despite how fast I could feel his heart beating, felt anchored, solid, despite his being sent to a country where he didn't belong, touching a girl he didn't know. I'd been right to want to be close to him in the pool, rooted low and deep as he was. When he had to leave, his curfew calling him from the perfect connectivity of our mouths, time to round the troops back up into the truck, we parted with surprising resistance and inappropriate quantities of tenderness given the circumstances.

He went back to the camp where they slept. I went to bed with earplugs in, blocking the rock show still raging above, depending on sleep to help me settle into my surroundings, however unsettled they felt. The previous night, one of the locals at the bar had tried to tell me how the earthquake had affected him, and had resorted to a rhetorical, unanswerable half-question. "When the very ground beneath your feet betrays you?" he'd said, shortly before trailing off entirely.

The next morning, I woke up early and had a roll with some butter on it and went out to work and something happened inside me, and whatever it was, however many years I would spend trying to figure it out, I wasn't the same anymore after that.

2.

As my early interviewees, and the Frenchmen, had said: In the dark, security-less tent cities, full of orphans and widows living under plastic sheets, rape was rampant and unchecked.

Marc called to say he was indeed picking me up. From the moment I got into his car, every conversation and every interaction centered on sexual violence and violation; dripped with horror and graphic details of bloody injuries. Of course the trauma didn't end—it never ended—with the rape itself, and I started the morning watching how it continued in ways that I had never anticipated. I was speechless during our first stop, when a female doctor turned to me during a consult with a rape victim and demanded: Did I understand the situation? Did I understand that this was what happened to girls like this one, who have children but are not married? That this wasn't one of those tragedies in which an *innocent* girl is raped?

"Remember when I told you that in Haiti people blame the woman when she gets raped?" Marc asked me quietly as we walked out of the hospital. Later, he said, "Some people say going to the doctor when you get raped is like getting attacked again."

And then, after we drove away from the hospital, I saw something.

That's all. I'm not going to say much about it. I witnessed something very suddenly. It had something to do with a rape. I was extremely startled by the scene and by the sudden screaming—not mine, but the closest I'd ever been to anyone's complete and abject terror. So close and so shocking that I lost myself to it.

The whole situation was immeasurably worse for those more directly involved, and they later decided they didn't want to talk about it. The exact details are as bad as you might imagine, or worse than you could imagine, and I won't share them so as not to risk retraumatizing anyone. Even if I did want to share them, I probably couldn't, the subject so raw and complicated that it spiraled out in ways I can't describe, with privacy and ownership debates and lawyers. Part of the chaos formed by trauma's wide path. I raise the situation because the next several years of my life were shaped by it. It was a witnessing and a sound but, more, it was the way it landed on me, the screaming and terror from just a few inches away penetrating and dispersing me.

That's what I'm going to tell you about. The dispersing.

For a second, I felt intense panic.

Then suddenly, I disappeared.

On a street in Port-au-Prince on September 17, 2010, just before eleven in the morning on a Friday, downtown was hot and bustling, and I lost myself in place and time and in my body.

In fact, I was in a car. *You're in the car,* something inside me said, and I knew that I was in the car, but I couldn't feel myself in it; I couldn't feel my body sitting there, or feel myself inside my flesh, since there was that screaming and screaming and terror and I burst into a deep, frantic confusion about where I was. Soon, the screaming stopped. In seconds, the alarm was over. I could see that, sure as I was still registering the rest of the scene, but all I could feel was a disembodied version of myself hovering somewhere behind me and to the left, outside my car window.

Who are those people? I could hear it asking about everyone inside. *What's that awful thing going on inside that car?*

I hadn't ever had my consciousness separate from my anatomy before. That made me lucky, I would later learn. But in the moment, though it was extremely disconcerting, I didn't have time to think or worry about it.

I had a big workday ahead of me yet. There were hours of interviews to do and people to meet—whether I was in my body or not. And so I got on with my work with my fixer, Marc.

Marc, stocky Marc, in his late thirties and wearing designer eye glass frames, who sweated his balls off in his un-air-conditioned jeep and jeans and polo, weaving through cars and rubble and constantly answering his phone—"I'm like an ambulance," he said. "People are always calling to say someone got raped." Marc also seemed disturbed by the morning's events. We went to the bank to withdraw funds to move the anti-rape activist we were going to pick up into hiding. Someone had threatened to shoot her for standing up for rape victims. While we waited our turn, Marc alternated between silence and shell-shocked exclamations about how terrifying the screaming and witnessing was.

Silence, silence, sitting in the bank lobby's plastic chairs. Then: "That was crazy!"

Silence, silence, his elbows propped on knees knocked wide, before: "I've only seen things like that in movies!"

My own continuing reactions to the morning's events were more internal. I thought I was doing all right, but I did notice some intermittent numbness and weirdness as we sped around Port-au-Prince. When we got to the headquarters of FAVILEK, whose Creole acronym stands for Women Victims Get Up Stand Up, I seemed fine enough to sense the force of Marc's colleagues. Rape survivors all, in their forties and fifties, their fierceness ended up being a principal subject of the print feature I eventually turned in.

"We had this rape problem before the earthquake," Yolande Bazelais, the president, told me. She was gorgeous and voluptuous, showing a lot of skin and sitting with the gravity of someone who didn't give a fuck what anyone thought, gesturing calmly, the weight low in her hips. Her organization was founded by women who were raped during the 1991 coup that ousted President Jean-Bertrand Aristide. "Now," she said, "we have double problems." That was a scary statement, given that a survey taken before the quake based only on *reported* rapes and sexual assaults put the number at fifty a day in Greater Port-au-Prince alone. More than half of the victims were minors. Marc and the FAVILEK founders said it had always been that way, with perpetrators that were neighbors or street thugs or police and paramilitaries, who used rape as a tool of intimidation and terror or who raped just because they could. Now, they said, FAVILEK's resources were stretched thinner than ever. They got three or four calls a week about new cases from the dozen camps the organization attempted to cover. There were 1,300 camps in all.

As we sat in a circle of folding chairs, under a tarp in the driveway of another organization's office because FAVILEK couldn't afford one, the women explained that they needed two agents in each of the 1,300 camps instead of the one dozen agents total. Then, if they had the agents, and could pay them, which they couldn't currently, they'd need the resources to help the victims. They said that the other day, a woman was raped and choked nearly to death; she called to say she was in hiding, but these women couldn't help her, because they didn't have the funds to pay for moving her someplace safe. They were struggling just to take care of their own, they said. The previous night, some hooligans who didn't like that they were trying to help rape victims had ripped down one of their agent's tents. As they talked, the women closest to me reached down to swat away the mosquitoes that landed on my bare ankles. One of them told me that in addition to being raped she'd had her legs smashed up. Another one had been shot.

The woman who had been shot became frustrated as I continued asking questions about the situation and what needed to change to improve it. "We meet with white people, and white people, and white people," she said. She started raising her voice, and two women beside her put their hands out to calm her, holding her back but smiling. White people make promises but nothing ever, ever happens, she said. She was tired. She was exhausted, and at least they could have given them an office, and if I, White Girl, thought I was actually going to make something happen, she would give me her goddamned e-mail address. . . .

I could feel that she was upset. I could feel my conversational paralysis, that I had ten reasons to be uncomfortable: because I had no answers for the race issues she was raising, because yelling equaled conflict (which I hated), because why *was* I taking up their time when, as a journalist, I *wasn't* there to help them, not exactly, so what the hell was my purpose? But at the same time, it didn't really seem like she was talking to *me*; I was made of air. Enter the weirdness. If I wasn't that real, it stood to reason that she wasn't, either. I remember that she felt real anyway. I remember that I was taking notes. I remember that nothing outside the square under our tarp seemed to exist. I remember that I did not bother asking if the police were helping them, because the woman Marc and I had picked up on the way there had gone to the police to say she'd been threatened by a guy who said he would shoot her, and the policeman told her he wished he would have. That he should kill all the rape activists. And because earlier today, when Marc and I drove past a man in a blue button-down shirt who'd been identified by a victim as a rapist, and Marc tore around the corner and jumped out of the car to go collect the license plate number of the nice car he was getting into, he came back and said actually he didn't know what he would do with it, since a guy who drove a car like that was probably friends with cops.

I did ask the FAVILEK founders about the UN. And the Interim Haiti Recovery Commission, led by the country's prime minister and Bill Clinton. Did they have any systematic plan for protecting the women in the camps at that time?

Their five heads shook instant, hard *No*'s.

The weirdness persisted. As dusk fell and Marc dropped me off at the edge of the largest tent city, 55,000 homeless people on a golf course turned displacement camp where a source lived, I felt extra spacey and flimsy. I figured I was tired from the long day. Marc didn't want me to go.

"I'm black, and Haitian, and I wouldn't go where you're going right now, in the dark," he said. He meant this: He would not go with me. So I got out of the car and walked to my meeting point with Daniel.

Daniel was built, serious looking, shorter than me, and sweet and in his twenties. We shook hands, and together we walked into the camp. My feet fell heavy on the uneven, dried-mud ground. But like the area outside the FAVILEK tarp, it didn't seem to exist, either. I felt like I was floating through a stage set. Or like none of it was happening at all.

This camp, unlike most of the others, was lit sporadically by a few floodlights on improbably high poles for security. I squinted into the glare as we walked down the central thoroughfare, before winding through the narrow passages between tents toward Daniel's house. "Did I call it a house?" he asked in his near-perfect English. He'd spent some time in the States, before getting deported. "I'm sorry, should I say 'tent'?" He laughed. He led me past row after row of stick-supported plastic. "And here we are," he said. "My piece of Tent City."

Daniel's shelter, like the rest, was several sheets of sturdy tarp cobbled together. The few floodlights didn't permeate here. The ceiling was uneven, low, and leaky, and the shelter was built on a steep dirt slope. Daniel said water got in from all directions when it rained. And oh, how it rained: hard, monsoon-season buckets pouring in through gaps in the roof and the sides, the earth floor liquefying, a mud flood forming under the higher-up rows of lean-tos until it collapsed under its own weight and slid fast downhill into the tents pitched below. Inside Daniel's place, the only source of light was a flashlight aimed at the gray tarp overhead. The dim beam illuminated the USAID decal printed on it—which announced the gift as FROM THE AMERICAN

PEOPLE—but little else. While I waited for my eyes to adjust to the darkness, a child materialized at my left thigh.

"This is my daughter, Melissa," Daniel said. "She's ten."

"*Est-ce que je peux te donner un bisou?*" she asked, barely audibly. I sensed the outline of braids in her silhouette, but couldn't be sure.

"*Bien sûr,*" I told her, she was welcome to give me a kiss, and I bent down to accept it, supersoft and tiny against my cheek.

Daniel overturned a bucket to offer me a seat and told me, as he, his fiancée, and Melissa sat on the ceramic tiles he'd placed over the mud, about the handicap-aid organization he was starting. He said that when the American soldiers came after the earthquake and set up this camp, he'd helped run errands for them, delivering babies, doing whatever he could to aid the aiders.

There was just enough room for the four of us to sit; my shoulder touched Daniel's fiancée's; my feet touched Daniel's feet. Melissa was sprawled across his lap.

"Fortunately," he said, "it's not that hot in here right now."

I nodded. All our arms were slick and our faces running with sweat. But this was nothing compared with the daytime, when being under the plastic was like being in an oven.

Daniel asked me if I was thirsty, and I was, but I didn't want to drink anything because Daniel had also said I shouldn't use the communal portable toilets. It was only eight o'clock, but dark, and plenty of gals before me had been assaulted on that trip to the bathroom. That was one of the reasons the inside of this tent smelled like urine. To avoid the communal toilets, Daniel's family used a bucket in a corner. The three of them kept their plastic-walled hovel fantastically neat, and emptied the bucket often, but at some point I inhaled sharply and breathed in too much of its stink. I puked into my mouth, and pretended I hadn't. I suggested that we go for a walk.

Outside, it was clear that plenty of other residents were improvising bathroom facilities, too. The air was still, and within seconds my nose and throat were coated with the reek of hot rotting shit. "People have a lot of needs here," Daniel said as we strolled along. The difficulty of getting around the steep muddy trail was one example of the trouble that disabled people, particularly recent earthquake amputees, were having. He introduced me to some neighbors, a woman who'd lost her husband, a tall smiley fellow who was deaf from rubble that had fallen on his head; he needed a hearing aid but couldn't get one.

The camp buzzed. People gathered in the wider paths, vendors cooked hot dogs and sold water, and someone had run long electrical cords to steal power to play a garish remake of "We Are the World" over the steady, chattery thrum. It was early on a Friday night, but the noise was already starting to die down, Daniel pointed out. People had to wake up early, lest they roast to death in their plastic ovens once the sun had risen. Suddenly, a skinny guy came tearing up the path. He was asking Daniel, he was asking some guy behind Daniel, he was frantically asking everyone nearby: What should he do? Some thugs were threatening his family because they wanted the space and piece of tarp his family occupied. The thugs said they would set it all on fire if he didn't move his family out. Was there anyone to talk to? Could he find a cop around here or what?

The peacekeepers you saw everywhere in Port-au-Prince had a presence in the camp. Nico and Jimmy, in fact, patrolled this one. But people complained that the troops didn't do much to protect camp residents or any other Haitians. There was a police substation in this camp, because Sean Penn, whose aid organization ran it, had fought for and won it, but we hadn't passed any police or soldiers or security on our long lap around. Daniel suggested to the panicked man where they might be. The man went running in that direction.

"You won't find Haitian police in the camps because they're at your hotel," Marc joked when I got back into his car. He had picked me up at the edge after my walk with Daniel, a couple of hours after we'd parted. And indeed, when we drove back to the Hotel Oloffson, through traffic that was less crazy that late at night, several men in uniform were standing guard at the high gate.

I was supposed to write a story, the daily online story. But by then, my whole body was vibrating and tingling and buzzing. The hotel felt like another stage set. I was unsteady and far from creatively capable; I couldn't even imagine working on a story. I sat down at a table on the balcony, ordered cold gin, and drank it fast.

I chain-smoked a pack of cigarettes I'd bought from the bar, though I'd mostly quit years ago. I at least wrote some necessary e-mails, again at the open-air tables, feeling hot and unmoored, but bizarrely not exhausted. Intermittently, I opened and reopened an e-mail from Nico, the reading of which was a strange and almost unbearable contrast to my day.

When I'd woken up that morning, I had the message from him. It appeared he had composed it with the painstaking help of a French-English dictionary at dawn; I'd read it before Marc had picked me up. There were a lot of lovely words, he said, to *described* me. He said that *when he came front my door he believed his heart will be explode.* Then, during the day, this intense, at times horrible day with Daniel and the hospital and the screaming, he'd sent some texts to my Haitian cell, too, the number of which I'd written on the back of the business card I'd given Jimmy.

Now that the day was over, we seemed to be online at the same time. We sent a few e-mails back and forth. What was my secret, he wanted to know. *How I had captivated him so?*

We continued corresponding the next day, when I had a hard time getting out of bed. For the first time in my life, I couldn't will myself to move around. Forgoing work, I confined myself largely to my room, texting and e-mailing from my BlackBerry and pacing. I didn't go out. I got very hungry but stayed behind my feeble wooden plank of a door. Nico and I wrote back and forth that we missed each other urgently, crazily, all afternoon. It didn't make any sense, to either of us, and it probably didn't help my persisting feelings of unreality. But neither of us could stop. Nico wasn't allowed out of base camp except to work and for all-platoon "free time" to blow off steam, like they were doing when we'd met. It was the first time they'd done something like that in the month since they'd arrived, a fluke that we'd caught each other at my hotel. There was no way he'd be able to get back out to see me again, or for anything else. Captain's orders, he said. I encouraged him to desert.

So when someone came knocking on my door after dark that night, it wasn't him.

One of the old rich locals who frequented the hotel, a doctor, apparently, had instantly developed an unwholesome fixation on me, always finding me if I was in the extensive restaurant-balcony-lobby—and, it seemed now, anywhere else on the grounds. The night before, when I'd returned from work, he'd arrived at my table with a bottle of baby oil in a plastic bag and an offer to give me a massage. All The Doctor wanted to talk about was that there were lots of reasons I should have sex with him, chief among them that he was a gentleman, in that he lost his erection if a woman started to fight him off. I accepted his invitation to join him at the bar now, in the interest of keeping him away from my room, and had one drink before retiring quickly.

When there was another knock at my door hours later, I was already in bed. A flush of panic and weariness went through me. Unsure of what else to do, I got up and crept to the entry.

"Who is it?" I asked.

No answer.

I looked through the curtain of my window, my heart racing unpleasantly.

And there, *there* was Nico, leaning his head in front of the glass so I could see his wide-smiling face.

To describe how he'd come to arrive, Nico seemed to have looked up the word "cunning." Somehow he had stolen a military vehicle and escaped the camp that served as the French UN troops' base, but we didn't share enough of the same language to discuss the process.

No matter.

When I opened the door, he kissed me immediately. I wasn't dressed, and I hadn't got dressed when I saw who it was, clutching a bedsheet to my front. When Nico realized this, he reached down for the trailing fabric and gingerly pulled it up to cover my backside. His fingers landed only so delicately on my skin, as if it were precious, or forbidden.

Something was wrong, though. I couldn't make sense of it, but when he climbed on top of me, he felt weightless, a feather, closing me in with biceps I couldn't feel.

"I wahnt to make love weez you," he had whispered the other night, that first night we'd kissed.

I'd laughed. "I bet!" I said. The response was a reflex; honestly, I was surprised. For some reason he didn't strike me, based on our extremely limited interaction, as the type to have sex with people he'd just met. In any case, I wasn't. But now that I had Nico with me again, two days later, it seemed like I'd been waiting for him for months, and even if I couldn't feel my limbs, or gravity, or the weight of him on top of me, I could feel that.

We lay next to each other for some time afterward, working our way through bits of conversation. Nico rolled over on top of me. "It's not possible," he said, shaking his buzzed head and struggling with both language and, now, sentiment. "But . . . I feel. . . ." he touched his forehead near my lips, talking into my neck. "I am a leet-tle bit . . . love. Why I feel that?"

I smiled at him.

Because you're traumatized, I thought.

Nico had been in Haiti for more than a month. The day I met him, he and Jimmy told me that that day they'd broken up a fight among children in camp who tried to break into an aid tent to steal food, like the gangs of rapists that sliced through the sides of tents to steal a woman, easy as pie. I couldn't really think of anything more dispiriting to do for a living than hold back a bunch of starving homeless kids desperate enough to break into an aid tent in the aftermath of one of the deadliest earthquakes in recent history. Also, as part of MINUSTAH, the United Nations' force of more than 10,000 peacekeepers, Nico was hated in most places he went. Haitians complained that the troops' orders seemed to be to drive around in fancy trucks pointing guns at people rather than to protect them. When the UN renewed its peacekeeping mandate the following month, people rioted.

But I didn't have nearly enough French to explain my theory, and this guy hadn't come here to get psychoanalyzed—or projected upon. So I said nothing.

He lay back down, and I squeezed him tight. Petting his chest, I fingered the thick silver chain around his neck. "This is very important," he said. "My father."

"Is he dead?"

"Yes."

He paused for a moment. "If . . . I . . . *make* myself?"

I tried to think of possible synonyms or words to fill in the blanks.

He tried a word in French. I didn't know it.

"If I . . . make . . . myself?" he tried again.

I thought about it some more. "I'm sorry," I said, shaking my head.

He made a gun with his fingers and mimed shooting himself in the temple.

I jumped up onto my elbow. "Jesus!" I said. "Your dad shot himself?"

"No," Nico said. He made a fist, upside down, and pulled it up in the air, as if he were grasping something that also was attached to his neck, his head dropping to the side a little as he yanked at it.

"*JE*-sus!" I said. "He fucking hung himself? Oh, my God, I'm sorry. How old were you? *Quel âge?*"

He counted in his head in English. "Seventeen."

"I'm so sorry," I said.

I hugged him a little tighter, and we held on to each other, trying to navigate conversation, or not. When he said he had to go after a while—if his AWOL were noticed, he'd be demoted, likely, and almost certainly sent dishonorably back to France—I pleaded for five more minutes.

"Of course," he said without hesitating, and I clung to him with my arms, even if, for mysterious reasons, they didn't feel like they were there.

Probably it would have been better, in the long run, if I hadn't gone to work the next day.

The next day was Sunday. But there are no scheduled days off on assignment, and I woke up feeling more solid, and Henri, my driver from the airport, had offered to act as my driver on Sunday. He suggested taking me to the beach on the outskirts of Port-au-Prince, to show me his Haiti, real Haiti, on the way to some interviews that I'd requested. The beach was lovely, crowded with music and people relaxed and reveling. Then we drove to the interviews and they were so far out of town, too far, much farther than he'd told me, and when we got there and entered the apartment where he said the interview would be, he closed me in a single, small cement box of a room with a bed. I sat down in the only chair and pushed it into the corner, away from him; he said the interviewee was still coming; he followed me too close. He had taken off his shirt to reveal the wifebeater underneath, and I found myself assessing his physique. *Could I take this guy?* I wondered abruptly, then my BlackBerry beeped in my pocket, the voice-command function activating when it brushed against the chair as I tried to squish myself into it to gain additional space between us, and Henri told me it was my father. He told me my father was calling to tell me to watch out, because I was about to get kissed.

It was my editors, I lied. They were looking for me and freaking out and poised to call the embassy, the UN, if I didn't get back to my hotel and my computer and contact them immediately. He ceded to my repeated assertions, although much too slowly, and eventually he opened the door he'd been blocking and we went outside and got back in the car. Throughout the interminable drive back into the city, he pawed at me in the passenger seat. I tolerated it politely, having no idea where I was and no idea what could happen, little pieces of myself shrinking and dying off as I said and did nothing.

I would have to worry about reviving them later. But for now, back at the hotel, I consumed a lot of booze.

The next morning, I went to the hospital again with Marc. After seeing a rape victim off to surgery, I sat slumped on the lobby floor while Marc, too, was quiet and tense. When he finally asked me what next, I shook my head and picked myself up, and we got back into the car to travel to a new displacement camp set up on the outskirts of the capital. "They moved all those people out in the middle of the desert," Marc said, "like Moses or some shit." A chalky, shadeless tent city on sharp gravel, where disaster capitalists had convinced already-disgruntled tent dwellers that the free Oxfam water was giving them stomach and genital infections so that they'd buy water with any money they could get. "We have nothing but misery," yelled one of the residents during our interview, a tall man holding a little bar of soap he said he'd bought on credit. Marc and I went back to the hospital on another rape-care errand afterward. It was late by the time I got home that night. And that night, when I got home: booze.

I took a two-day trip to the Central Plateau, to the northeast, through green and rolling terrain with distant cloud-shrouded mountains, where impoverished residents were excited to have temporary jobs through an international aid program. They sung gorgeously while hoeing together, clearing the way to build a road, but then asked the visiting Mercy Corps representative worriedly when the program would end. After that, for me: booze! More booze, after a day of interviewing domestic-development advocates. At the office of the Haitian Platform to Advocate Alternative—that is, non-foreign—Development, the program director fumed across the conference table in a breeze-cooled room that aid was a self-serving interference of foreigners who hijacked rebuilding plans and tried to control Haitians' destiny. From there, I went to a training seminar for teachers trying to handle students' post-quake trauma ("My students are very afraid of noise. Any rumbling truck passing by shakes them up. . . .") in their classrooms, and after that, I had booze again, and booze again after all the other days.

With each passing night, I got increasingly drunk. Extremely, almost falling-down drunk, stunning myself with how much whiskey I could hold. I got drunk and locked myself in my room and called my dad or my best friend Tana or my other best friend Alex, incessantly clutching my Black-Berry, whether I was on it or not, in my palm or sometimes against my chest like it was an infant or an important medical device. One afternoon, after I'd finished working but before I started drinking, I started crying.

This crying, I couldn't control. For two hours. Embarrassed but desperate, I wrote an e-mail to my editor about my declining mental health. I cried so hard that when I called my dad, my dad started crying, something that I'd seen him do so few times I could count them on my fingers.

"I don't feel good here," I wailed. "I don't know what's wrong with me."

"I'm so sorry, Mac," he said, his voice breaking. The sound of it made me cry harder. I was being such a baby over nothing, alarming everyone and myself. "I feel so terrible," he said. He could barely talk as he started weeping. "I don't know how to help you. I don't know what to do."

When we hung up, I kept crying. Inside those two hours I was unfortunately scheduled to give a phone interview to a media outlet from the States, and I cried through the whole thing, then asked the reporter quoting me please not to mention the crying.

In bed, at night, I listened for every sound. Each one hit my eardrums like a knife, painful and startling and sharp, my eyes so wide open my face ached. As the rain came and went, the power went out frequently, and in the darkness, it was easily 100 degrees in my room with no fan or air-conditioning. I thought about the people in those airless, hotbox tents as I sweated, too scared to open the windows though they weren't the kind someone could fit through. Whenever I dozed, I woke up fast, wet and heart racing, from nightmares that someone had got in, or had grabbed me there on the mattress.

It wasn't much better while I was awake. Not having my eyes closed didn't stop me from picturing it, the men involved in what I'd witnessed, or men dragging the FAVILEK women out of their homes so hard they nearly tore their arms off. Men coming out of no place, to hurt the women I'd met, or me.

The sky opens up fast and spectacularly in Haiti. One minute you're sitting in dusty, broiling traffic, and then the car is being assaulted by wind-split leaves and hard-driving rain. In the camps, the gusts ripped the tarps from their tethers. Outside, rivers of water and garbage ran through the streets. With three days left in town, my two weeks almost up, I went to visit Daniel in camp again after one of these storms. Though it had rained for only half an hour, at least five camp dwellers in the city had died, and thousands of shelters were destroyed. Daniel showed me that his was one of them. The back half of his "house" was a collapsed pile of plastic; inside, under the remaining shelter, everything—clothes, sheets—was soaking wet. His fiancée was wiping and wiping at their ceramic tiles, but when anyone moved, more mud oozed up from beneath.

"I guess it's actually good we don't have electricity," Daniel said. "All that floodwater and all these people, with downed wires?" His daughter, Melissa, wasn't radiant anymore. The storm terrified her, Daniel explained. If only that were the scariest threat to her here. At ten, she wouldn't be the youngest reported rape victim from the camps. Not by eight years. She sat on a rumpled, fallen tarp, legs tucked up under an oversize white T-shirt, quiet and distant. "She was shaking like a leaf," Daniel said.

Back at the hotel, the power was back on. It had gone out in the biggest rain, three days earlier, and for a long time; I'd been pleading a combination of exhaustion and Internet unavailability as my defense for failing to file any more Web stories. But I was on track for the print piece. Marc and I sat at a table on the hotel balcony, as we often did after a long day, fact-checking details. That day, we additionally needed to discuss some e-mails I'd got from the American lawyer and charity founder who had granted my access to parts of the story the night Marc and I had met. I'd been sending updates via Twitter about everything I was reporting, partly by force of habit and partly because I was contractually obligated to for work, so she was aware of all my observations—at the hospital, driving around with Marc—so far. She wanted me to leave one source's real name and some specifics of her background out of future stories, which wasn't a problem. I changed sensitive sources' names all the time; I'd only used this one because Marc had specified that the story had been on television before I'd arrived and locally was old news. I apologized profusely. But the lawyer also asked me "not to demonize" the doctor I'd seen blame a rape victim, which would require me to pretend I hadn't seen a lot for possibly questionable reasons.

Marc and I discussed the lawyer's objections for a while—she'd said she might want to use the doctor again in the future. Afterward, our conversation meandered. We were both thinking about ordering chicken for dinner. Then at some point the conversation turned, suddenly and via his steering, to why we weren't screwing.

He was an attractive man, he said out of nowhere. I was an attractive woman. So, he wanted to know, what was the problem?

I would tell almost no one about this. Later, I would write about it only in an unrelated story and without names or context. How many sexual harassers could I have, honestly, and for fuck's sake, before the problem was not them but clearly me?

And *Marc*. Marc who'd made a couple of comments recently about my looks but Marc the ambulance, the rape-victim hero. Marc who'd been shook up, too, by the screaming that one morning.

I was sitting sideways in my chair at our table, my back against the wall. I couldn't bring myself to face him head-on. I gathered all my energy to enumerate, as forcefully as possible, the reasons this conversation was completely unacceptable.

"I am your employer," I said. "Also, I am in a relationship"—I'd told him I was in a relationship; I always told everybody I was in a relationship to help avoid this kind of scenario. "And anyway, regardless of the inappropriateness of your having raised the question: because I'm saying no."

But I couldn't look him in the eye. As I spoke, I directed my face and stern voice at the table.

Marc didn't find my answer satisfactory. He repeated the reasons he thought we should have sex, which seemed mostly to consist of his finding me sexy.

Years later, I would get in touch to ask him about this, and he would say he didn't remember the conversation. But I remember so clearly the way he said, "I know your room is just over there," pointing over to where my room was, eliminating the possibility of my feeling that I could safely retreat to it. Not that he was dangerous. But I felt paranoid and paralyzed. I continued to protest from my seat, and it went on for more than half an hour. How could it go on for so long? He continued to protest my protestations, Marc who had called me partner. Marc who was finishing law school in preparation for a career in human rights advocacy, so he could cut through the corrupt government—Marc who was outraged that the whole previous year, only eighteen rape cases had been brought before a judge in all of Port-au-Prince—Marc who hoped to find a way to make a difference and get justice for women.

Marc, who, despite all that, wouldn't take no for an answer.

Over Marc's shoulder, I saw one of the hotel regulars walk in, a big guy who always kept a .45 in his waistband. I called him The Robber Baron, because he seemed to drop hundreds of dollars on his bar tab nearly every night; he carried the .45 because he was paranoid about getting robbed and shot, having once been robbed and shot. I jumped up, saying I had to go to the bathroom, and grabbed his arm as I passed, whispering fast that I'd give him $500 to come sit down with us, not leave until the other guy at the table left, and make it clear that he wasn't going to leave for the rest of the night. He seemed amused, but after I returned from the bathroom, he came to our table. He refused to take my money, as he'd been looking for someone to drink with anyway. He brought glasses of whiskey *and* a bottle of vodka.

That night I got so drunk I was almost blind. Marc made irritated faces in The Robber Baron's presence for a while, but then went home. When my impromptu bodyguard finally left as well, also plastered, he hugged me, and I held onto him for too long. For life.

Locked back in my room, I called my friend Gideon, who was in a time zone I could dial at 2 A.M. Haiti time. I rambled at him, slurring wildly and tearing up. Just having some trouble, I said. I didn't sound any worse talking to him than I had talking to Tana or Alex or my father, telling them again and again, about the witnessing and screaming, about feeling threatened by Henri, while they panicked about how bad I sounded but had no idea what they could do.

Gideon, however, had been part of reporting teams in Pakistan and Colombia. "You're done," he said.

No, no, I said. I still had three more days.

"Mac, you're done. You are clearly not handling yourself. You're not handling things that you might otherwise be able to shrug off, so you're done."

This infuriated me. *I* was the problem? The problem was that I was over-reacting, and I shouldn't be this upset, and if I was my usual self I'd just be breezing through all this? It infuriated me because I agreed with it. Nothing had happened, really. Not to me. I'd only been scared. I had no reason to be flipping out.

That wasn't what Gideon meant. He was making the argument that fleeing for safe-feeling ground, whether within the same city or outside a whole country, was a necessity on any assignment. He said that the news corporation he'd worked for had mandatory rest periods for a reason. When you were working away from home, if you couldn't take care of yourself and had no support network, regardless of the reason, or even if you could but had been out too long, time to go was time to go.

"Admit that you cannot do it," Gideon said, "and get the fuck out of there."

"No," I said. I wasn't a loser who couldn't do my job, I said. I pointed out defiantly that I was still in fact successfully doing it.

Plus, now that the subject of leaving had been raised—it had never even occurred to me—I thought of an additional argument against it. "I met this guy," I said. "If I leave now, I won't have even a chance of seeing him again."

Gideon was flabbergasted by the absurdity of this. But Nico and I had continued to stay in constant touch. I missed him with astonishing fervor, and couldn't imagine leaving the country he was in just like that, no matter what else was going on, or how unlikely it was that we'd be able to meet.

"I love him," I told Gideon, weakly.

I'm not stupid; I know how stupid I sounded.

"No, Mac, you don't. He's just the only thing that's made you feel human recently."

I had considered that, too. I'd even inwardly accused Nico of the same thing when he'd asked me why he felt in love. But it didn't seem like quite the right explanation. It couldn't be sufficient to explain the efforts I'd made to reconnect in person. I'd offered to visit his camp, professionally, just to be in the same room with him, but his superiors refused to assume the liability for an American's safety, however briefly. And though I'd offered to find a car and a driver to come pick him up, he said it was impossible for him to get away again; it was a miracle it hadn't cost him his career the first time.

But Nico did get away. The next day, when I e-mailed him to say I was leaving early. This time, when I answered the door, half-dressed in a bra and cargo pants, he kept using the word "pretext" to explain how he'd come to knock on it again; I couldn't follow what the pretext was but that it involved the word "shirt." Anyway, we had "ten minutes," he said, indicating that this time limit was military-tight, pointing at his military watch. We kissed, and I grasped at him, at anything concrete, my palms on his ass muscles through his uniform, my pelvis against the gun at his waist. This time, there was no denying my dysfunction. Even after I had him take off his gun and his shirt, my bare arms around his chest, my hands on his back, it wasn't just that I couldn't feel my limbs again. They felt like active absence. I could feel only something static and empty in the places they usually occupied. The sensation slapped me with an onslaught of volatile emotions; I couldn't tell if I was more shocked, or nervous, or excited, or panicked, or terrified. I had no idea what to do. What was I supposed to do?

"This is crazy but. . . ." Nico said, standing with his forehead against mine, his hands on my hips. He shook his head at the craziness of it. "At this moment . . . I want . . . to say you . . . I love you."

My torso disappeared to wherever my arms had gone.

"I love you, too," I said.

He thanked me. And then he turned to leave. "I really hope to see you again," I half-called after him, loading as much earnestness and sincerity as I could into one sentence, shirtless and barefoot and alone. He turned his head over his shoulder as he took the last step out my door, one last flash of green eyes and a smile, and was gone.

As soon as I'd locked the door behind him, I broke down. The gasping, hyperventilating, doubled-over sobs seemed dramatic and unrecognizable to me, making me curse myself. *Who cries like that? Why would I cry like that?* I couldn't say what I was crying about.

Within an hour, I'd packed my things. I put on some Justin Timberlake and pulled myself together, and acted normal on the way to the airport, but once I was on the plane, whatever last semblance of stability I was mustering was over.

A couple of weeks earlier, as I'd flown into Haiti, the Haitian woman sitting next to me had started weeping just before we landed. She said it was "not a good sensation," but couldn't explain how come, and started crying harder. Now, approaching San Francisco, it was my turn to cry, for my own inexplicable reasons. Landing in a city where I wasn't an obvious foreigner all alone and with no allies, where appearing strong felt less crucial to survival, I dissolved into a pile of public tears, awash in relief, but also something ominous.

3.

Four years earlier, in 2006, in a cramped, dingy room serving as an office in Mae Sot, Thailand, I sat with a refugee from Burma in between summer rain showers. I was there as a volunteer, recently out of grad school; I'd been stalking information about the Burmese refugee crisis as best I could for a couple of years, since stumbling upon it accidentally in an Internet search before a vacation to Asia. Explanations had been difficult to find and then unsatisfactory, and so there I was finally, living with some of them on a quiet residential street tucked behind the whizzing motorbikes and grime of a small but hectic border town. My housemates were runaways from refugee camps. Their organization had responded to my e-mail queries and invited me because they needed to practice their English. It was about a day after my arrival that I realized most of the 150,000 refugees were from an ethnic minority fleeing state-sponsored genocide, and this day, a few weeks into my trip, one of them was showing me a video of it on his computer. A pile of dead bodies, a line of murdered children on the ground. Close-ups of a kid with a land-mine wound, a woman crying that she would like her kidnapped daughter back.

"I can't believe I never heard of any of this before," I said.

"So," Lah Lah Htoo said, nodding, spiky black hair standing up from his serious, caramel-colored face, "you will tell everybody in America."

It was another accident that, four years later, I had a job as the human rights reporter for a national magazine. I had applied for a paid internship as a fact-checker there when I got back from Thailand, figuring it would be difficult to make the connections to publish a book about refugees as an adjunct college composition instructor. The internship program didn't want me, but then it found itself in need of an extra intern at the last second. I moved to San Francisco. *Every* move I made was in the service of one goal: to tell as many people as I could in America.

My refugee housemates' story had taken over my consciousness. It was all I talked about—for years. If you didn't want to talk about genocide, you did not want to get stuck talking to me, my talking about the story only a mild antidote to its kicking around my insides. I wasn't entirely sure why. It wasn't as if before that moment I'd been naive about atrocity. I was liberally educated and aware. Even as a child I'd watched *Unsolved Mysteries*; I knew people did horrible things to each other. More personally, when I was six, my Aunt Karen and Uncle Tim were killed in a car accident, and their four-year-old daughter and eight-year-old son became my siblings almost overnight. I was excited about them—my other sister, Jessica, was ten and had long ago grown tired of looking at my boring face—but it robbed me of my illusions that the world was an untragic place. If I'd had any. Another of my relatives had randomly been murdered by a stranger. As a collegiate adult, I was friends with the type of people who put Darfur posts all over their MySpace pages. But there was something about these refugees that obsessed me. Combined with my love for them—my hilarious, brave, sincere housemates-cum-friends—their tragedy lived and grew and stirred inside me.

My housemates' story was that they snuck back and forth over the Burmese border collecting information—videos, photographs, interviews, proof of a genocide they were stockpiling until the day someone might care enough to look at it or prosecute their government for war crimes. When they asked me to tell more Westerners about their cause, I didn't have any more of a platform than they did, but they of course recognized my increased access to one. I had citizenship—anywhere, for one, but in *America*, of all the magnificent places. I had education, and perfect English, the Language of Important People. I was white. I'd grown up working class in Cleveland, and we didn't have any extra money—my father confessed to me once that when my grandmothers sent birthday cards to me as an infant, my parents took the money inside with elation that they'd be able to buy *good* beer—but we'd had enough. The largest point of my personal disenfranchisement, my sex, was hardly an obstacle to be discounted, but it was outnumbered by the refugees' many. Total lack of citizenship. Zero access to higher education. Non-whiteness. Obscure native language. Inability to legally work in any country on Earth. My childhood hadn't been flawless, and my early adulthood, even less so, but my life was never destroyed by the invasion of a racist marauding army. My privileges, a constant point of conversation in the refugee house, gave me the luxury to do, to pursue, so much.

Once at the magazine, I wrote a couple of little stories. One of them got me an agent. Four years after Lah Lah Htoo had been sitting in his organization's office showing me videos, the book came out, in 2010.

By the time it was released, the magazine had offered me a writing job. Though I hadn't had any specific ambitions beyond publishing the book, that was great by me. I'd spent huge portions of my life writing and rewriting sentences in my head for no reason. When I was five, I got lost on a family vacation to the North Carolina coast when I was walking along the ocean writing mental sentences, so absorbed that I wandered far off. They had to form a search party to find me. I'd briefly fantasized, as a teenager, about being a documentarian, voraciously consuming social-justice films, so an appointment as a journalist was beyond ideal.

Six months before I went to Haiti, I spent a month on a book tour blathering about refugee issues. My dream.

A month after that, I went to New Orleans, where I'd gone to grad school years before, to do a story on the public defender's office.

The Deepwater Horizon oil rig exploded in the Gulf of Mexico shortly before I arrived. One morning before I was due to leave the city, the other story done, I was looking at the *Times-Picayune* over breakfast, with a map of the growing slick from a well that had somehow failed to be plugged for weeks. I thought oil might make landfall on Grand Isle, an inhabited barrier island to the south; I made the two-hour drive to check it out. The oil and I seemed to get to the beach at about the same time. I didn't even realize it until I was standing in it, that the brown dots all over the shore were balls of tar. I couldn't wash them off my feet, and they burned my skin. They were still small enough then that the tourists and local families hadn't noticed, either. Little kids were splashing around in the water.

I started reporting stories about the oil spill. After several weeks on the Gulf Coast, I went back to San Francisco for a few days. But within a week, I was back in Louisiana. The tar balls that washed up were replaced by entire sheets coming ashore, and I wouldn't leave the South for the next three months.

It was in that time that any ignorance I had about my vulnerability to other people's suffering had started to dissolve.

* * *

In St. Bernard Parish, Louisiana, in a cool, shaded plantation house, I sat in on a mid-oil-spill therapy group with a cluster of fishermen's wives. As I took notes, they hollered out their panic that their newly unemployed husbands were suddenly drunk all the time. Or abusive. Or threatening to find BP oil executives and hurt them. A toddler sat on one of the women's laps, watching. Their oil-spill claim checks weren't coming, they said, and the charity grocery vouchers weren't redeemable for necessities such as toilet paper. One of them kept announcing, and you could feel it from her across the room where she sat eight months pregnant and husky-voiced and dressed in white, that she was a nervous wreck.

After I left, I called back to San Francisco for a phone-counseling session with a brilliant specialist named Meredith Broome.

I'd seen Meredith for a while when I first moved to California, which coincided with the falling apart of a brief marriage—and a subsequent search for therapy. My husband and I were best friends and excellent partners, but even before the nuptials, we had been more an affectionate team than a romantic couple. As honest as the mistake was—he was bright, hilarious, and thoughtful, someone I loved and could easily picture living with forever—and as young as I'd been when I made it, I'd still felt conflicted about the divorce. And guilty, in the way that one, especially one who went to Catholic school for thirteen years, does. I'd been to therapy as a child, when the adoption court that handled my orphaned brother and sister's entrance into my family had automatically mandated it for all of us. It had made the idea perfectly natural to me: When you were going through a major life event, you could seek emotional guidance from a professional.

Meredith had helped me process my divorce transition. Now I reached out because I, like the fishermen's wives, was finding myself to be a bit distressed, too.

And I was alarmed about it. Hadn't I spent six weeks living with refugees who talked about and showed me pictures of genocide all day, no problem? It was hardly a meal that went by without one of them pointing out how slowly I chewed my food, when *they* had been taught to chew as fast as possible in case soldiers came to murder them and burn their house down in the middle of dinner. But by the day I spent with the fisherman's wives, I'd called Meredith for advice from the Louisiana assignment once before, having been unable to stop a weepy fit from coming on after a white oil-spill cleanup worker told me to notify him if any black cleanup workers hit on me, so that he could organize a lynching. That day, I'd been huffing crude fumes in near 100-degree heat for days, and also it was my birthday. Plus, Deepwater Horizon wasn't my first run-in with apocalyptic misery on the Gulf Coast. When I was working, living, and going to grad school in New Orleans, it was 2005—when Hurricane Katrina made landfall. So though in retrospect some light weeping doesn't seem unwarranted, I whined to Meredith then that I was a loser. All my complaints were obviously meaningless compared to my subjects' strife.

"It's OK to cry," she said.

"Everyone's going to think I'm not tough enough to do my job."

"You don't know what Anderson Cooper does when he goes home at night."

He was in town, too, eventually. Tons of reporters were. There was a lot of newsworthy wretchedness going around the single largest accidental oil spill in history, with the companies' malfeasance, the collusion of local police guarding oiled beaches and moonlighting as BP's private security, hospitality and marine livelihoods ruined, and crude-drenched birds and turtles washing up. When I called Meredith about the fisherman's wives, she suggested that when immersed in trauma I do exercises to prevent absorbing and keeping trauma. Visualize breathing in people's distress, she said, and exhale compassion.

It was similar to the advice the fisherman's wives had been given about weathering what their husbands were bringing into their houses. Breathe in your favorite color, said the clinical coordinator running the group therapy. She was part of a local nonprofit that was trying to mobilize resources around the uptick of depression and domestic violence. She had the wives practicing *iiinhaaale, one, two, three, four, five, six*—hold for a second with your abdomen, not just your upper chest, full of oxygen, then just as slowly imagine you're breathing out black smoke.

Try to stay grounded so your husband, who will not go to touchy-feely therapy meetings like this, will stay more grounded, she said, as the oil well was still gushing, as it gushed away for eighty-seven days. Stay calm so maybe he will be calmer, to better protect yourself and your children.

That was about the extent of my professional training on the matter. And that was more than a lot of reporters got—despite some studies showing that journalists exhibit far greater rates of post-traumatic stress than the general population. I did have life experience that I thought should contribute to my adaptability in tough work situations. I'd traveled frequently, long trips to Europe, or Asia, or short ones to Micronesia or the Caribbean, half a year around the South Pacific. I'd been comfortable being uncomfortable. I considered myself highly resilient. Yes, I had cried about the idea of a lynch mob in Louisiana. And yes, I ultimately cried another day there, too, after spending the morning in a helicopter over the oil spill and seeing the sheer, uncontrollable size of it, sucking in vapors from the black clouds where they'd set it on fire to burn it off, then getting home and finding an e-mail that my coworkers in San Francisco were having a "disaster-themed" potluck at the office, dishes named with oil-spill puns encouraged. But toward the end of my time on the Gulf Coast, on top of my other work, I took a side reporting trip to Oklahoma for several days to do a story about the vigilante economy that thrived on Indian territory.

And I'd handled it well, I thought. Under the circumstances.

My central source was an immense guy named Ruben. People paid him to beat up people who'd wronged them in lieu of calling in the lax local justice system. The only cops with jurisdiction over America's 56 million acres of Indian land were 3,000 Bureau of Indian Affairs officers—and tribes couldn't prosecute non-Indians, who were responsible for the majority of violent crimes against Indians. Late one night, Ruben took me to meet some of his friends, and then abandoned me to them as he went to flirt with the girl across the street. Since I was busy interviewing the guys, I hadn't minded at first, though they were drunk, and historically dangerous—scars and cauliflower ears all around, and one of them who was even bigger than Ruben confessed that he, too, had been paid as a punisher, breaking a guy's arm for $500. I'd known they would likely also be criminals. And I knew the statistics, that violent crime among Native Americans was twice the average national rate, and on some reservations, twenty times higher, and that at least one in three American Indian women was raped in her lifetime. Earlier that very day, a former tribal police chief I interviewed told me that if a woman bothered reporting a rape around here, he "guaranteed" she'd be raped again in retaliation. But I'd walked into that party assuming the best of everyone until I had a reason to do otherwise. Alert, but totally unafraid. Until the conversation turned to how fun it would be to pass me around for sex.

As Ruben had pointed out to me just two days before, when we'd been joking around and I'd told him I wasn't afraid of him: You don't have to be afraid of someone to lose the fight.

When one of the guys got handsy, I bolted. When I found Ruben, he refused to leave the girl next door's house. I had his car keys, because I'd driven us there (his license had been suspended for DUIs—and he was actively drinking on the way over); he told me to just go to sleep in his car with the doors locked. Instead, I stole it. Driving lost around the rural darkness in the middle of the night, black roads, black sky, black Oklahoma nothingness on all sides, my phone's mapping function useless in an area that apparently wasn't on a map, I started worrying that I would run out of gas. Gradually, I became scared that I would be stranded, murdered and/or eaten by coyotes, and never found. It wasn't entirely rational, but rationality didn't lessen my fear—and also, the whole point of the story I was working on was that tribal and county police agreeing to share jurisdiction over the checkerboard of tribal and non-tribal land I was currently wandering amounted to neither type of police taking much responsibility. And that federal prosecutors, who had to handle serious crimes on reservations, turned down 65 percent of those cases referred to them. One of the men I'd just run away from had had a murder charge fall through the cracks.

"Do you know what time it is?" the clerk at the motel I finally found at dawn sneered when I told her I wanted to check in, as if I were some all-night floozy.

"Yes," I sneered back. "I do."

It wasn't like I'd simply shrugged this whole thing off. The next day, when Ruben was calling and calling my cell to ask where his car was, I finally answered to holler at him for reneging on his promise to watch out for me. He was unmoved. I later appealed to his mother, who had chastised him the moment I arrived about taking care around the parts—and people—we were planning to visit. ("Mom!" he'd yelled at her, protesting like a little kid. "This isn't the first white person I've had around the reservation! And there's never been any casualties!") "I didn't want to turn my back on those guys, much less when asleep," I said to her, looking for solidarity, when I saw her at his house that next day. "Nooooooo," she said. "I wouldn't." When I found out that some of them, as a group, had once beaten a guy to death with their bare hands at a party just for fun, I kept shaking my head at the potential closeness of the call.

But I didn't go all crying and crazy. Because of my work with Meredith, I did notice that I'd been affected. Meredith was a somatic practitioner, which meant that she focused on the physical when trying to heal her clients mentally, addressing what was happening with their bodies as well as their emotions. The method was concerned with wholeness. I hadn't chosen it purposefully at first; I'd simply asked my friend Alex whom she saw that she loved so much, and made an appointment. *Somatics* has the Greek word for "body" as its origin, and a unified body and mind as its defining goal. In my world, which prized thinking above all else, even this stripped-down and sensible-sounding objective smacked of mysticism, and though I went to yoga sometimes, I was from Cleveland, for God's sake. I rolled my eyes right into my cerebral and practical head the first several times Meredith had talked about how stress and emotional suffering shaped a body into contortions and contractions that could have long-term ramifications if the "energy" wasn't released. Though this hadn't necessarily been what I was looking for, I'd stuck with Meredith, seeing her for some time, and ended up learning a lot: that, for example, I hunkered down and carried my stress in my chest. So after I got to the hotel I'd fled to on that warm Oklahoma morning, I was keenly aware that, despite the triple-locked door and the sturdy walls of the room and the exhausting night, I couldn't coax my body into relaxing. I was tenser in my shoulders and pectorals. More hunched.

But it didn't last. The next day, I went with Ruben to "church," a low and tight sweat lodge made of tent and animal furs on a hill in Ponca City. Stripped to a sports bra and sweating buckets, I sat in total darkness close to a handful of old men singing in Sioux around twenty steaming boulders that had been engulfed in flames all day. The leader, the oldest, reminded us that we were there to suffer for a couple of hours, to restore balance to ourselves and the universe, and while Ruben called out under the noise of the songs that he was thankful for the old man, who'd taught him that not all Indians were drunks or fighters, and prayed for his life and that he might do better in it, I lay down and put my mouth to the earth. Sucking air, they called it— trying to pull oxygen from the dirt that was cooler than the air in the tent, which was so hot it singed the inside of your nose and throat as you consumed it. The heat was suffocating, forcing any tension out of my chest just so I could breathe. When church was over, and everyone's best intentions collectively aspirated into the inferno, I crawled out flush and dripping, reborn and *open*, even as I could hear the coyotes, the ones I'd earlier feared would disperse my carcass, screaming in the surrounding plains.

So I'd been less than invincible on assignments before. But I'd regained my equilibrium. I'd always been human, but rebounding, on my assignments—and in my life—before. Never once had I completely fallen apart, or felt incapable, or stopped functioning.

No, I'd never experienced anything like that.

4.

Dissociation. Noun. An altered state of consciousness. Characterized by "partial or complete disruption of the normal integration of a person's psychological functioning." In which cognitive, psychological, neurological, and affective systems interact in a complex process triggered by an event. A common response to trauma, a defensive psychological retreat, a trick of detachment as coping mechanism. An escape from feelings when feelings are too much.

If only that were all it was. "Terror leading to catastrophic dissociation," as clinical psychologist and NYU professor Ghislaine Boulanger puts it in her book *Wounded by Reality*, "leaves a lasting biological impression with profound psychological reverberations."

The morning after I got home from Port-au-Prince, I cried while I was checking my e-mail before work. I cried when I got to work and one of my coworkers said, "Hey! How are you doing?" I went to see Meredith—I recognized a crisis, even if I didn't know what it was—and I cried on my bike on my way there, the Golden Gate Bridge in my blurred periphery, and I cried from the beginning to the end of our session.

This wasn't like me, I sobbed to her. This wasn't like any sane person. I told Meredith I had no idea what was happening and no idea what to do. I'd experienced stress and fear for brief periods like anyone else, but now it felt like stress and fear were the only things holding me together. And only tenuously. And remarkably unpleasantly.

Meredith said that I was exhibiting symptoms of post-traumatic stress disorder.

I said that that was absurd.

My symptoms would need to persist for a couple of more weeks for an official PTSD diagnosis according to the thirty-days rule of the American Psychiatric Association's *Diagnostic and Statistical Manual of Mental Disorders*. But given their severity, it certainly appeared they were going to.

And that they certainly did.

I cried in the shower. I cried through most of a one-and-a-half-hour yoga class. Several times. The crying was at least better than the gagging, which was similarly unpredictable and sent me running into bathrooms and heaving over the garbage can underneath my desk at work. I had flashbacks of things I'd seen in Haiti, so that suddenly I was seeing them again, and they made me want to curl up into a ball and gouge out my eyes. Anything could trigger it. A smell vaguely reminiscent of the raw sewage at the displacement camp where I'd thrown up and swallowed it, or a smell—or a sound or a sight—I hadn't even registered. Or nothing. Triggers, I was learning, are often senseless, impossible to pin down. I was scared, and I was humiliated. I was joyless, and I couldn't sleep. Relaxing my body, even a little, shattered my tenuous emotional stability, possessing me of an instant certainty that I would die. When I went to a steam room to try to unwind, I ended up panting out loud to myself, naked in a San Francisco spa where people get $155 facials, "It's OK. It's OK. Shhhh, you're OK."

On the way to and from work, I walked down the street looking around with a wild-eyed disconnectedness, watching reality unfold like a video game, and not the one I was supposed to be in, and where all the colors were too bright and the noises too loud. Standing in line with my best friend Tana as she got coffee once, I became so confused by what was happening around me that I took to reminding myself quietly, with the pace and nervousness of a tweaker while her drip brew filtered, "This is San Francisco and you live here. *ThisisSanFranciscoandyoulivehere.*"

As the weeks went on, and I didn't get better, shaky all the time—*all* the time, whatever I was doing, and I didn't want to get out of my bed or even from under the covers, though staying there afforded me little relief—Meredith kept reminding me in successive sessions that it was all just the normal course of a not ideal but perfectly common response to a terrible thing.

"You have PTSD," she would say.

"I don't see how that's possible," I would say, though I could match my symptoms to the *DSM*'s criteria plain as day. PTSD was for veterans. For people who had seen a lot of people killed, and who had nearly been killed, or for people to whom other actually terrible things had happened. I kept shaking my head at Meredith. "That just doesn't seem right."

Psychological trauma is an experience or witness of threatened or actual death, serious injury, or sexual violence.

Though these scenarios are generally associated with feelings of extreme fear and helplessness, a victim needn't experience them or even be in danger to become traumatized; emotional disasters, such as the death of a loved one, can also produce traumatization. Further, hearing about any of the above happening to a loved one can be traumatic, as can being consistently exposed to details about any of the above for work. *Post*-traumatic stress disorder is simply a nervous system's inability to return to its normal baseline after the trauma is over, a body perpetrating or suppressing memories of the incident long after the fact and firing life-or-death stress when those reactions or survival mechanisms are no longer necessary.

It's actually pretty straightforward. But given trauma's complicated relationship with the world, and even within psychology, the discipline to which it belongs, perhaps some understanding could be extended to my profession for its lack of openness and regular conversation about it. (One might feel less generous toward the Committee to Protect Journalists handbook at the time for including advice about such extreme scenarios as smearing oneself with mud and leaves to hide from rebel forces—but not a word about sexual harassment and sexual violence on the job.) In a 1992 book that was crucial—to psychology, to humanity—clinical psychiatrist Judith Lewis Herman documents how political and controversial the very study of trauma is and always has been. Because, she explains in *Trauma and Recovery*, it can't be done without naming and confronting the people who perpetrate it and acknowledging its victims' experience. Without belief in victims' stories and self-reported symptoms—and an investment in their fate—the study can't exist. Unfortunately, given the frequent demographics of oppressors and the oppressed, one key to the study's advancement has been one of the least credible and most dispensable populations of all: women.

Ugh, women. Plaguing society with their hysterics. In Freud's day, the young Sigmund vowed to solve the mystery of what made them act so crazy. Incredibly, after hundreds of hours of diligent, sensitive interviews, he figured

it out. In a breakthrough 1896 paper, he announced that he had finally determined the root of the severe psychological symptoms of the women he was
treating. It was one no one had anticipated, and no one turned out to want to
know.

It was sexual abuse. Hysteria wasn't an innate psychological weakness,
Freud found, but a result of horrors inflicted on its sufferers. According to his
studies, the strongest, smartest minds were susceptible to it. In fact, one of his
books posited that they were especially susceptible to it. His argument and
evidence encapsulated the same findings of some of the best research done
today. It was not well received.

Given the prevalence of hysteria, the implication of Freud's work was that
someone, a *lot* of someones, were sexually molesting women and children, at
all levels of society. Statistics would bear that out to be the case a hundred
years later, of course, but the Establishment didn't seem to be ready for it. It
certainly didn't embrace it. Freud was ostracized. It wasn't until after he
switched course, finding that the origin of his patients' sickness was inside
them rather than in their surroundings, that he was on the path to eternal
fame. His original theories are as good as forgotten.

During World War I, it was the soldier's turn to become hysterical. The
similar set of symptoms popped up with a prevalence that was impossible to
ignore, and again, great minds set themselves on trying to solve the mystery
of an invisible but incapacitating ailment. Must have been the shock of ex-
ploding shells on soldiers' systems, doctors concluded. When that didn't pan
out, evidence-wise, they moved to calling traumatized men "moral invalids."

In 1943, when Lt. Gen. George S. Patton met an American soldier at an
Italian hospital recovering from "nerves," Patton slapped him and called him
a coward.

In 2006, the British Ministry of Defence pardoned some 300 soldiers
who had been executed for cowardice and desertion during The Great War,
having concluded that many were probably just crippled by PTSD.

This tendency to blame a victim's faulty wiring or physiology wasn't new
(and would never get old). During the American Civil War, it could hardly
escape the military's attention that soldiers were suffering from . . . something. Never mind that the Greeks had long ago put it together that perfectly
good men could become "out of heart" and "unwilling to encounter danger,"
and discharged them honorably; Civil War doctors, who couldn't think of
any other thing that might be unpleasant about fighting the Civil War but

homesickness, diagnosed thousands with "nostalgia." Eventually, a physician named Jacob Mendes Da Costa nailed down a solid explanation for their inability to carry on with daily activities, the uncontrollable panting and sweating and palpitations and fatigue. The symptoms Da Costa observed are today recognized as PTSD; many of his subjects were having panic attacks. But he saved the government—and the affected soldiers—a lot of trouble and embarrassment by assigning the blame to the circulatory system in his 1871 paper "On Irritable Heart: A Clinical Study of a Form of Functional Cardiac Disorder and Its Consequences."

As Herman explains, there's good reason to befuddle and forget and muddy the conclusions of trauma studies, challenging the world order as real results do. *War*: Was there any justification for subjecting people to it? *Women and children*: Should they *not* be voiceless slave-toys? When trauma studies don't find that the fault lies with the victim, and when they create space for those victims' realities to be validated, an entire society becomes responsible. More specifically, usually, men do. And so the study was picked up for a time here and there with new wars and new waves of feminism but then, until recently, abandoned again as quickly as possible.

Psychology got it together, in the face of a flood of Vietnam vets experiencing persistent mental issues, to make PTSD an official diagnosis in the *DSM* in 1980, uniting soldiers on the same page with traumatized civilians—who'd previously been assigned labels such as "accident neurosis" and "rape trauma syndrome." Psychologists started to note that the symptoms were similar regardless of the cause. But popular awareness failed to follow suit. Ditto in the fourth estate. Certainly, I had not learned in school, or at work, the signs that you've experienced something that has affected you seriously or might precede a nervous breakdown. Had I any sort of cultural or professional knowledge about trauma, I might've known that the conditions of my assignments were risk factors for journalists' developing PTSD: the number of traumatic assignments, and the height of their intensity, and low perceived social support and high organizational stress. I'd fought the date of my Haiti assignment, protesting on the ground of my exhaustion, but I might've *insisted* on more time off before leaving. I might've known that one of the strongest predictors of long-term PTSD is entering a dissociative state during a traumatic event. And that my continuing failure to adjust afterward was a normal, if not great sign. It is a true testament to national ignorance about PTSD that before I was diagnosed, I'd never heard of the concept but in passing reference to soldiers.

It's not a testament just because at least 4 billion people in the world will survive a trauma at some point of their lives, or because 89.7 percent of Americans are exposed to trauma by the *DSM-V*'s definition, and an estimated 9 percent of those develop PTSD. Or because being in a war isn't even close to the most common cause of PTSD in America. Violence against women—including sexual assault and domestic abuse—is. Among the civilian population, car accidents also top the list, and they could happen to anyone. My ignorance was a testament because I'd been part of one of the more collectively traumatized civilian populations in living American memory.

The Saturday before Hurricane Katrina started destroying New Orleans, my husband made me evacuate our house. That time, I had resolved to ignore the order; hurricane evacuations were expensive, with the driving and the hotels, and always for nothing. But my husband, an ecological engineer specializing in coastal geomorphology, knew damn well the open secret that the wetlands and levees wouldn't hold in a strong storm, and his expertise won him our debate. We were all the way back in our native state of Ohio when it hit, having first gone to Mississippi and then realized we hadn't gone far enough, and that it maybe was going to be a while before we could go back to Louisiana.

Our displacement lasted several months—evacu-cation, some of us called it, because we were so funny, and since our jobs had ceased to exist. But after months of couch surfing and guest-room shuffling and not being sure if we could still graduate or reclaim employment, we returned.

In December, after Christmas, we arrived back in a city like a war zone, bombed-out-looking empty houses everywhere. Even those four months later, in our miraculously unscathed duplex, the water rarely ran properly. Even by the next Mardi Gras, six months after the storm, we were collecting pots of it from a painstaking dribble of the kitchen faucet to put on the stove for a bath, since the pressure was too weak to run a shower. Phone service hadn't been restored. We lived on the second floor of a house in a neighborhood that had largely been, along with 80 percent of the rest of the city, submerged, and mostly abandoned. Tree lawns and neutral grounds—that's New Orleanian for a grassy median—were piled with moldy refrigerators and drowned cars, and the National Urban Search and Rescue's spray paint was all over the houses, codes for the date and time and unit of the search-and-rescue plus the hazards (RATS) and number of bodies found, written in quadrants formed by a giant X. Plus the tags advertising the findings of the Louisiana SPCA, such as TWO DEAD CATS. There were greasy black stripes drawn across almost every building, waterlines from the flood. There was no mail. My best friend and neighbor, who I'd tried to calm from paroxysm on the sidewalk, gasping and shrieking after shoving in her flood-warped door and finding her belongings ruined with black mold, was drunk all the time, and so were some of my professors. Some people felt renewed and reinvigorated by the challenge of rebuilding after the storm, but most everyone I knew was bloated from booze and weeping and junk food, anxiety and uncertainty even under brave faces and good times.

Natural disasters, unsurprisingly, are a reliable source of PTSD. New Orleans then was like a case study of it. There's the horror of a disaster itself, but also the sense of continuing, imminent danger. Some of my interviewees in Haiti whose houses hadn't fallen had slept in their yards for months after the quake for fear that an aftershock would bring it down on them after all. In New Orleans, with tens of thousands of homes destroyed and nearly 2,000 dead, we were reminded, with every step down the street, that the Earth we walked on could not be trusted. (Being reminded of it again with news and footage of Haiti's earthquake proved unbearable to many residents; the non-profit that would soon offer therapy to the fishermen's wives during the oil spill registered a huge upswing of calls after the Caribbean quake.)

As it turns out, New Orleans then *was* a case study of PTSD. Harvard and Columbia University researchers descended dutifully upon the city, find-ing that about a quarter of the population was exhibiting symptoms—a rate that for, say, measles would qualify as a full-scale public health crisis.

On the ground, we heard nothing about it. I even participated in a study, conducted by I don't know whom, in which I answered a survey about whether I was drinking more, crying more, exercising less and eating worse food, get-ting fatter because I was depressed or displaced, and/or losing my will to live. (I wasn't.) The researcher had recruited us through someone at the university, but didn't bother sending us the results. We heard nothing of the assessments people were making of us, unless we went academic-journal searching for them, much less how to get help for a serious but treatable condition. There were public health notices not to drink the water on certain days, but I never heard any suggesting that we should be on the lookout for symptoms of trauma.

And so, no one was. And almost no one did get treatment. Nearly two years later, in 2007, when the East Coast researchers checked back in on New Orleans's psychological progress, they found that there was hardly any. Further, they found that, though PTSD rates almost always decrease within two years of such an event, Gulf Coast residents overall had got worse, regardless of race or sex. More than 6 percent of the population's members were actively thinking about killing themselves. Two and a half percent had a suicide plan. Statistics in 2008, in 2009—three years after the storm, four years after the storm—would later bear out suicide rates 56 percent higher, then 85 percent higher, than those before Hurricane Katrina.

"Everyone's saying this knocked us on our knees?" one of the fishermen's wives had said in the oil-spill therapy session, in 2010. "We were already on our knees. I used to say I was a Katrina survivor until Gustav, and I realized I hadn't really survived, because I couldn't deal with Gustav."

"Did you know that there are whole neighborhoods in New Orleans that are still destroyed, where it looks like the storm was five weeks ago?" I'd asked Marc on the balcony of the Hotel Oloffson, just weeks after Hurricane Katrina's five-year anniversary. After asking me if I was *sure* that the people in charge of *the United States* had failed New Orleans, had still not got their shit together, so had evidently couldn't, or wouldn't, he sunk back as if he'd been punched in the chest.

It's not possible to start recovering from trauma, they say, until a sense of security and safety has been established.

"The majority of people in that one-year and certainly the two-year window's time recover," the Harvard Medical School principal of the post-Katrina PTSD studies said, "and in very bad situations you fail to find that, that there is not as much recovery or in some extreme cases no evidence of recovery. But we virtually never find an increase, and we are finding a doubling in the prevalence of PTSD in most of the area affected by Hurricane Katrina," he said. "That's really quite striking."

It really is. Compare it, for example, with the other biggest traumatic domestic event in recent history: September 11, 2001.

Five to eight weeks after the World Trade Center attacks, researchers found that incidences of PTSD in New Yorkers who lived close to Ground Zero reached 20 percent. That's around the same as New Orleanians' after the storm. Six months later, though, researchers (some of whom also conducted New Orleans studies) found recovery rates of 30 percent in the city in general. And they found "resilience" rates—that is, people whose mental health improved beyond mere recovery—of 65 percent. Even among the most exposed and largest PTSD populations—people who had a friend or relative killed *and* saw the attack happen; were physically injured in the attack; or were *in* the World Trade Center—recovery was between 20 percent and 40 percent. Their resilience was between 30 to 50 percent. Like other PTSD survivors, these New Yorkers would be susceptible to their symptoms recurring later in their lives, from continuing fallout from the original event (which caused health problems, job loss), under great stress or after death or divorce, new traumas that can agitate old, even healed PTSD indefinitely. But a surprising number of them had rebounded. Politicians hailed it as a triumph of human spirit.

Of all the things New Orleanians have been accused of, lacking spirit has never been one of them. So what accounts for the disparity, then? One quantifiable difference in the disasters' aftermaths was logistical and professional support: After 9/11, crisis counselors provided more than 40,000 free sessions to troubled New Yorkers in five months; the fire department sextupled the number of full-time counselors; employers and community centers offered therapy. In New Orleans, some people weren't even delivered food and water for as many as five days. After the flood had been drained and the residents returned, the barely functioning city eliminated nearly a quarter of its in-patient psychiatric beds.

But another major difference was social. As Bessel van der Kolk, one of the nation's preeminent trauma specialists, has pointed out, after 9/11, most of New York still looked like New York—a reasonably safe place to live. People retained, and returned to, their homes. After Katrina, with so many communities destroyed, communities couldn't band together, with many residents dispersed for months, or forever. They also lacked a wider kind of cultural support: Following 9/11, New Yorkers were represented in commercials and newspapers and political speeches as heroes. Survivors of Katrina? They were hapless victims. Sad, sweating, standing helplessly on a bridge or roof or sidewalk waiting for a helicopter or a bus. Or worse, criminals. They looted, and later, when the crime rate skyrocketed, people didn't think about how New Orleanians had been failed by emergency services and the Army Corps of Engineers and leaders of various levels of government both during the storm and long before, but shook their heads at the poor, or black, animals who didn't know how to behave in an end-of-their-world scenario and made bad life decisions—to not leave the city earlier; to be poor in the first place. As

New Orleanians returned and walked around an Armageddon whose levees had been compromised—and remained that way for years—certain to have everything leveled again if another big storm came through, they were not nationally celebrated, or congratulated for having survived.

If validating the experience of the traumatized requires regard for the victims and the culpability of responsible parties, in the case of poor, Southern, mostly black New Orleans versus a New York City besieged by brown terrorists: trickier on both counts. And validation is another crucial component of healing. So after Katrina, not only was the first requirement for healing—security, safety—not in place, neither was the second.

On my return from Haiti, having reestablished safety behind the two double-locked doors of my apartment in beautiful, highly structured San Francisco, Meredith mounted a one-woman validation campaign. It's OK to have PTSD, she kept telling me. Your symptoms are normal for PTSD.

I did not believe her. A year later, I would have Herman's *Trauma and Recovery* always on display at my house so I could look at it, and sometimes touch it, to remind myself that trauma is a real thing and that my symptoms, weird and outlandish as they seemed, were literally textbook. Later, I would go digging through libraries of universities I didn't attend and see the similarities to traumatized Civil War vets, but for now, I felt like an overdramatic emotional freak show. Meredith was a single voice, and one I was paying to talk. I'd seen the world react to traumatized people before, even if I hadn't known what I was looking at, and I'd learned that even a great national catastrophe wasn't an acceptable excuse to fall apart. Even under the grave, multiple-disaster circumstances of the fishermen's wives, the sympathetic nonprofit clinician trying to help them never uttered the word *trauma*, using instead the less-validating words "stress relief"—as if the problem were just that they weren't relaxed enough. As far as I could be convinced, there was no space for accepting So You Dissociated While Witnessing Mortal Terror in Haiti and Then Were Sexually Terrorized as an excuse for meltdown in my culture.

"Nothing bad ever even happened to me," I told Meredith, over and over.

"OK," she said, shifting in her seat in a way that struck me as frustration. "If you drew a picture of what happened to you, it might not look that bad."

OK. If I did that, in one picture, I'd be backing away from a guy in a wifebeater in a tiny concrete room with a closed door. In another, there'd be the events of the witnessing and the screaming. In a thematically related frame, perhaps, I'd be sitting alone in the dark in the middle of the American Southwest with several enormous drunk men with fight scars holding Budweiser cans while one of them was sliding his hand up my thigh.

OK. Maybe those would look bad even as illustrations. Maybe as a series, they'd justify why it was reasonable for me to have developed a conditioned response of fear and terror that refused to turn itself off. Either way, there was no protocol in my community for supporting a person with PTSD; nobody was going to bring me casseroles or send me cards and flowers. But just because my culture didn't acknowledge it, Meredith said, one seemingly small, isolated incident could be plenty to give a person crippling PTSD. No matter what she said, though, I couldn't agree that I had earned the diagnosis.

"I can't believe I'm so weak," I cried. I knew other people thought I was, too. One of my coworkers, and two superiors, suggested that I needed to consider whether I could handle my job.

Growing up, I'd had a paranoid schizophrenic aunt who couldn't take care of herself. I still had a schizophrenic aunt, but when I lived back home in Ohio, I saw her a lot more often, on all family birthdays and holidays. I was a little bit scared of Aunt Terri when I was little, the way she always talked to herself. Or probably more accurately, I was afraid of being her, of not being able to tell the difference between real voices and voices in my head, of being pulled so deep into my imagination that I'd never get out—and of then becoming a burden. Before her psychotic break, Aunt Terri had been a straight-A student and a talented artist. When she was sixteen she'd appeared in the backyard one day, pacing and flailing and screaming-babbling incoherently, and as for her normal functioning and living, that had pretty much been that. I saw how my friends who came over looked at her; how I continued to see people look at, and fear or hate, crazy people on the street. I saw how Aunt Terri mostly sat off to the side of family gatherings talking to her voices, how everyone in my family but a few seemed uneasy around her. Though no one admitted it to me explicitly until I was an adult, there was no way I didn't pick up on it as a child that some of our relatives thought—despite her legal diagnosis—that she was faking, or lazy, or just spoiled and wanting attention.

A lot of people are afraid of the mentally ill. But most people take their own mental health for granted. I, having watched Aunt Terri, actively cherished mine. When I was a sophomore in college, I was asked in a sociology class to write my No. 1 goal in life on a piece of paper, and as the anonymous responses were collected and read aloud, I was definitely the only one who had written "To be happy AND SANE."

But here I was, a blind and staggering baby. What was I to do with or make of this gagging, sobbing mess of a person I was now?

5.

I'd brought my Haiti drinking habits home with me.

In fact, I'd got drunk at San Francisco International Airport as soon as I landed. I'd begged Tana to meet me for my rough homecoming, and we headed directly to the TGI Fridays in Terminal 1.

"Where are you ladies headed?" two businessmen seated at the next table had asked us when our drinks were delivered, assuming we must be in transit if we were getting drunk in an airport.

"Nowhere," we'd responded, staring them down. "We live here."

After workdays, I dragged Tana to more bars around town to tell her, and tell her again, what had happened, while I pounded cocktails, though I'd already hashed out and rehashed it with her in drunken phone calls from Port-au-Prince. What the terrified screaming had been like. What Henri had done. What Marc had said. No matter how much whiskey or gin I swallowed—I usually never drank gin, but since that night I'd ordered it at the Oloffson, I craved it—it didn't stop that awful gagging from coming back as I talked. I leaned over the side of our outdoor bar table, spitting, constriction in my throat and roiling bile in my stomach.

It made me so mad. At myself.

"Why don't I get some real problems?" I demanded. "What kind of fucking pussy cries and pukes about getting *almost* hurt or having to watch bad things happen to *other* people?"

"Dude," Tana said. "Marines." Tana, tall and brilliant, who made excellent points about everything. "Marines get PTSD even when they don't get hurt and only see bad things happen to other people. When you hear about that, it's not that they got shot but, like, how they saw their buddy get shot."

I wasn't hearing it. Tana, like Meredith, was too biased of a source to be reliable.

Soon after my homecoming, I figured out that I could consume almost an entire 750 milliliter bottle, some 25 ounces or so, of hard liquor in a night and still work the next day. I weighed 125 pounds. But I had a six-spread magazine feature about Haiti due. I forced myself to work on it sober until at least early evening, but come six, and then five after a couple of days, and then four, I couldn't bear it any longer, my shakiness worsening as I wrote about rape activists and rape survivors and the earthquake-displaced, so I continued working from home with a small drink in hand. Once, on a day I had to go into the office, I left in the middle of the day to go to a bar, did a shot of whiskey, and then returned, going around to ask my coworkers for gum. One night, I arrived as a judge at a literary competition drunk, having had five or six cocktails, and then had two more when I got there. At a fund-raiser where people had paid up to $50,000 a table, I took the stage as a speaker, and I did so hammered. I was invited to an even higher-end fund-raising dinner and got hammered there also. "I almost got sexually assaulted in Haiti," I leaned over and slurred, tearing up, to the millionaire stranger seated next to me.

Fortunately for me, she'd had a nervous breakdown herself once, after her prominent husband left her and their children in spectacular fashion. "You just tell as many people as you want as many times as you need to," she said.

I recognized my level of tolerance and dependence as a red flag for an issue I would have to reckon with at some point. But at the moment, I considered it the least of my problems.

A trigger, in the parlance of the trauma community, is anything that fires a PTSD gun. Anything (or a nothing) that sparks an episode, or any moment in a firestorm of symptoms. That was what it was called, I learned, when I was going about my business, la-la-la, and then all of a sudden, not doing that anymore, but crying or gagging or having a flashback instead: being triggered. Sometimes it was something vaguer—an overwhelming agitation that could last for a moment, but more often hours, and sometimes days. It was a noun, and a verb, and a psychological phenomenon. It was nonsensical and unpredictable.

Logistically, the randomness of my triggers made it difficult to make plans. Emotionally, the inconsistency was its own form of terror. But worse than not knowing what could set off an episode was knowing one thing that always, always, unfailingly would: sex.

Historically, my assessment of my sexuality had been positive. A serial monogamist, I was rarely interested in having sex with people I didn't know, and the loving people I did have sex with tended to describe me with embarrassing but healthy words like "sensual."

"You talk about sex a lot," one of my boyfriends in college had always said. That was true. But only by comparison with the puritan silence surrounding it in suburban Ohio. I talked about sex the way some people went on about soccer, or their kids, and only more so the further I got from the Catholic Diocese of Cleveland's educational institutions, which kept the hallways and lunchrooms spied for punishable language about it. "Petting Is A No-No" was a section in my junior high "sexuality" textbook. In high school, certainly no one was trying to facilitate my honest sexual expression when the faculty got word that I had, since the age of sixteen, been dating a twenty-year-old lesbian from Ashtabula. They instituted a special rule my senior year so that we wouldn't be able to go to prom together. Even after we'd broken up and I'd fallen in with a male member of the hockey team, they suspended me—*me*, in the top five of my class—for "some complaints that you are gay." So yeah, I often exercised the validity of sexuality through language, gave it a stretch and took it out for a walk, letting it stake its claim in discourse, in the open, in the land of things people could admit out loud.

I'd come from a long line of perverts, anyway. In my grandfathers' day, it regrettably manifested as philandering, but my parents—not that I wanted to know—appeared to have cultivated a relationship where mutual lustiness could thrive. When my dad came home from work, there was a lot of hugging and mouth-kissing. Since my childhood, they'd gone on vacations without us, and my older sister Jessica and I theorized that they were sexy vacations, stacked as my mother's bedside bookshelf was with Anaïs Nin books; as adolescents, our suspicions were confirmed by suggestive notes they left each other and didn't hide well enough. One Christmastime in high school, my dad handed me a shopping bag and asked me to wrap its contents for my mother, then had to awkwardly apologize for handing me the wrong one when I dumped it out on my bedroom floor and found it contained sex toys.

The (evidently) above-average libido I'd always felt, and that people like my (practicing Catholic) college boyfriend accused me of, seemed like my destiny. By the time I moved to New Orleans, and still more by the time I left for San Francisco, I was long proud that I'd overcome my mean religious indoctrination to be able to enjoy sex. To love sex.

Now I couldn't even think about sex. Or rather, I could think about it, but it made me wince out loud and scrunch my face and eyes and mouth up watertight, because it was invariably accompanied by rape imagery.

That was unfortunate, because heavy drinking wasn't the only new thing I'd brought home with me. Since the moment I'd left Haiti, Nico and I had been continuing to exchange e-mails at least once a day. Usually more than once a day. Fifteen in the first four days after I left. And my sex trigger was turning out to complicate our burgeoning epistolary relationship. Nico was still in Haiti for another month, and said everything there reminded him of me and made him miss me and my eyes—and my body. The letters weren't all dirty; he labored to venture outside the conversational English he barely knew with Google Translate on hand, saying *excuse me for my english*; mine contained details about my life in San Francisco and the weird awfulness of suddenly struggling to cope with it, in sentences stripped of complex tense and advanced structure. Mostly our letters were sweet. He'd never been to my country, much less my city, but I told him I missed him like he'd always been there, biking to work looking over my shoulder as though he'd be biking next to me, picturing him with me at every restaurant, in my apartment, at the grocery store. But when the correspondence took a graphic turn, I responded in kind, about his beauty, about his body, about missing his tongue. In theory, I wanted those things. But I couldn't picture them without making myself sick.

As the weeks went by, this effect failed to lessen whenever sex crossed my mind—a memory of having it, the very idea of the existence of it, made every muscle in my body tense painfully, my eyebrows knitting together to keep the bad pictures out. I made some timid and quickly abandoned attempts that soon became a desperate determination to touch myself like a normal, wholesome person. One time, I managed to keep the rape thoughts at bay all the way until the end. But then, even with the dazzling sunshine flooding the walls of my safe, locked apartment, flashbacks of the screaming incident in Haiti burst into my head and I lay there, soft and failed, choking on instant hard sobs.

I could not process the thought of sex without violence. So, I started picturing orchestrated violence against myself. The moment I thought about sex, I thought about having sex while simultaneously having a fight. Someone nice, someone I knew, but someone forcing me, while I struggled, with my permission, to have sex with them. My choices were to picture violence I controlled, or to picture the abominable uncontrolled things that had happened to rape survivors I'd met. I pictured the former often.

"All I want," I told Meredith, sitting down for a session one day, "is to have incredibly violent sex."

I thought about getting slammed against a mattress, getting slammed around. During the night, I dreamed of the Haitian women, or of men attacking me. During the day, I thought about getting choked and hit, and having sex while fighting mightily.

Meredith didn't even blink. She'd been working with trauma clients and running a sex-abuse support group for years, and I was hardly the first person who'd come at her with something like this.

"Being aware and understanding what's going on in your system and then literally working it through your body, like retraining your body how to calm down, is really useful," Meredith explained. Somatics works on the assumption that your body and nervous system and emotions and any kind of spirituality you might have are all connected. You don't just talk and talk about your asshole father until you think you've resolved something; you let surface the sensations you've buried—sadness, disappointment, shame—letting them out of lockdown in your stiff hip or that knot behind your shoulder, letting them run their true painful course so they can become a part of you that is integrated, not compartmentalized or denied.

For many of Meredith's clients, it was a long and horrible process. But not as painful, ultimately, as not going through it. "A lot of people don't heal, and it manifests in a lot of different ways throughout their lives," she said once. "Because when trauma doesn't get to work itself through your system, your system idles at a heightened state, and so getting more really intense input calms your system down." Which is why, Meredith said, "A lot of folks who've survived trauma end up being really calm in crisis and freaking out in everyday life."

Personally, I had a lot of fear and helplessness to start working through at the moment, among other things. I wasn't looking for violent sex as a matter of recreation. For whatever reason, it was what my body felt like it needed. Experts had different theories for why people were driven to reenactments—Freud's contemporary Pierre Janet, who never abandoned his own conclusions that hysteria was caused by abuse (and suffered controversy and obscurity for it), saw it as a means of restoring agency, or power. Some practitioners used "flooding," a controlled re-creation of traumatic events, with their patients. Rather than analyze, pathologize, or categorize, Meredith simply supported me.

"Do you have anyone who can do that for you?" she asked.

I had an ex-girlfriend who would have been into smacking me around, I told her, but I wasn't having rapemares about women. I did have an ex-boyfriend I thought would be amenable. We hadn't slept together in a while, and although we were a terrible couple, we loved and respected each other et cetera. We'd had aggressive sex before, anyway. This was going to be a whole other story, but I guessed he'd still be up for it.

"Isaac," I told Meredith. Isaac could do that for me.

In an expensive pizza restaurant with exposed-brick walls, Isaac got a little more than he'd bargained for when he accepted my invitation to catch up.

"So, apparently, I have PTSD," I told him, voice quaking.

We were in the San Francisco Mission. I felt embarrassed. I felt alienated, surrounded by supereducated white people with tattoos. I, too, was a supereducated white person with tattoos, but since I'd been back, I'd failed to for one second achieve the feeling that I was of this city, or the rest of the human species. It shouldn't have been so surprising, since I'd also yet to feel like I was of my own self.

I treated Isaac to the same spectacle Tana had been party to so many times: watching me drink while I recounted, thin-voiced, heart racing, some of what had gone down. When dinner was over, and we were back out on the sidewalk, I was a little calmer. By which I mean drunker.

I proposed tequila. And a sleepover.

My new general anxiety, that too-heightened idling state and incessant hyperarousal, returned full force as soon as we got into bed at my apartment, tequila or no.

What, I agonized, *was my stupid brain going to do?*

The moment we started making out, my violent feelings welled up. I stopped for a moment, and looked at him.

"I'm gonna need you to fight me on this," I said.

He paused, weighing that.

"OK," he said. And because I was different, and the stakes were different from those of any fun tussling we'd done before: "I love you, OK?"

I know, I said. OK.

And with that, he was on me, forcing my arms to my sides, then pinning them over my head, sliding a hand up under my shirt when I couldn't stop him.

The control I'd lost made my torso scream with anxiety.

I cried out desperately as I kicked myself free. With all the strength in my limbs, I managed to knock him over to the other side of the bed. And then again, when he came back at me. But it didn't matter how many times I tossed him off and escaped. He had sixty pounds on me, plus the luxuries of patience and fearlessness. When I got out from under him and started to scramble away, he simply caught me by a leg or an upper arm or my hair and dragged me back. By the time he had pinned me by my neck with one forearm so I was forced to use both hands to free up space between his elbow and my windpipe, I'd largely exhausted myself.

It had taken less than ten minutes. Just like that, I lost. It was what I was looking for. But with no free hands to defend myself, my body—my hard-fighting, adrenaline-drenched body—exploded into panic. The comforting but debilitating blanket of tension that had for weeks been wrapped around my chest solidified into a brick. Then the weight of his body, and of the inevitability of my defeat, descended on my rib cage. My worn-out muscles went so taut that they ached. I stopped breathing.

I did not enjoy it. But as it became clear that I could endure it, I started to take deeper breaths. And my mind stayed there, stayed present even when it became painful, even when he suddenly smothered me with a pillow, not to asphyxiate me but so he wouldn't break my jaw when he drew his elbow back and slammed his fist into my face. Two, three, four times.

My body felt devastated. But relieved. I'd lost, but survived. When Isaac lay down and gathered me up in his arms, I shattered into a thousand pieces on his chest, sobbing so hard that my ribs felt like they were coming loose.

"One tried-and-true impact of trauma is people just really shutting themselves down," Meredith told me when we talked about it. "Also, stuff comes up for people like the way it came up for you: Folks can have a counterphobic approach, moving toward fear instead of away from it. And sometimes people have fantasies like that after trauma, putting themselves in dangerous situations, almost to try to confirm with themselves that they were not impacted. 'Look, I did it again. It's fine. I'm fine.'"

Isaac pulled my hair away from my wet face, mustering a supportive mantra and repeating it to me while I cried. "You are so strong," he said.

"You are so strong."

"You are so strong."

I didn't believe him. Not that day. Not anymore.

The flashbacks of the witnessing and screaming every time I thought about intercourse did stop. Isaac and I went through a miniature renaissance, celebrating, happily and filthily, the successful safe space we'd created.

As exes, we weren't beholden to each other, and my reclaimed sexual functioning seemed to extend beyond him. That year, between the book tour and reporting trips and holidays, I was out of town for seven months. I didn't become celibate or start sleeping with strangers; instead, I'd inadvertently cultivated a collection of geographically scattered sex partners with whom I shared no obligations but was in regular and affectionate touch. In the Southeast and in the North, in Cleveland and New York and California, we'd get together whenever I was in town. Even after Haiti, I forced myself to go through with planned short trips, to the East Coast, to Ohio, to work panels and family obligations. When in the interest of full disclosure I informed one gal who was clearly trying to seduce me that she was about to join what my friends had come to call The Roster, she seemed taken aback.

But after a second she shrugged. "As long as it's more like, a basketball roster than a football roster," she said.

Everyone knew about Nico. A picture he'd sent me of himself and some other soldiers shirtless in the jungle had become the background wallpaper on my phone. And Nico was busy with another romantic life, too. When he returned to France, he went back to the girlfriend with whom he'd been on and off for years. He was giving it another honest shot. Therefore, since the unifying theme of our correspondence was how in love we were and that we couldn't live without each other, we had to stop talking. He knew I was hardly saving myself for him, but he asked me not to get married until we figured everything out.

I thought that sounded good, if admittedly insane.

In the meantime, I was inconsolable. Not like I didn't have bigger problems to worry about. Nor was I lonely by any stretch. But the days without Nico's grammatically disastrous notes felt additionally isolated and empty. I missed him as if we'd been together every day for years. I described my sadness about it with such weight and frequency to Alex that she composed a fake letter from Nico, complete with a broken-English haiku about the quality of my blow jobs, and sent it to me to help fill the void.

The rest of my friends thought I had lost my mind. As though more evidence of my instability were necessary during the great sobbing drunkenness of late 2010, here I was babbling about how my soul mate was this guy I'd fucked one time in the middle of a mental health crisis. Who didn't speak English. Who lived in France. Who—let's not pretend class was no major issue here; a foreign software engineer or architect or fellow journalist would have sounded more viable—was a soldier. Who was, frankly, too young.

"How old are you?" Nico had asked me almost immediately after we'd had sex, when I was still on top of him and everyone was still panting and we were staring at each other, dumbfounded: *What just happened?*

"Thirty," I'd answered.

"*Thirty?*" he'd exclaimed. "*Thirty?*"

Oh, my God, I thought. *Oh, no!* Had I just had sex with a teenager? He hadn't looked young, but *did* you have to be an adult to enlist in France? Hadn't they told us in school that the French were allowed to start drinking when they were like, six?

"How old are *you*?" I asked, eyes wide.

He answered in French. I guessed the translation (correctly) out loud in English, but as he didn't know the English words for the numbers, he couldn't confirm whether I was right. He traced some figures on the wall with his finger. Twenty-four. No, wait. Twenty-five; he'd just had a birthday there in Port-au-Prince.

I didn't care. As I'd told Gideon, I told everyone else: I loved him. I felt the absence of his letters every day, while I was doing everything.

So when he e-mailed me again after nearly a month of silence, it was all joy and heart-stopping relief. He missed me, he said. He couldn't stop thinking of me *all days*. From there, we were back to our old routine.

Things were looking up, then. I remained extremely shaken by the experience of the sex-related flashbacks even after they were over, the memory of the way they had cringed and twisted and closed my body down lingering like a misery hangover. But now I could think about sex, and write e-mails about it, and have it. My faith in almost everything else remained shaken, too, but it was soon rare that a movie rape scene triggered immediate, whiplash-inducing weeping. Within a couple of months, the gagging fits seemed for the most part to have ceased. One month, I told myself I was allowed to drink on only five days of that month; I ended up drinking on way more days than that, but on some of my days off, I managed to do something other than lie in bed watching *Grey's Anatomy* reruns for fourteen hours at a time while eating heaps of popcorn, like my parents used to make when we all watched TV together. My dad and I had liked to eat the half-popped kernels at the bottom of the bowl. We called them "burnt seeds" and hunted for the best ones, each handing them to the other. I looked for them alone now while bingeing on medical dramas, finding it comforting, though sometimes painful, to crack them between my teeth.

Three and a half months after I returned from Haiti, I was assigned to go back. In January 2011, my editors called me in to discuss coverage strategy for the first anniversary of the quake.

And to discuss something else. "Are you . . . *ready* to go back?" they asked.

I still drank too much. I almost always got drunk to have sex, with Isaac or anyone else, but I didn't drink every day, and I could get out of bed in the morning.

"I think *so!*" I said, assuming that my most obvious symptoms had abated because I was better and they were gone, not because I'd possibly transitioned into the next phase of symptoms. "I feel pretty good."

6.

Back in Haiti, things looked mostly the same. It had only been a few months. But I had a better lay of the land than I did on my first arrival. And this time, I fantasized incessantly about having sex at gunpoint. There was absolutely nothing in the Western Hemisphere I wanted so much as my back against a wall with a friendly gun to my throat.

Whatever. I considered an inability to think about sex without thinking about guns a huge improvement over an inability to think about sex without picturing rape. Maybe it was the guns I encountered every day—shotguns on the security guards in front of banks and gas stations. Rifles on the peace-keepers, who slung them carelessly across their laps in the backs of UN trucks, barrels pointed inadvertently at your face while you drove behind them in traffic. Rich people talking about the handguns used to kidnap other rich people who were bartered for ransom, rape activists talking about gun threats, and gunpoint rapes, too. Whatever the source of the fantasy, it nearly became reality when a regular at the hotel bar got desperate one night and, asking for the eighty-seventh time if I would sleep with him, grasped for anything that might change my mind, trying eventually, wildly, "We can do this at gun-point if that sells it for you."

It did.

That was a lucky guess on his part. But the plan was scrapped as quickly as it'd been conceived when I asked him if his firearm had a safety, and he said no.

I—even I—was not that crazy.

Although, when he offered to unload the gun, I declined, because then I couldn't see what the point would be.

At the one-year mark since the quake, that January, sources I interviewed said that the idea that the country had made "progress" was a joke. They complained that the rebuilding was happening only for the rich; people in the displacement camps were becoming more desperate and dispirited. Part of my reporting plan was to check in with FAVILEK, the fierce group of rape survivors whose efforts I'd profiled in my previous feature, to see if the safety conditions in the camps had improved at all. They hadn't. FAVILEK's president told me that the number of reported rapes weren't the same as last time I was there: They were worse. And since people had been so hungry for so long, she'd been seeing more child prostitution.

This trip, I'd insisted on taking a male photographer along with me as a man buffer. The propositions I'd been getting from men over the past few assignments were only what lots of women, and lots of female reporters, experienced everywhere, all the time. But I didn't have the spirit to go through that again right now. There was a reason that during the oil spill in Louisiana, I'd taken a very tall and broad male reporter with me when I went to cover "female oil wrestling" night at a club frequented by BP cleanup workers. As one of the only (non-stripper) women in the rowdy crowd, I'd been safer with him there. Arriving in Haiti the second time, the moment my photographer-escort and I landed, I'd felt doubly justified in doubling the magazine's travel budget when wouldn't you know it the first person I ran into, just outside the airport, was Henri. We made surprised faces at each other. Though I continued on my way, I went so stiff that my photographer could apparently see it. "That's the guy?" he asked, turning around to look.

I entered the country more prepared, better rested, and less friendly this time. Much as I liked to think I could sufficiently project fuck-off-ness on my own, the photographer's presence made me feel like I didn't have to spend all my energy keeping my back quite as far up. While having him may not have deterred every proposal—he wasn't by my side every second; while we were standing on just opposite sides of FAVILEK's driveway, I of course ran into Marc, who took the opportunity to tell me how delicious I looked, acting injured that I hadn't called him to tell him I was back—he did keep threats down. But even my photographer wasn't safe from the language violence that pervades the global rape culture. We'd only just got our dinner the first night at the Oloffson when my old friend The Doctor sat down with us and started explaining to him that if you were trying to rape a woman and couldn't stay hard, you'd have to resort to violating her with a bottle, or a piece of wood, or maybe even a pen—which he helpfully pulled out of his pocket for demonstration.

My photographer promptly slid his tumbler full of white rum across the table to me.

I drank more than I did on the last trip. I was quite practiced, after all, by this point. But there was no crying. No nightmares. I can't say if I ever dissociated, because I was so drunk or post-drunk at all times that I wasn't particularly connected or self-aware in general. Every morning, I woke up early, pulled my hair back, put sunscreen on, and jumped in my new fixer's car. I was more than a week into my trip when Baby Doc Duvalier surprise-returned from two decades of post-overthrow exile in France—big news— and I accepted my editors' proposal to extend my stay. Even though I'd contracted a parasite. Intestinal fortitude was a bragging point I brought up more often than was decent—I'd never got sick abroad, from Asia to Micronesia to Mexico. "I can digest anything," I would always say, then add obnoxiously, pointing to whatever table I was sitting at: "I could eat this table."

But suddenly I couldn't digest a single food product. For the last several days in Port-au-Prince, I stopped consuming almost everything but bread, whiskey, and Barbancourt rum. And, while I was at it, cigarettes.

The wisdom of my nutritional decisions aside, I felt good about my apparently vastly improved emotional functioning this time around. During the last trip, I'd managed to file exactly one dispatch while I was in the country—on the morning after I'd arrived. This trip, I posted nine. I wrote about the concept of recovery after such a disaster; I wrote about rebuilding efforts, and the scrappers around debris-removal sites. I covered a protest against MINUS-TAH, and a one-year-anniversary ceremony at a mass gravesite. I saw Bill Clinton. The unveiling of a new market. A tent-city shack that opened up as a tiny movie house, one of three in that camp, showing ninja movies and porn for about a quarter. I chased newly arrived Baby Doc through the airport and around his hotel with a swarm of other reporters, and went to multiple orphanages. I spent one muggy Saturday with The Robber Baron, who'd been trying to convince my photographer—his newest drinking buddy— and I that if we were going to cover all that disaster business during Haiti's most disastrous time we had to make time for the best of Haiti, too. One morning, he spirited us away to Jacmel, a historic waterfront city in the south.

On the way out of town, we drove through slums where the crush of humanity got heavier, the piles of garbage higher, taller than a man, with naked children picking their way around flaming mountains of trash. But as we continued west, the Caribbean to our right, the population thinned out, and as we cut due south across the peninsula, we blasted Billy Squier and Billy Idol and Britney Spears along the narrow, climbing switchbacks over the mountains. The pavement cut into the hills like California's Highway 1, but with rolling green valleys instead of ocean below. I stuck my head out the window, happy but carsick. When we reached the port city, we feasted on whole grilled fish seaside, plus lobsters, and Five Star Reserve rum. On the beach, one of The Robber Baron's other rich friends showed up on a Jet Ski. They told us to come back for vacation sometime.

On the way home, back up and over and down the mountains, my photographer and I dozed in The Robber Baron's truck, drunk but having to get up early the next day. Haiti Part II was sweating and running and working nonstop, and I remained tired but wired throughout, exhausted at the end of the day but with a restless energy that I poured into getting plastered and then, in bed, playing gunpoint-fuck scenes in my head.

Never any crying. Passed-out fine sleeping. Parasite-eaten insides. Still, one of the most important differences between the two Haiti trips, to me, was the absence of Nico. I'd spent a combined total of four hours with him on the first one, but they had been consuming; we'd met, we'd slept together, we'd said I love you. This trip, we reached another big milestone.

By the time I was back in Haiti, more than three months since the last time we'd seen each other, Nico and I had exchanged hundreds of e-mails. We were ready to take our relationship to the next level. The highest level that long-distance couples can attain: a video chat. On the same Gothic mansion deck where we'd first laid eyes on each other, we finally came face-to-face again one night through our respective MacBooks. I stared at him for two hours, sitting outside there at the Oloffson. We regarded each other with something approaching awe.

We Skyped another time while I was working in the courtyard of a hotel downtown, where lush plants overflowed their decorative pots and "La Vie en Rose" came over the speakers. We Skyped yet again before I left the country.

After I got home, we graduated to Skyping from my apartment in San

Francisco. We didn't actually talk, as we still didn't share a language; we just looked at each other while we typed, looking up translations as we messaged along. We Skyped while he was in barracks, and on long journeys in the backs of police trucks; I saw his face in the various cities where he'd been deployed, in the morning before guarding the embassy, at night before going out with the other guys. We talked through the eight weeks after Haiti II before my next two back-to-back assignments, to the Democratic Republic of Congo and Uganda, while I was putting together the complicated plans for them.

During those two months, I told Alex at the time, I felt great. Alex was my going-for-long-walks friend—whereas Tana was more my long-bouts-of-drinking friend. Both of them were deep-talks-about-feelings friends, and what I told Alex about my feelings during our strolls was that I felt great. I felt a little out of body, but I attributed it to the fact that I was starving; I was still getting over my Haitian parasite for weeks after coming home. But maybe I should've given more credence to the fact that when the IT guy at work told me they were shutting down the company server that supported my Black-Berry, I was still habitually, fanatically clutching it. When he said he would have to take it away from me for another model, I begged him not to. When he took it anyway, I started crying. Clutching the new phone, I registered its shape only in terms of its difference from my BlackBerry's, emptiness on the sides of my palms where the boxier BlackBerry had been when I held it all through Haiti, and I felt empty, too, and nervous.

Or maybe I should have seen a tell that I wasn't a hundred percent cured during an NPR interview I did about rape gangs and displacement camps and personal threats, when the host asked me how I coped with my fear and I responded, so faint with parasite famishment that my ears were buzzing, "Whiskey."

But I wasn't thinking about what percentage better I was, just that I was much better than I'd been before. I was functioning. Those two months, I had a momentum, piecing together the logistics for the extremely complex Africa assignments, calling embassies, even planning a stop in New Orleans on the way to cover the one-year aftermath of Deepwater Horizon. After work, or on breaks, I chatted with Nico for hours at a time. Every second of which was transcendent joy.

"I have to stop in The Hague for a couple of days for interviews," I typed to him one day. "You know, the Netherlands is only a six-hour drive from France."

He laughed, saying he didn't know his deployment schedule yet.

During any free time I wasn't spending talking to Nico, I would head out to connect with Alex at our designated meeting point. Confidently, exuberantly, I would beat my way down the San Francisco street toward our walking rendezvous, blasting my iPod. I saw Meredith only three times, for post-trip decompression and pre-trip maintenance. I didn't feel like I needed more professional help than that.

I felt prepared. I felt informed. "There are six physiological responses to crisis," Meredith had kept reminding me after Haiti Part I. They were instinctual means of survival: flight, fight, freeze, collapse, dissociate, become hypervigilant. My shocking introduction to dissociation, in the car in Port-au-Prince, did strike me as wholly out of my control. And now I understood what it was. But my instinct to freeze—like a deer in headlights—was the object of great self-disgust, and of Meredith's repeated lessons.

Lots of people—and animals—freeze, she'd continuously reminded me. Information about the world comes into one part of an almond of multistructured gray matter in your brain called the amygdala, which sends it to another part of the amygdala that administers instinctual responses. Mine was to freeze. I froze when Marc wouldn't stop propositioning me, when I might have made a scene. I froze for too long, impotently watching it escalate to touching, when the guys in Oklahoma had started talking about what merriment it would be to gangbang me. I froze in front of Henri, retreating into myself when I sensed the problem, trying to disappear into my chair when it was confirmed, then demurely lying my way out, in all cases failing to engage, paralyzed like easy prey, spending all of my valuable energy and time to react being still and just wishing it wasn't happening, wishing it would end and it was over.

It wasn't my fault, Meredith had been trying to tell me. It was innate. Further, the instinct was reinforced by socialization. Hardly anyone is taught how to set her own boundaries; add a crisis or conflict to that mix, and it becomes drastically harder to enforce them. I was no debutante. But being bisexual and capable and hardworking didn't necessarily make it any easier to make "No" come out of your mouth without a polite smile or adding a "thank-you" or even "sorry." Not without practice. Especially not when as a girl, you'd been raised to practice the opposite your whole life.

So Meredith had qualified, many times, that it wasn't my fault for feeling powerless. And that there were, granted, countless situations in which no amount of proactivity prevented a woman from being beaten or raped or killed.

Still, I wanted to burn down her house when she pointed out that a woman who forcefully engages a harasser has a better chance of shutting down the situation. That a woman who fights an assailant increases her odds of not getting raped. Probably, anyway: The studies didn't take into account your outlying but very real misfortune if *your* rapist turned out to be a sadist. And one study suggested that this might apply primarily to attacks by friends or strangers, since it found that fighting an attacker who was your intimate partner increased your chance of sustaining injury, horrifyingly, by double. One thing that was not in dispute, though, was that people who've been victims once often find themselves victimized again—that I'd basically been lucky that nothing worse had happened to me, because some human predators, like mountain lions, are more likely to confront a target that isn't strong and active.

Some evidence shows that pleading with an attacker actually makes your chances of escaping without rape and injury worse.

I hated all these statistics. I had, and I felt every other harassed and assaulted person had, the right to feel zero percent responsible. Experts said it was important to make victims understand that only the perpetrator was responsible for a crime before urging them to examine and accept their own role in what happened, and I couldn't see how these opposing sentiments could be reconciled.

I thought of the second day I'd spent at the hospital with Marc, several days after our first together and the day after my scary day with Henri. How after the victim we'd been with had gone off to her operation, I'd sat crumpled on the tiles of the lobby floor, demoralized. How weak I must have looked to Marc then. Broken girl. Vulnerable girl. Not a girl who, if you sat at a table asking her repeatedly to take your dick, would upend that table into your face.

Thus did I take it upon myself to get up at six in the morning three weekends in a row after Haiti Part II to drag my ass to an Oakland dojo for a "full-force" personal safety course Meredith had recommended. This particular class was inspired by a black belt in karate who had found, one horrible day, that despite all her training, when it came down to it she couldn't defend herself against being beat up and raped. She was an expert at fighting—in theory. But all the highly skilled kicking and chopping she'd done had been in controlled spars, not under the influence of survival adrenaline, which can overwhelm cognitive function.

In other words: She froze.

In general, the people who came to Impact Self-Defense had either experienced a similar paralysis or anticipated that they might. There were thirteen other women between the ages of twenty and sixty in my class, which was built on the philosophy that though you can't stop your instinct to freeze— your instinct to not move, to hide motionless in plain sight, which can be a dangerous way of hanging out—you can learn to overcome it and transition to proactivity in about a second. If you get enough practice.

In this case, practice was spending eight consecutive hours each week with a guy wearing astonishing amounts of padding. This was not the light play-acting assault of my self-defense elective in college. Though the instructors poured all their energies into creating a safe space *around* the practice, they couldn't change the fact that this practice was unnerving and uncomfortable and terrible. This was a guy approaching me, when it was my turn, in front of a bunch of other people and exploiting my social training to be nice. He was polite and friendly while inching into my personal space, then kept talking to me even after I'd said I wasn't interested. He chatted me up like a normal person, then refused to go away when I tried to end the conversation.

And then, suddenly, he attacked me. Or he did go away, but then ran at me from behind and tackled me to the floor. Or came at me from the front. Or body-slammed me from the side or grabbed hold of my hair. All day the first day, we alternated between running down drills of strategies to defend against these assaults, and getting assaulted. Practicing "full-force" defense meant that we were not allowed to pull or mimic our punches; the assailant fought us until we struck him as hard as we could, multiple times, and he thought he could've been legitimately knocked out if he weren't padded. Or until we called a safety word (which in this class, no one did).

Otherwise, the fight continued, whether very bad memories came up and overwhelmed you or not. At one point in the afternoon, those of us whose turn it was not to be assaulted watched our assailant attack a young woman who was unable to fight him off with her initial suite of standing moves (throwing a palm into his nose, slamming a knee up into his dick). She started crying while she continued to struggle with him on her feet, failing to get away from his heavy bear hug by swinging a punch behind her into his groin, or extending her arm and slicing it back to elbow him in the solar plexus, or extending it again but palm down for the windup to a backward elbow across his face. We all winced, some of us turning our heads, as he dragged her kicking and screaming to the ground.

"How was it, my baby?" Nico asked when I get home, inquiring about my day as if we were a normal couple, his little face peering into my computer screen after he'd typed the question.

It was the single worst thing I could think of voluntarily doing with a day. That is, until the next week beat it with the "what to do in the incredibly unfortunate position of being on your back and seconds away from getting raped" module. That would be the one where you lie alone on the floor with your eyes closed, and all of a sudden a guy pins your arms to your sides. When your eyes flash open and you start to struggle, he holds you tighter and barks, "Behave!" You do, because you haven't figured out what else to do, and because he's put all his weight on top of you and put his nose to yours. His fingers are tight around your wrists, and he's crushing your chest.

You go completely limp, which can be a self-defense strategy itself if you use it to plan your next move. A fake-out. But in this particular case maybe you have simply been shattered by the awfulness of what's happening and his breath on your face. "You thought you were tough, didn't you?" he coos. "But look at you now with your weak, hot ass."

Because some experts suggest that women can be triggered into paralysis merely with words—if they elicit enough fear and a sense of entrapment—our assailant employed them liberally, and disgustingly, in Week Two. Even more unpleasant than being under him, somehow, was being witness to his climbing on top of the other gals in the class. One of the students was in her mid-fifties or so, like my mother but much shorter and frailer. She went perfectly still when the big young guy pinned her arms and mounted her, telling her gently, assuredly, that she was going to like what he had for her, rolling her slowly over onto her stomach. When he pushed her legs apart with his knees, telling her to "relax, you disgusting slut," and settled his groin in between them with a low and satisfied groan, something inside my chest crumpled. For the better part of an hour, the monstrosity repeated and repeated itself with different women on the floor in front of us. We all cried silently as we watched.

But every time, after the initial freeze, something would change in the woman on the ground: Eventually, she would get her wits about her, and gather the fight in her, and activate the tools she'd been taught. Essentially all the options in that module led to a dirty ground fight in which you had to free your legs from his grasp with a move called pistoning so that you could kick him in the face enough times to knock him out.

Oh, but that wasn't all. Week Two also included more intensive drills about how to verbally de-escalate situations, including setting boundaries with people who weren't strangers and sessions of customized assault, in which Impact instructors deliberately reenacted your personal nightmare.

I used the opportunity to get a redo on my scene with Marc, that scene also a proxy for plenty of similar ones—nonsexual pressures from people I knew, conversations with bosses, even—that I wanted to go differently next time. The guy in the padding pretended to be my translator. Our conversation started friendly enough. We were just hanging around, chatting, until it turned ugly as he asked me when we were going to screw.

No, no, I said. We weren't doing that. That wasn't happening.

He persisted, and persisted, reminding me that he knew where I slept. The guy in the padding, who'd been given just the most basic parameters for this scene, was making up his end of this universal conversation easily enough. Plenty of American gals put out, he said, and I had been acting as if I was going to, and weren't we friends, and it was time, and I was hot, so what was the problem?

No, I said. No. We were just friends and this was totally inappropriate.

But just as when it had happened in real life, I hated this conversation so much that even my body language was trying to escape it. I stood at a ninety-degree angle to my antagonist.

Another therapist, when my symptoms got much worse later, would show me how this would not help my chances with a potential adversary, as Meredith had also been trying to explain. The new therapist would turn her body away from me in her seat across the room, legs to the side at a ninety-degree angle, whole body facing the wall to my right but her head turned back to me to say, with something of a side-glance, "No." When I saw how unconvincing and unserious I found her in that position, my heart would sink.

In my Marc reenactment, an Impact instructor had to put her hands on my shoulders and forcibly turn me toward him, because I was physically incapable of facing him straight on even though she was standing right there the whole time saying, "Hold your ground. Hold your ground." It wasn't until I did so, and raised my voice forcefully enough to make my "This conversation is over" sound believable, that he said, "Fine." And left.

I won! The other women clapped, as we always did when someone won. I was free to rejoin my place in the peanut gallery, though the adrenaline and

memories had made me so sick to my stomach that I inched away from everyone in case I had to go throw up. I wasn't sure that even if I had been taught
to break my paralysis when feeling threatened, to aggressively enforce my
boundaries, I would've have had the energy to do it in Haiti with Marc. But
the next time it was my turn in class, I was able to fully face the guy and bark
him down faster, and I was slightly less nauseated. Which was good, because
that time, the instructors had decided that after I talked my way out of that
threat I would immediately suffer a surprise assault by a different guy, who
attacked me from behind as the other was walking away. An instructor had
to reprimand me for instinctively trying to escape at one point during the
ensuing fight, because in this hypothetical scenario, I had no safe place to go,
and so had to continue fighting until one of us gave up.

Every fight you won further embedded in your body the possibility of doing it again. So we kept doing it again. Until our bodies performed the physical and verbal drills automatically. Until our bodies had broken the habit of
not yelling at dudes who were being assholes. Until our bodies weren't so
shocked by a physical attack that we could respond fast. I had far from nailed
it, even after the third, final day of training, with "extended" fights—where
you struggle with an assailant who . . . Just . . . Won't . . . Quit. Usually only
one of your blows had to be hard enough to knock out the mock attacker, but
these fights required landing five or seven knockout blows, since, as my instructor described it, they were "meant to simulate scenarios where the assailant is either on a psychotic break or high, and thus not receptive to a 'pain
knockout'—and requiring a 'structural knockout.'" As in, he must be kicked
or punched in the head so that his brain knocks against his skull hard enough
for him to lose consciousness.

Those fights were "also meant to provide students the opportunity to continue fighting even though exhausted," the instructor said, "so that you know
you are capable of doing so. And because we don't hit students in our class,
fighting through that exhaustion is the closest we can get to safely giving you
the experience of fighting back through pain or shock if you were hit in a
real-life scenario."

Even at the end of the third day, with all that fresh practice, I failed to
prevent an attacker from knocking my legs out from under me. With all the
things everyone had seen so far, my back still hit the mats from such a height
and so hard as to draw gasps. I could hear them while I lay there, temporarily

stunned, the air knocked out of me, really preferring not to have to get up and engage that guy in hand-to-hand combat. Really, I preferred to lay there forever.

People that I knew, I had found, were for some reason under the impression that I was a brawler. I speculated that it must have been because I was opinionated and independent, supporting myself with a job that was hard, or with a job that was usually done by men. Or because I rarely wore skirts? But being adept didn't mean being violent. I'd landed my job because I'd wanted to write about a hidden war in Asia, not because I was an adrenaline junkie. I'd taken it because my father had told me, every day, that I could be and do anything. Not because I'd hoped I would get in fights. I hated fights. More precisely, since my childhood home was run by two adults who loved each other—and, frankly, pot—I was never exposed to, and never developed tolerance for, fights. The only big fight I'd known of between my parents had happened when my father said something out of line once—when I was about four years old. And the only reason I knew about it was because I was there when my mom got the flowers he sent from work the next morning.

But as conflict-averse as I was, I did get good at fighting during the training. Despite the exhaustion of many highly adrenalized hours in a screaming-and-assaulting environment, I could generally drop the assailant in two blows in five seconds, even when the timing and style of the assault were a surprise. Over the past several months, I'd so often felt so overcome with my post-traumatic fear—and this practice made me feel less afraid.

I couldn't know if the training would translate into results the next time my emotional or physical space was violated, or if it really would have made a difference in, say, Oklahoma, against that many fightin' men full of beer and darkness. Or if my odds would improve further yet if I took the next, knife-and gun-fighting course. I was there less for the fight moves than for the practice making my boundaries clear and heard by any means necessary. At least I understood that I hadn't just *felt* powerless. I had in fact been powerless, sure as if I'd been sent into battle with a weapon I'd never learned to load or fire.

"Now I know that if I got attacked, I would definitely fight back," one of the other women said before we left class. When we'd first arrived, she'd said she couldn't even scream if something bad happened. But here we were hours of training later, and she had changed her tune. "I don't know if I'll win," she said. "But at least I know I'll do something."

I wasn't anticipating getting attacked on my next assignment. But I felt stronger in general, more able to stand my ground. It was the first time in my life I'd had an extensive discussion of even the idea of standing my ground, enforcing my personal boundaries, like that. Talking to Nico about it in the days following, he, too, seemed less concerned about my fast approaching departure. He looked proud.

Eight weeks after I'd landed in San Francisco, I left again. From my first stop, where I attended town hall meetings between angry crowds and the government's oil-spill compensation czar in New Orleans, I went to Mississippi to speak at a panel about the state of the oiled gulf a year after the spill. It was there, in a drab hotel, that I was settling in with a Styrofoam box of takeout dinner when Nico called with big news.

"It's good," he typed simply when his face came up on my computer screen.

"What?" I asked. It was three days before I was to embark for The Hague, where I had appointments at the International Criminal Court. "What?" I asked more loudly, as the realization of what he was saying sunk in.

I started shrieking excitedly.

"*What?*"

He wasn't due for any missions that week; he was free to take some time off. He was going to hop in his car and meet me in the Netherlands. We were going to see each other again.

I could not stop screaming and laughing, but he was playing it cool. "It's good" was all he would say. He shrugged as if it were no big deal, but smiled slyly.

7.

Nico walked into my hotel room using the key I'd left at the front desk on a Tuesday afternoon in April, seven months after we'd met. I'd finished my meetings and war-crimes trials for the day, so had been trying to nap off some jet lag. He climbed into bed. When he kissed me, his face was cool from the cloudy Dutch skies.

He was shaking.

"Hey, baby," he said nervously; it was how all our Skyping chats had begun in type.

I said what I always said, too. Elated to say something to a face that wasn't separated from me by two computer screens and 6,000 miles, I sighed, smiling. "Hi, gorgeous."

It was a little bit awkward.

I'd had my concerns, obviously, about the language barrier, telling Tana and Alex that I didn't know what the hell we were going to say to each other, or how—since even when we typed, in the easier mode of reading rather than listening, our dialogue still moved at the excruciating pace of a sentence per minute. Nico hadn't tried *speaking* my language, the one we'd chosen as our primary, since the few sentences he'd choked out when we'd last seen each other. When he opened his mouth now, his words came with the thickness, slowness, and hesitation of a person who hadn't used his voice in years. As if his throat were full of syrup.

We were, additionally, strangers to each other's presence. No matter how many e-mails we'd sent about our love, our textures and smells and airs were entirely foreign again. Pleased as my fingers were to land on the smoothness of his skin and the strength of his arms, amid the further disorientation of being in a country that was alien to both of us, my body hesitated at his unfamiliarity, asking, *Who is this person?*

We didn't mind so much. That would all pass. We stowed ourselves away in bed at the Hotel Ibis Den Haag, a slick chain with Ikea-looking furniture about as charmless as the city's weather, with nothing but a glass of water and a French-English dictionary. Nico pressed on bravely and undiscouragedly, without verb tenses and articles, looking up or pantomiming nouns as we talked in simplified sentences, repeating ourselves repeatedly. That first night, after seven or so hours of sequestration, we left the room only because we'd become dizzy with hunger, going downstairs to order a pizza at the bar before the kitchen closed. We looked up *pineapple* together in his dictionary, and chatted over drinks while we waited for our Hawaiian to come out.

For a couple of days, I went to work, interviewing the chief prosecutor of the International Criminal Court, or mean-mugging the Congolese politician who was on trial for multiple counts of crimes against humanity and war crimes. I sat a few feet from him in the observation gallery while he watched the proceedings against him with his cantaloupe head sunk calmly into hunched shoulders. Then I came back to the hotel. And there was Nico.

Since Haiti, I'd been having sex with members of The Roster, but I'd entered nearly all of the encounters inebriated, and occasionally so disconnected that it was as if they hadn't happened at all, or at least not to me. Now I was having sex daytime-sober. It was not cloaked in the savvy city-person irony and cynicism of the elites I knew, but savagely earnest—*European* earnest—involving more eye contact than I'd had with everyone I'd ever slept with in my life combined. I could feel that it wasn't perfect, the uncomfortableness of unknown bodies. I could feel that *he* wasn't perfect. He looked like a romance-novel cover, but I didn't perceive him naively; I noticed a guardedness that I hadn't before, an edge that could fast turn him cold. It struck me as artificial, impermanent—as if I knew the real person inside this person I barely knew. But I could finally feel my limbs. And his weightiness. I managed to remain mostly present through the raw naked weirdness. Maybe I couldn't attach my feelings, the good ones as well as the questions about this highly improbable relationship, completely to my body, not get them permeated all the way down to the cellular level. But at least I had them.

I fell asleep overwhelmed with gratitude that when I woke up, he'd be next to me. I woke up ecstatic that he really was.

Didn't I think I was on top of my game, those couple of days in The Hague! Waking up early, walking with a purpose, pressed suits and morning meetings following efficiently ordered omelets, sober sex, no nervous break-downs. It's easy to feel that way when you're moving, strutting through inter-national airports on your way to a country you won't stay in long enough to ever feel like you've really landed, and then it's time to get in Nico's car so he can drive you to Belgium—rather than your taking the train in the wrong direction back to Amsterdam Airport Schiphol, for the next flight, to Africa—on his way back to France.

During our fourth and final dinner together, in the dining room of a con-verted seventeenth-century inn in Brussels, Nico told me he was disappointed in the way the trip had turned out.

We'd both been drawn to the white house, which was down the street from our B&B, by the ivy growing over its face. Inside, the ceilings were wooden, beamed; the room was warm and tight. Though Nico handled the ordering in this country—I'd been in charge of public interactions in English-fluent Holland—our waiters and fellow patrons, old and stuffy all, could hear enough of my native tongue to compel constant looks toward our table.

One moment, Nico was sitting next to me huddled close, sneaking kisses to the bare shoulder my shirt left exposed, and then the next, he was backing up, one forearm on the table and one at his side, head cocked back, chest tilted away from me in his chair.

"I hope[d] . . . you were . . . not amazing," he said, watching me from the distance he'd created. Glasses of wine and our translation dictionary clut-tered the table between us.

Before he'd arrived in the Netherlands, Nico had got his hopes up that things would go a certain way: He would drive to my hotel, be reunited with me, and be underwhelmed. He'd wanted, he explained, to be disappointed. He'd prayed that I was lackluster and overhyped, that once in front of me, he'd realize his love was baseless, founded on temporary insanity or a hormone im-balance or whatever it was that made him write me e-mails saying he felt like he could leave his whole French life for me. He didn't need to say the reasons he'd wanted that, because they were obvious. We lived in different countries. Language, plane fares, citizenship, employment, family, roots, cultural divides.

He looked sadder than I'd seen him yet when he uttered, defeated, "In fact, you are more amazing zhan I think before."

In the morning, we went to the Brussels airport for my flight to Kinshasa. Our despondence showed. The clerk at the ticket counter who couldn't find my reservation for a minute shrugged like it was no big deal that I might not have a ticket, nodding toward Nico, "He would be happy."

We hugged and kissed for so long that Nico got a parking ticket. But it was unsatisfying. Sad, fleeting kissing, the sort you couldn't give yourself all the way up to and that you couldn't count on having again. When we finally parted, I stamped out my disconcertion on my way through the terminal. As it bubbled up in a panting kind of cry, I resolved not to talk to him much anymore. It wasn't right that I felt like myself around him when he hardly knew me, and that he felt like home though I barely knew him, and certainly neither of us was anywhere near home then. Even if he for some reason felt inevitable—my main emotion in his presence was relief, *relief* that we were near each other—I couldn't continue to get wrapped up in someone I never knew when I would see again. If ever.

But it was only a month before I saw him again. After both assignments in Africa, I stopped in New York for work; once I got there, it was determined I had to go back to The Hague by the end of the week for the International Criminal Court unveiling of an arrest warrant for Muammar el-Qaddafi. I had a few days to get there. I flew into Paris.

Nico hopped a train from his region, in the east, near the German border. He arrived shortly after I'd installed myself in a borrowed apartment. Pacing the carpet of the petite bedroom, I happened to stop and look out the second-floor window toward the street just as he turned his green eyes skyward.

Every hour after sunset, the Eiffel Tower exploded in a glittering light show for the spring tourists. We walked the narrow streets behind Sacré Coeur in search of gelato, and stopped in a dark basement bistro for cassoulet. The staircase we scaled to get back to the flat wound past an ancient-looking mural of fleshy nude women and peacocks. But I didn't have any reaction to that. To that, or to the history dripping from the apartment, which I'd rented from an acquaintance of my father's named Peter Salk. It had belonged to his father, Jonas Salk, curer of polio and husband of Françoise Gilot, the painter who'd been Picasso's muse and the mother of his children. I'd noticed my indifference almost immediately, reciting the facts about the place to Nico but not caring. Then while watching Nico, gorgeous, passionate, his face alive across dinner tables but far away, his body sturdy but somehow insubstantial to me, arched on top of mine like a picture or projection. It became downright absurd when I woke up one morning to find him crouched bedside and shirtless with a bowl of strawberries he'd washed and lightly sugared. They were so tiny and delicate. He'd been to the market while I was asleep. He held one out to feed it to me as he placed a rose on my chest, and I couldn't make myself have any feelings about *that*. Not even when I tried.

At the very least, I thought, watching his muscles flex as he tended to me, *you could react to the fact that YOUR LIFE IS AN ABSURD SCENE IN A HARLEQUIN PAPERBACK.*

"You weren't there with me," Nico would say when we talked about this moment later.

My body, my desire still worked in a perfunctory way. And I wasn't upset, or crying, or melting down, which as of eight months ago always seemed like a victory. But no, back in Europe, just four weeks after I'd seen Nico there before, and though we had decided in the interim over a series of Skype conversations from Uganda that we would be exclusive—the ridiculousness of that be damned—I didn't have any feelings at all.

"[A] rapid and dramatic return to the appearance of normal functioning," Judith Lewis Herman warns in her book, though I hadn't read it yet, "should not be mistaken for full recovery."

Throughout the trip in Africa, where I spent the time between the Netherlands and Paris, I'd kept my cool and continued to feel good. In the Democratic Republic of the Congo, the assignment was to stalk a warlord, Bosco Ntaganda. He'd once led his own rebel group, but as part of a 2009 peace treaty had been incorporated into the national army. All along the way, Human Rights Watch and the International Criminal Court, which held an outstanding warrant for his arrest, had tracked his alleged atrocities: 800 civilians massacred in one town in 2002; 150 civilians massacred in a province in 2008; ongoing assassinations and disappearances; ongoing conscription of child soldiers. He'd recently disappeared a man who told researchers that Bosco had murdered his sister. His men had threatened some UN peacekeepers; his troops, several years ago, allegedly killed one. All my major Congolese sources were on the run from Bosco, who was so powerful and employed so many spies that I couldn't use Congolese translators for the interviews because of the danger both to them and the sources. Since Human Rights Watch had suggested that translators from actually any nearby countries in Africa weren't preferable, I hauled one named Joey all the way from the United States.

So it was still an intense trip.

After a long interview about assassinations with several guys in hiding one day, Joey was shaking. Understandably: The guys were under assassination threat as well, and toward the end, they'd begged us to help them by giving them money or getting them repatriated. Certainly you must know people who could help, they said. They said they'd certainly be murdered if we didn't.

"I might need you to hold me later," Joey said, nearly in tears, as they were leaving. But then looked at me more closely. "How are you so calm?"

A driver in Goma, eastern Congo, having also escaped a Bosco abduction, almost tossed me off the back of a motorbike while executing a hard skid to turn because he thought soldiers were following us. Another day, when an aid worker and I drove past Bosco's heavily guarded house, we indeed appeared to acquire a tail of a truck full of soldiers. One night, I met with one of Bosco's colonels at a bar. It gave me pause when he guessed that I usually drank my whiskey straight; I couldn't tell if he meant that I seemed like that kind of girl, or if he knew for a fact how I drank my whiskey because his people were following me. But unlike Joey, I didn't start having nightmares, even after we learned that another American reporter had been chased all over town after witnessing something he shouldn't have, spending his last night before he fled the country with all the furniture in his hotel room pushed up against the door, barricaded behind it, sleepless, with his eyes wide open and a knife in his hand. When I told one of my sources that I wouldn't publish any stories I wrote about Bosco until I arrived in Uganda, he shook his head. "They could easily kill you in Uganda," he said, not because he was being dramatic but because there were a lot of alliances there, and he'd been chased farther than that across the continent himself.

"I know Congo is hell," the same source said. "But better to stay in *this* hell. I feel that I have to help my country."

"I gotta get the fuck out of here," Joey said at breakfast on one of our last mornings, nightmare-frazzled. I laughed at him a little bit—me! Of all people!—but then Colonel I Know How You Drink Your Whiskey called my cell unexpectedly. When I asked him what he wanted, he said he just wanted to say hello. Just to see what I was up to. After we hung up, I put my earphones in and my iPod on shuffle in my hotel room, and it randomly picked "Private Eyes."

They're waatch-ing you. They see your evvvvveryyy moooove.

I stopped in my tracks on my way into the bathroom, feet on cool tiles, toothbrush in hand. *Oh I see you, oh I see you. Private, private, private eyes, girl.* I looked around the room, which was worn down but bright and airy; I looked out the wide window for anything suspicious in the field next door. It was still and grassy as usual. I turned toward the door and watched it hard, trying to intuit what might be on the other side in the dark hallway where the lights never, ever worked, for a second—before laughing and congratulating myself on not believing in signs or letting paranoia, and Hall & Oates, paralyze me. Even if it was justified: Human Rights Watch later assured me that I really was being followed.

Right. It was an intense trip. And being cool and prepared did not necessarily mean being well balanced.

"You are so calm all the time!" my Congolese fixer said.

"You are *verrrry* adaptable," my Ugandan fixer, Geoffrey, said, too, when I arrived in Kampala via Rwanda for the next assignment. I took both these statements as supreme compliments. But what kind of person should be calm all the time, anywhere? Much less on the human rights beat? In East and Central Africa?

One day I interviewed a Uganda expert at a café while riots raged down the street. We could hear intermittent gunfire, the bursts followed by people fleeing past us; that afternoon, the police killed two protesters. Later that night, I watched the news footage of men being bashed in the head with police batons on a projector screen at Sappho Islands, Uganda's only gay bar. That was why I was there: to cover the Kill the Gays bill on the table in Parliament. It proposed upping the penalty for having "aggravated" gay sex (with a minor, with an HIV-positive diagnosis, or with any frequency) from prison time to a death sentence. The good news was that no one I talked to thought it was going to pass, and the stories of the gay activists I was profiling were remarkably inspiring; they had either never been in the closet or had come out despite their knowing that it would cost them friends and school expulsions. They maintained offices for their activism organizations in the face of murder and arson threats. They gathered in this tiny bar, lit by Christmas lights inside and with a rainbow sign out front, for karaoke night. When the news was switched off and the karaoke started, I watched a couple slow-dance up front, near me, the boys so tender—unconcerned, for the moment, about being arrested. I recognized it as heartbreaking. But I couldn't feel my heart break.

I felt the brief clench in my chest for a second, and thought I would get misty-eyed. But I didn't. And in an instant, the feeling was gone, though I could still hear its logical iterations in my head. *That is so moving,* I thought. *That is so heartbreaking.* But feelings: Gone.

It wasn't that I had *no* feelings. It wasn't that I felt cheerless. I had a good time at karaoke. I performed a rendition of ". . . Baby One More Time" that earned me the nickname Britney Spears among members of Uganda's gay community who weren't even there. In Congo I'd had a lot of laughs with Joey and with my fixer, who called himself The Congolese Jack Bauer and called me Madame President, which was a *24* reference I didn't get. I felt an affinity for the Ugandan activists, and when Jack Bauer said, "There are few journalists who behave like you," and I had no idea what that meant, he added: "Your boyfriend must be the happiest." So I must have seemed delightful. But something was missing.

If there was any assignment I would've expected to overwhelm me emotionally, it was this one. Gay rights had always caught at something especially deep. The gloom I'd felt as a college kid at a Matthew Shepard vigil, like my organs were filled with thick blackness. The same heavy sensation had crept inside me when I was fourteen and a carful of guys whipped a screwdriver at my head from the window of a passing car, yelling something about fags, as I went for a romantic walk along the road. Ironically, the person I was snuggling then was a guy, but I was so butch-looking that they thought we were gay men. At sixteen, when I started making open displays of coupledom around northeast Ohio in a relationship that actually was gay, I entered places—restaurants, parking lots, Old Navy—proudly, but with my back up. My girlfriend, who had a blunt manliness to her but a feminine-pretty face that made people feel confused, and subsequently angry, had got in fights about her sexuality more than once. She'd had her car windows smashed in. When a guy at my school asked me out but I wouldn't go because I was dating her, he threw a locker door into my face.

In Uganda, I'd had to carefully vet my fixer for the assignment, feeling him out when I hired him, asking him what he thought about all of this antigay hullabaloo. After he'd considered for a moment, and said that it seemed a bit wild and unnecessary, he asked me what I thought, and it was my turn to consider my answer. An honest one involved the disclosure that I was bisexual, and I sat with it in my mouth, trying to remember the last time that particular anxiety had arisen, wondering if someone would refuse to work with me, or stop being nice, or start being weird, or hostile. I remembered: It was in Oklahoma. Not that safe passage was guaranteed even in San Francisco, famously the world's most gay-friendly city, where more than 200 incidences of antigay violence had been documented the previous year. I had two seconds to decide if I owed it to my convictions to tell Geoffrey the whole truth or if that was idiotic and unnecessarily reckless idealism. I chose the former.

Geoffrey didn't care. Mostly he got curious, and started asking me questions about whether a gay couple had to choose which one was going to be the man, and if so how the couple went about deciding that.

In Uganda, I could still sense it a little, the gloom. I felt it while I was sitting at Sappho Islands with Kasha, the bar's owner, a lanky, ropy dyke with dreads, asking her if she wasn't worried that someone would come in and hurt or arrest people, and she said that we weren't doing anything wrong, though she knew the penal code. The simultaneous fearlessness and danger about her. I felt it, too, when I walked into her gay-rights organization's secret office and into a meeting of dykes looking as unabashedly dyke-looking as any dykes, with polo shirts and baseball caps and squared shoulders. I felt it when I imagined them walking around outside that way.

But I didn't feel it as much as I should have. Not when I met Dennis, from another organization, and he had a scar near his eye from having had a bottle broken across his face, and it reminded me of my old boss in New Orleans, who was beaten so badly when he left a gay bar one night that he lost his right eye. Not when I saw the boys slow-dancing. Not even when I was leaving karaoke, and the lesbian who walked me to my taxi outside gave me her cell number. She said it was so I could call her when I got back to the hotel safe because "it happens" that a taxi driver would rape a girl out by herself, particularly "correctively" rape a girl who he just saw with a bunch of lesbians. I sat in the taxi still and ready to fight, waiting for the first move with a detached and matter-of-fact dauntlessness about battling until one of our last breaths. I was confident it would be his. But if this guy did manage to strike nonconsensual carnal treasure that night, he was going to be prying it from my cold, dead thighs.

A lot of folks who've survived trauma end up being really calm in crisis and freaking out in everyday life, Meredith had said.

There were other hints that I wasn't running on all emotional pistons. Though I drank on only a few nights—I wasn't going to *not* drink at gay karaoke night—I spent as much of the trip as I could as checked-out as a person can be while sober: watching TV. I'd started doing this to some extent toward the end of my Deepwater Horizon deployment, sitting down on days off for three hours or four at a time, tired, ultimately watching every episode of *30 Rock*. Then between Haiti I and Haiti II, there were days, everyone knew, when I did nothing else.

In Uganda, my TV binges were epic for a person on a work assignment. The third-rate movie station in my gleaming, ultramodern Kampala hotel played the same film almost constantly, in which Alec Baldwin lives on the bayou and gets caught up in a murder mystery. It was boring—though I did like that the characters were realistically doused with Southern Louisiana sweat. I did my job when I had to, but my reluctance to leave my room was becoming pathological. It wasn't that I couldn't, as in Haiti; I just didn't *want* to. A couple of days into Uganda I was struck down with some African flu that Joey, my translator, had been puking all over the Rwandan roadside as I escorted him from Goma (which had no international airport) to Kigali for his flight back to the U.S. before I continued on. It was horrible crawling back and forth to my hotel toilet, alone, with no company for days but the maid who kept threatening to tell her boss and force me into the hospital if I didn't get better soon because if I died in one of her rooms, there'd be trouble. I was in agony. But I was really glad to have the excuse not to go anywhere.

Maybe I was burned out. Maybe something in my body didn't want to do any more of the type of witnessing that going out entailed.

"Where were you?" Dennis, of the under-eye scar, hollered at me when we went to a bar's unofficial Gay Night a few nights later. ("We're the biggest clients," Dennis explained of the establishment's tolerance.) Geoffrey, who'd driven us and a couple of other homos to the club, was by then taking gay company in stride, feeling that he'd learned some things. "They are just like any other human beings, with feelings and entitlements," he remarked to me sagely. Also: "They are so courteous!"

So I'd felt comfortable leaving him and Dennis together, wandering away from our table to interview the patrons, all soap-and-cologne-smelling, wearing impeccable jeans. There was dancing and flirting, and the occasional lip gloss. Over by the bar, a toned and sanguine gentleman commented that I stood too much like a man not to have sex with women; when I confirmed that I did, he asked me if I was "free" to disclose it to my parents. I admitted that I hadn't been, since before I could decide to come out I got caught, at sixteen, the immediate aftermath of which involved my father telling me how twisted and fucked up I was. When I asked the gentleman the same question in turn, he dropped his head and smiled.

It wasn't always as free as people thought it was for gays in the States, either, I told him. At one point in college I'd had a roommate who was also queer, and I remember the day her mother called our apartment at six in the morning, demanding to speak to her. "She's still sleeping," I said when I answered the phone, laughing because most people would still be sleeping. "Do you want me to wake her up?"

Her mother, who'd somehow discovered evidence of a lesbian relationship, was not laughing. "*Yesss,* I want you to wake her up," she said, "so I can tell her how DISGUSTING she is."

I wasn't talking to the boys at the bar for long. But when I returned to Dennis, he was hollering. "Where *were* you?" he demanded.

I told him where I was.

"I couldn't see you! I thought you were kidnapped for corrective rape." When I made a horrified face, he grabbed my arm and yelled, "Just kidding!"

"Do you know a lot of women that has happened to?" I asked.

"Nooooo, not a lot," he said. "Like, five."

One tried-and-true impact of trauma, Meredith said, *is people just really shutting themselves down.*

Two transatlantic flights and ten days later, Uganda to New York to Paris, in the curtain-filtered morning light of Jonas Salk's apartment, my sweater draped over Claude Picasso's childhood desk, there was Nico with his sweetness and his bowl of perfect strawberries. And I did seem to be having some trouble responding to it, yeah.

I seemed fine enough to me. Both in Paris—if I wasn't having any feelings about Nico, that was Nico's fault—and when I finally returned to San Francisco, after seven and a half weeks away. I had never freaked out, or been crippled by sadness, though everyone I'd interviewed was under threat of being gay-bashed or murdered. I had not been afraid. Because fear is a normal response—something to overcome, not something to stop experiencing entirely—I might have been concerned about my lack of human emotions.

Instead, I congratulated myself. I was not hysterical. This was not, as far as I was concerned, constriction, the name for post-traumatic emotional anesthesia, a concept I hadn't heard of yet. This was—I was—an awesome feat of efficiency.

I didn't think therapy was in order. I didn't have time, anyway. In less than three weeks, I would start a monthlong assignment living with a married couple in Columbus, Ohio; they were, like me, Ohio State graduates, and they were likely about to be laid off by the new governor's budget cuts.

In the meantime, I got ready, and resumed my walks with Alex. We labored up the hills in bright but crisp Pacific air, the city's abutting, painted houses looming above us, as we puzzled over how weird it was that no number of shared gelatos or café conversations on cobbled Paris streets had evoked any feelings for Nico. Unable to find another explanation, I chalked it up to failed and fleeting chemistry. I took a break from packing, and called him up on Skype to tell him we had no future together.

8.

I could have lived like that. For a long time. People do it. Like a piece of cardboard, walking around tall and flat in the world, without nerve endings, sinews stiff enough to keep any weakness they're holding safely twined up. It keeps the good things from getting in, too. But you barely register emptiness when you only have two dimensions. People do it, keep their constriction mostly intact; except for the moments when they don't.

"Equally as powerful as the desire to deny atrocities is the conviction that denial does not work," says Judith Lewis Herman. "Remembering and telling the truth about terrible events are prerequisites both for the restoration of the social order and for the healing of individual victims." I had no such eloquently realized agenda when I wrote an essay about how PTSD had ruined my life and my sex life. Pieces of it had floated around my brain for months, and they started coming together while I was pacing the patio out behind a café in Congo where I was waiting all day in case my warlord, a regular patron, might appear. While Joey dicked around on the Internet inside, in the same place where one of our sources had been found by and escaped from would-be assassins, I took to an abandoned stretch of the meandering, scrabbly yard, attempting to march some energy out back and forth under the blinding sun. I put the rest of the notes together in the few weeks I was home in San Francisco before leaving for Ohio. Sentences about it wrote themselves across my consciousness while I was trying to fall asleep, and the moment I woke up.

"I don't think you should write about this," one of my friends said. He wasn't the last.

"Yeah," I agreed. But it seemed like a foregone conclusion that I would. I felt like it was important. I felt like I had to, though I wasn't entirely sure why. One of the worst things about having PTSD—worse even than the symptoms oftentimes—was feeling that no one understood. If someone else had written a piece like the one I was composing and I'd been able to read it, I would've felt less alone those hard months after Haiti I. As a writer, how could I sit around wishing someone else was writing about it? I wanted to write about it, anyway. When I presented the gist of the story to a friend (and groundbreaking feminist) who edited a magazine, I told her I felt like it was a conversation that needed to happen. She agreed, and assigned it.

I worked on the essay between Africa and Ohio, forcing out sentences about how I'd gone to Haiti from the Deepwater Horizon Gulf, where one moment had also got a bit hairy in Oklahoma, and that I'd lost track of my own body in the car during the rape-related witnessing in Haiti. It was harder than I'd thought. I encountered a severe and extremely uncharacteristic case of writer's block.

"I can't do this," I told Tana, calling her from the back steps of my apartment.

"OK, I know you know people are going to attack you," Isaac said when I called him the next time it happened. "People hate when journalists admit they're human, and ladies who like having sex." Or lady journalists who touched the subject of sexual assault: A few months earlier, CBS correspondent Lara Logan had publicly acknowledged that she'd been brutally raped and beaten by an entire group of men while on assignment in Egypt, and her disclosure still garnered jokes, dismissals, and blame in the media. I was unlikely to get any breaks for getting *not* raped. "But fuck 'em," Isaac said. "This is important to you, and you've got this."

I wanted to do it. I didn't want to not do it just because of the consequences. I thought I could handle them.

I wrote about Henri and The Doctor. I admitted that when I'd gone to Haiti again I became sexually obsessed with guns. I admitted that when I'd been with Nico there I couldn't feel his weight or my arms. I admitted to all the crying, and the gagging, and the self-hate. I talked about my talks with Meredith, and some of what I'd learned about trauma and my nervous system, and how devastating it was that I hadn't been able to touch myself without appalling flashbacks. I admitted what I'd done with Isaac. That when he held me

down and punched me in the face, it had helped with the screaming-flashback
sex problem, and the not-being-able-to-see-rape-on-TV-without-going-
apoplectic problem, and the ultimate abatement of many of my symptoms.

It was a lot to cop to. As I polished the sentences before sending them to
the editor, I leaned on tequila—they seemed impossible to read back over,
and made me feel like I couldn't breathe. But once I'd turned it in, I largely
put it out of my mind and went on with the rest of my work.

Sober.

The Ohio assignment was a dry assignment. For one, the married people
I was living with, in their guest bedroom, were near teetotalers with a baby.
For another, who needed daily booze when your own insides were a veritable
wellspring of numbness? Even without that, my circumstances would have
kept me plenty distracted: I had to report and file three stories a week on the
decline of the middle class, the governor's proposal to slash local government
budgets by 50 percent, and the fight to reinstate the union rights he'd recently demolished. At some point during that time, I also had to write the
feature on Congo. And I had to find some time for video dates with my
boyfriend, stationed in barracks somewhere in France.

Yes, I had told Nico that we had no future. But that conversation turned
out to be more of a heads-up than a breakup. I didn't want him thinking that
we were, say, moving toward marriage or anything, but something held me
back from a full good-bye. Though recalling images of us in Paris together still
jogged zero loving emotions, I kept remembering one afternoon when we'd
lain on the Salkses' couch, chatting, our faces touching, the left side of my
nose against the left side of his, nose tips into each other's cheeks. As I
could feel myself drifting off, I'd thought, *No one falls asleep like this*, that
close, breaths mingling irritatingly, even if it looked romantic from the outside. But I wasn't irritated. I was full of a deep kind of peace spread outward
from my belly button, and in tandem we'd sunk into sleep.

Other than that, though: nothing. So I'd issued a caveat as a courtesy.
Don't rely on me. I can't imagine my life without our continuing to talk, so it
doesn't have to end right now, but it will. It seemed like the right thing to do.

Watching his face, small on the other side of the computer screen, I saw a
few tears escape his little eyes.

"Don't cry," I said. Since our rendezvous in Europe, we'd evolved to talking out loud.

"Don't tell me we have no future," he said.

He asked me if I generally informed people that I knew a relationship was going nowhere but that I didn't want to break up. I admitted that I didn't.

So, he wanted to know, why was I doing that with him? He told me I didn't know what I wanted. He told me I was wrong.

"You will see," he said. And he'd looked so sure, I couldn't help believing him.

Now, at any spare moment in my Ohio sources' house, we resumed our conversations.

"Hi, gorgeous," I would begin when he appeared on my screen. "How was your day?"

I spoke very slowly, perfectly enunciating each word, with a space between every one.

One.

Word.

At.

A.

Time.

Whenever he still couldn't understand, even after many tries, I would type the sentence or word out in English.

I'd aborted my few determined forays into French lessons over the past months. It was a miracle I was mustering the extra energy to do my laundry, much less tackle fluency of a convoluted tongue. Nico didn't want to talk in French, anyway. He wanted to *live* English. His bravery about it leveled me with admiration and made me envious enough to strangle him. If he didn't know a word, he merely ventured forward with a guess. "I want to make love with you on the workplan," he said to me once, because he thought that might be the word for *counter*. I never could have been so fearless. If I didn't know the word for *counter*, I would have excused myself from the conversation, looked it up in the dictionary, called a French expert to verify the pronunciation, practiced the sentence out loud at least a dozen times where no one could hear me, then maybe have been ready to try it on him next month.

Nico took my corrections utterly unself-consciously. He improved every day. One day when I was in Ohio, he heard me use my regular, all-syllables-strung-fast-together English to say something to someone in the house, and he got that I was talking about shoes. Brown shoes. It was a major breakthrough.

So every moment in Ohio was accounted for. I was hustling. I was working, or I was talking to Nico. Or I was spending time with my source-host family. The wife had just finished her school year as a junior-high teacher and was celebrating her transition into summer vacation with hours upon hours of my second-favorite self-medicating activity: television! At night, everyone sat around watching *MasterChef*, we women attempting and failing to distract the baby from pulling the power cord out of the husband's laptop while he tried to apply for jobs in the run-up to his impending government layoff. During the day, between reporting gigs and interviews, I could spend a break joining mother and child in front of TiVo episodes of *Toddlers and Tiaras* or *My Big Fat Gypsy Wedding* or *The Bachelorette* or *Tosh.0*, my whole universe either reality TV or running around working, for weeks, humming and vibrating like a hologram, feeling like I might start shaking with energy and tension but remaining blissfully if unsettlingly numb.

Not everyone thought I was doing as awesomely as I thought I was. I drove several hours to Cleveland one weekend to report on the trend of people squatting in the city's multitude of foreclosed homes. Specifically, to report how one of those people was my sister Jessica. I hadn't seen her in a while, and we hugged hard when I arrived at "her" house that drizzly June afternoon. Having followed her through the kitchen, its walls ripped up, I sat down to talk to her on a couch among piles of discarded crap—hers or the former owners', I wasn't clear—and found myself the object of her concerned gaze. My sister, who, at thirty-five, waited tables at a fancy restaurant in Shaker Heights but had been living in this abandoned house with her boyfriend for nine months because he couldn't find a job (and what was the point of paying rent when there were all these perfectly good empty houses?), was generally not much of a worrier. Definitely she was not prone to worrying about me. Now her pale eyes stared at me intently, expectantly, as if she was waiting for me to do something drastic though I sat calmly. "How are you *doing*?" she kept asking me. "Are you O-*K*?" She took me upstairs to show me the laser-sighted Kimber .45 handgun she kept in her room given the neighborhood's crime stats, and told me that because she often drove home alone at night she kept knives in her car. But of the two of us, it was she who kept saying that *I* was scaring *her*.

She could see me. And when I could see her seeing me, in that instant, I wanted to curl up in a ball and never stop crying.

I told her I was fine. But I couldn't wait to get out of there.

I hemmed it up and hemmed it in. Kept it compartmentalized. Kept myself busy enough not to have a second to feel. So what if it was only skin-deep, the cold functionality? It served its purpose. It didn't last anyway. It might not have lasted regardless, since, I would later learn from literature and experience, the post-traumatic-stress-disordered often vacillate between phases of symptoms, moving from intrusion—the crying and howling nightmares and other asylum-worthy behaviors—to constriction and back, without predictability or reason. It's one of the many things that undermine their credibility with the outside world: People seem fine for a while, but then they're not fine, or they go from one extreme set of symptoms to an opposite one. But either way my tidy detachment couldn't have lasted one second after the essay I'd written about my PTSD was published.

When the editor texted me that it had gone live, it was National PTSD Awareness Day. I was parked on a leafy side street in Columbus. It was about a month after I'd returned from Europe and Africa, and five months after Haiti II, and whatever was holding my emotions broke and let loose a flood of grief and alarm and the most toxic sludge of all: shame. There it was, all of it out there, and I couldn't take the vulnerability I'd created back. I started hyperventilating, but had just a few minutes before I had to get out of the car and walk to my interview with an Ohio state representative. I took notes with shaking fingers.

Everybody knows that sad people often drink too much. There's a conventional wisdom that grants recognition and some sympathy along the lines of "Oh, she was abused as a kid" or "lost a child" or "had a really rough marriage, and drinks a lot," even if the *extent* of the relationship between trauma and substance abuse remains less acknowledged—that, for example, raped women who develop PTSD are 26 times more likely to become substance abusers than the non-crime-victim population. That 75 to 85 percent of veterans with PTSD turn to booze. I didn't feel too embarrassed about having announced publicly that I'd had some drinking problems. But going on the record about trauma-related sex dysfunction was a whole other thing. No one ever said anything about things like that. I sensed that I probably wasn't the first person in history to experience it, and Meredith had made comments that supported that notion, but I didn't personally know any of these other supposed people, either. Of all the unlimited crap online, support groups and information dumps and chat rooms, even Internet searches didn't turn up much. When I'd disclosed the gunpoint fantasy, the *less* weird PTSD-sex thing I had going on, to one of my friends, she'd looked at me wide-eyed and yelled, "You're completely nuts!"

The editor had headlined my essay "I'm Gonna Need You to Fight Me on This: How Violent Sex Helped Ease My PTSD."

So I felt like throwing up, vomiting distress and degradation over every surface, the moment the essay became public. That sickness did not improve when a coworker I barely knew wrote an e-mail to someone at one of the biggest media organizations in the world clarifying that I'd "had psychological issues" way before Haiti, and then forwarded it to me. Later, another coworker e-mailed me the advice that I could consider it a dire learning experience and still save myself from "career kamikaze." Other reporters and bloggers wrote articles about the essay, but though they were positive at first, I couldn't bear to read them. I heard from the editor that there were hundreds of comments of support—some from PTSD sufferers with similar experiences—posted on the piece, but I couldn't look at those, either. My stability had been thoroughly compromised from the inside, even before, several days later, I woke up to find my face on the cover of a major Web magazine in connection with an article titled "Mac McClelland: What's Happening in Haiti Is Not About You."

I'd known the essay would go over poorly in some corners. Trauma was a tough enough topic on its own, much less a woman's trauma, much less trauma coupled with sex. And Haiti, I knew from having written about it, evoked particularly strong feelings and territorialities, even from other outsiders. The previous year, when I'd published a piece about Daniel, the source I visited in his tent camp—who happened to live in the camp managed by an aid group founded by Sean Penn—I immediately started receiving scary e-mails from Penn. He excoriated me for not being responsible enough to include Penn's perspective, and for damaging the country by quoting Daniel on his dire assessment of his own life in camp. So while Sean Penn didn't "want a war with" me, he would "go ALL THE WAY DOWN on this" if I didn't go back and rewrite the story.

But I'd still underestimated how poorly the essay would go over. "[A Haitian victim's] violent rape feeds McClelland's need to feel victimized," the aforementioned article said, calling me "shockingly narcissistic." "I mean all of Port-au-Prince is suffering from PTSD and I'm supposed to care about some woman who parachutes in for a couple of weeks and has the luxury to leave whenever she wants because she's been inconveniently traumatized?" "If being in Haiti, or Bosnia, or Egypt, or Syria, or Libya is so damaging to these reporters' psyches, perhaps they should stop reporting from these places."

"She makes use of stereotypes about Haiti," said another piece that a group of (mostly non-Haitian) women who'd lived or worked in Haiti collectively published, "that would be better left in an earlier century: the savage men consumed by their own lust, the omnipresent violence and chaos, the danger encoded in a black republic's DNA . . . . Ms. McClelland's Haiti is not the Haiti we know. Indeed, we have all lived in relative peace and safety there. This does not mean that we are strangers to rape and sexual violence."

I was surprised that because I'd mentioned having sex with Nico, a *New York Times* reporter questioned whether I was a reporter or a UN prostitute, though having gone to Catholic school I should have been the last person caught unprepared for slut-shaming. I was surprised that writing about FA-VILEK's rape cases, being threatened, and the visibility of guns in the country led to accusations that my real problem was that I was a racist who was afraid of the lust of "savage" black men. My fellow journalists waged a war of articles and Twitter tirades, one side calling me sensationalist, self-glorifying, exaggerating, irresponsible, colonialist, and self-involved, and the other calling *those* people bullies, victim-blamers, hypocrites, silencers, racism-projectors, and PTSD-deniers.

There's a weird but common misperception about how trauma works that was illustrated by the fight they were having—that trauma exists only in the realm of those who have it worse than anyone else in the world. I myself held this misperception, the way I'd argued with Meredith that it was impossible for me to be traumatized. First, I hadn't suffered anything serious. Second, the circumstances of my life generally caused me little suffering. I was in the bottom of the right-to-suffer caste system; it makes a kind of sense culturally, if not biologically.

"Wowww," Alex said, calling me in Ohio to check on me, her speech slow and distracted as she scrolled through the controversy on her computer screen. "This is why guys like my dad never say anything." Her dad served as a naval officer in Vietnam, a combat adviser to local forces. He did, well, "God knows what he did," as Alex generally put it; "I don't even want to know." Whatever he did, he came home amped up but closed down. And though he was extremely high-functioning, working and earning well for his family, he stayed closed down and tightly wound after Alex was born and, in some ways, forever. It wasn't until she started going to therapy herself as an adult that she realized how impacted she remained by having grown up with a dad like that, and started begging him to go to the VA for assessment.

It turned out he was one of the estimated 30 percent of Vietnam veterans with PTSD. Forty years after his military service had ended, his psych evaluation showed such severe PTSD that the government rated him at 80 percent disabled. By then, PTSD had been in the news plenty regarding vets from Iraq and Afghanistan, but *no one*, Alex's dad told her, could know about his diagnosis. The military at the time of his service hadn't made any secret of its disdain for traumatized soldiers. And when a gunnery sergeant told him to change out of his uniform as soon as he landed in the United States before facing a public that hated him for his involvement in the war, he couldn't be left with any doubt that he wasn't going to find much understanding anywhere else, either.

Alex had used to think that her father's refusal to acknowledge his condition wasn't necessarily in his best interests, as he had always claimed. Alex's dad had been through much worse than I had or could even imagine, but though our situations weren't comparable, she felt she understood his secrecy better now. "Maybe that was smart," she said over the phone, laughing, sadly and only half-joking.

Judith Lewis Herman discusses in her book why people are so resistant to sympathize with a traumatized person. Traumatized people are saying, if inadvertently, *Share the burden of my pain* when they admit what's happened to them. *Do something—acknowledge it, at the very least.* Share the experience of knowing—while eating cereal in the morning and putting one foot in front of the other out the door on the way to work—that it is an atrocious world where something heinous could happen to you at any moment. Traumatized people are victims, of time or place or circumstance or evil, and nobody likes victims. It sounds counterintuitive at first, but it's easier to identify with a perpetrator. A rapist, a child molester. People who are in control, who are in power, who have power, who are on the winning side. People love stories about murderers. Not the sad-sack families they leave in their wake, needing everyone to remember what happened to their loved ones while they take years and years to get over it, keeping in mind the dreadfulness and injustice, or in the case of veterans, guilt. Victims ask you to uphold human rights and decency and help. Repression and denial allow you to do nothing, which is inarguably easier.

Consequently, the thing about character assassinations of victims was that they weren't exclusive to people whose traumatic incidents were of questionable seriousness or who had as many advantages in life as I did.

"Why don't they just *leave*," a culture communally asks of abused women—siding, by default, with wife-beaters. In 1964, a study of battered women determined that they had personality disorders that caused them to need and provoke battering. A 1988 study of a major hospital emergency room showed that doctors regularly described battered women as hysterics and masochists. In the eighties, some psychoanalysts tried to add "masochistic personality disorder" to the *DSM* to describe what's wrong with women in abusive relationships.

I would've avoided that situation, victims make people think, self-defensively. *Or handled it better. That wouldn't have happened to me. Not like that.*

In 2003, when a teenager named Elizabeth Smart was found after nine months of captivity with the man who'd abducted her, raped and tortured her, and threatened to kill her and her family, all everybody wanted to know was: Why didn't she just run away? At the time, I was sure that I would have. I was a twenty-three-year-old post-college feminist then, and I remember thinking, *What was her deal?*

"Denial, repression, and dissociation operate on a social as well as an individual level," Herman says. Even in her field, even a hundred years after Freud, she and other trauma researchers and practitioners found themselves sometimes shunned or sidetracked and invalidated by questions of PTSD victims' faking it, asking for it, or being untrustworthy—and therefore, as subjects, void. They found themselves harassed for taking victims' sides. "In spite of a vast literature documenting the phenomena of psychological trauma," she wrote in the nineties, "debate still centers on the basic question of whether these phenomena are credible and real."

A public debate about whether my own symptoms were credible and real wasn't doing great things for my stability. My already precarious condition had been steadily deteriorating since the moment the piece published, and I wasn't up to weathering much without my happy if not-so-healthy numbness intact anymore. By the end of the week, I reacquainted myself with daytime drinking, to the concern of my Ohio hosts. When the second phase of the backlash kicked in a couple of weeks later, taking a turn from calling me racist and narcissist to malicious and unethical, no amount of booze made my symptoms survivable, and I asked a friend to drive me late one night to the house of another friend who had benzodiazepines.

When I'd been in Haiti the previous fall, and the American lawyer for whom Marc worked had e-mailed me asking me to not include certain details in the final story, I'd offered to call her. She was unable to schedule a chat but sent two more e-mails, including one that asked me not to demonize the victim-blaming doctor. Then, suddenly, she e-mailed my editors saying that before I started to report the story, I'd assured Marc that I'd give her final approval over everything I wrote. That was news to me. I would've remembered it, since that wasn't how journalism generally worked, and she hadn't mentioned the supposed agreement among her other concerns so far. Since she didn't like the direction of the other Internet coverage my tweets were getting, she informed my editors, she was hereby instructing both Marc and another source, a rape survivor, to stop talking to me and revoking their consent to do a story.

Marc, who I saw daily for the duration of the trip, denied any such revocation and continued doing interviews with me. Five weeks later, after I'd returned to San Francisco, after the lawyer had not returned e-mails and phone calls from my editors, she made good on revoking the other source's consent, e-mailing a scanned written note from the rape survivor saying that I didn't have, and had never had, permission to write about her.

The magazine feature I'd written about her and FAVILEK and everything I'd seen and all the interviews I'd done was about to ship to the printer. There was no way I could contact the note-writer, though we went to great lengths to try. So we pulled the story. I stayed up late rewriting large portions of it, and just a few anonymous references to her case appeared in the final print. But when I published the PTSD-sex essay, which contained an anonymous description of a moment when our stories became entwined, during the witnessing and terror and screaming of that first, life-altering morning, the lawyer apparently made the note revoking consent available for publication.

My detractors were elated. Here, finally, was proof that I was as integrity-less as they'd been claiming all along.

Even as psychologically weak as I was, I couldn't agree with most of what they were saying. I didn't feel like the reason I'd felt threatened in Haiti was because I was racist—I'd never said all my sexual harassers there were black, because they weren't. I didn't think that a devastating natural disaster had managed to devastate Haiti only because it was populated by black people. And I knew, because I was there, that what had happened wasn't that I'd just never had consent. But those disagreements aside, and however absurd and obtuse some of my critics were being on some levels, the main idea they were peddling was one I'd thought was probably true for a while now, and lately was feeling unconditionally convinced of.

I was a disgusting person.

DSM-V Criteria for PTSD, Criterion D, number 2: "Persistent (and often distorted) negative beliefs and expectations about oneself or the world (e.g., 'I am bad,' 'The world is completely dangerous')."

Other people were making up wrong reasons why I was a disgusting person. It didn't matter; I knew that there were real ones. I couldn't say exactly from where my overwhelming sense of shame was coming, but I also couldn't say that I wouldn't find any deserving origins if I went looking for them.

I mean, where could I even start? I was mercifully unconvinced by the *Times* reporter's theory that I was a "geisha to the NGO republic" posing as a reporter. But the argument could definitely be made that I was an adulterous whore.

Look at my marriage. My ex-husband was a good man. A better man has never lived, and he deserved the best. Any woman could have, should have, been fulfilled being married to him. But I wasn't. That alone was evidence that serious things were wrong with me. Then, when our marriage started falling apart, we'd agreed to try seeing other people—in retrospect, a last-ditch grasp that made things worse, not better. It had been my idea. And I had ended up with a mistress, and though it was technically allowed within the rules we'd set, I could tell that my husband wasn't happy about it. And I did not, I could not, let her go. I spent every second with her that I could, switching my wedding band from my left, dominant hand to my right when I would put my fingers inside her.

And I was the one who'd talked him into jumping into the marriage in the first place, when he'd been concerned that we were too young and were rushing.

And my divorce—getting divorced, period—showed that I made bad decisions, and hurt people, and was a failure.

And, OK, all the reasons people were saying I was a monster weren't wrong. I absolutely agreed with their contention that I didn't deserve to have PTSD.

How *dare* I cry about my life, as a white person who lived in America and had a good job and hadn't even been hurt, they demanded. I'd spent hours demanding the same of Meredith, and my friends, and myself. I had never come up with a satisfactory answer. And Meredith's and Tana's had sounded like cop-out bullshit.

And even though I hadn't earned it, now I had a mental illness. Not because of genetics or hormones, but because of some little outside events, and as far as that was concerned, nobody thought I was more weak and disgusting than I did.

Also, when I was in grad school, I worked for a literary festival, and one time, on the last day, a patron gave me one or two twenties (I forget) for some merchandise after we'd closed out all our receipts, and I pocketed it.

And one time, in the course of my fifteen-year sexual history, I fucked around with a married guy.

And by one time, I mean several times.

And by one married guy, I mean two.

When I was in junior high, on a couple of occasions I made up elaborate stories and told them to my friends as though they were truth, even crying at the sad parts. About this same time, there was a girl who'd been newly integrated into my friend group, and I don't remember if I found her boring or annoying, but I convinced my best friend that we should dump her, and we did. She was so heartbroken that her older sister came and yelled at us at recess the next day.

And the semester after the semester that Hurricane Katrina had ruined, when school was back in session, I had one student in my freshman composition class who kept failing to turn in his assignments. "But I live in a FEMA trailer with my entire family," he would say when I wouldn't take his paper because it was weeks late. "It is so hard," he pleaded with me. But I refused to grade it.

Life is hard, I told him. Lots of people have to figure out how to write their papers in bad environments.

And now, if the spin were accurate, I had upset a rape survivor who'd already been through a lifetime's worth of too much—and I couldn't know how upset she was, or if the people saying she was upset had even told her what the essay said and didn't say, since she couldn't read English any better than I could Creole, and since no one would let me talk to her or, as far as I could tell, even ask her if she wanted to talk to me.

Marc had refused to give me her contact info. He said he wasn't allowed. I thought about flying to Haiti. I would continue to consider it for years. It hadn't been my intent to ignore her wishes, much less to exploit her for personal glory, which was why I hadn't written even 1 percent of the memories or material I had. I thought I'd not talked about her story but for the intersection where she was unavoidably one of the biggest parts of mine. But now I couldn't tell if I had traumatized her anyway. Had I retraumatized her? The article in which she was briefly quoted said that she was angry, and that was the writer's word, not hers. When I had written the offending piece, I had considered that moment when we were in the same place a story that belonged to me, too, because the rest of my existence had hinged on it. If the moral and ethical breach in writing it was not a gray area and was in fact as clear and evil as some people were saying, it could only have happened because I was too sick and disgusting to understand that. Even if they were wrong, the possibility remained that I had angered a person I had fervidly wanted not to.

In any case, when I said *No*, I wanted people to respect that without qualification and no questions asked. And I had failed to do that for her. I hadn't been able to figure out a way to disconnect us, a way both to own my trauma and do that for her. It would remain my strongest and most convincing point of self-disgust for a very long time.

There were those examples. There were other examples. Anyway, I could point to a general, nagging certainty, from deep within my bowels, that I was vile. I didn't think it was because that's what people with PTSD think. I was sure it was because I was right. I was nowhere near emotionally lucid enough to see those processes clearly, and it would take many months for me to be able to recognize and name them. In the meantime, I just knew I was incapable of any kind of peace. My shame was real and physical, and the pervasive fear I'd kicked after my first assignment in Haiti was back with a vengeance.

Having returned to San Francisco from Ohio, landing this time in the worst shape yet, I shook, always internally, and often visibly to outsiders. My stomach felt like it was full of stimulants, agitated and edgy like I'd throw up anytime I opened my mouth. I slept with the help of chemicals, and still woke up in the middle of the night panicked, sick, jolts of bad electricity passing through me, doubling me over, nerves sparking like my skin would catch fire. I arranged shifts with my friends to come babysit me. When I left the house, if I wasn't a numbed-out zombie, I sometimes started crying when I was talking to people, like a maniac, and if I didn't, even people who weren't very intuitive could tell I was on the verge of crying at any time.

"Oh, yeah, I've heard of you," a massage therapist whom Alex had recommended said at the beginning of our appointment, as the articles continued piling up. "And not in the good way."

There was a tiny flickering inside me, a flinching pilot light that said that my intentions were good and important; that my truth was valid. I found it impossible not to feel attacked. And sorry for myself. My sorrow extended far beyond my own suffering: Sorrow for Alex's dad. Sorrow for anyone who'd been traumatized and now heard trauma called narcissistic or weak because of me. I was worried that all I'd succeeded in doing was making them feel worse about themselves.

As it turned out, the concern between me and other traumatized people was mutual.

> To: Mac McClelland
> Date: Tue, Jul 5, 2011 at 6:17 PM
> Subject: "I'm Going to Need You to Fight Me on This"
>
> Dear Ms. McClelland,
>
> I'm writing because your piece really resonated with me. I have never been in the kind of extreme situations your work involves you in, but I was physically abused by my father from the time I was two until I was nineteen. He was a guerilla fighter in Africa while still in his teens so no doubt he played out his own trauma in this way; not that I forgive him. My family copes by pretending it didn't happen and also by implying that I am either malicious or nuts—or both—whenever I referred to it. Not surprisingly I stopped trying to get them to admit to it. I went away to college and pretty much didn't go back.
>
> Flash forward to me thirty-three years old, married and working at a church, trussed up on a dentist's chair *on stage* in a bondage club, taking a beating from the house dominatrix. I did this for about a year—never really engaging in the BDSM community

and never taking any sexual pleasure in it. I just felt compelled
to do it. After a year I stopped going and seven years later I still
feel no need to go back.

As to why I did it, I needed to take a beating and know that I
was totally in control of it. At any time I could have used the safe
word and gotten out of what was happening. It's not the same
thing that you did, but I think it came out of the same impulse.
My husband (now ex-husband) and my friends thought that I
was sick and sleazy, but really I was trying to get better. I don't
claim that it cured my PTSD, but while I was doing it, it definitely
seemed to help, and until my husband left me and then I had a
relationship with a sociopath (yeah—I know how to pick 'em) I
felt a lot stronger and less traumatized by the violence in my
childhood. I don't think the same thing would help me now, but
it helped me then.

I hope you don't end up feeling sorry that you published this
piece, because I was really glad to read it.

Best wishes,
Paula

To: Mac McClelland
Date: Tue, Jun 28, 2011 at 7:49 AM
Subject: Thank you.

Hi Mac,

I developed a submissive sexuality after being raped at thirteen.
I've spent a lot of time in therapists' office trying to figure out
exactly why, but you put it perfectly.

While I enjoy the simple sensation of pain as well as being
dominated, what's most important is the pushing of boundaries,
knowing that I can handle the violence I've asked for. I feel

relieved, loose, sane afterwards. It's really the only stress relief technique I know. The best kind of therapy.

I am also active in feminist communities, where it's often difficult to discuss incorporating violence into sex without being criticized for perpetuating patriarchy and violence; I fear for what comments will come your way. It's even worse outside of those communities, where people think you're really fucked up and damaged (which we may be, but it's none of their business anyway).

But know that there are many of us who support you in writing this. We totally get it.

Sincerely,

Emma

For days—and weeks—and, ultimately, years—many dozens of e-mails poured into my in-box from strangers who told me their stories. Many of them were wishing me well and telling me to keep my head up, because they knew from experience that sex-and-trauma disclosures were not well received. And many of them, to be sure, wrote about having, or wanting to have, certain kinds of sex after being traumatized. And feeling awful about it.

> To: Mac McClelland
> Date: Sat, Jul 2, 2011 at 11:31 AM
> Subject: a thank you for your PTSD article

Dear Ms. McClelland,

I had to find a way to tell you that you are not alone. I was raped when I was 21, and immediately afterward I found myself having risky, dangerous, violent sex. Except I didn't have the good sense that you did, and this was mostly with complete strangers. I'm so lucky that I survived that time period, because I could have easily been killed or hurt. I swore off this behavior when I was well enough to return to school, but I'm now 24 and I still have rape nightmares, flashbacks, daymares and think a lot about rape. I always thought I was a terrible person to have some kind of urge to be raped again. I feel dead inside because I walk dangerous streets alone at night, and when people tell me something is not safe, I feel like it doesn't matter anymore because the worst has already been done. In some way I feel protected because I think nothing can really touch me anymore. I became a serious self-injurer, bulimic and attempted suicide, and I told myself that no one could hurt me because I wasn't scared of pain or death.

Now I am 24 and I have recently come out of residential treatment for my problems and diagnosed with PTSD. I am making a lot of progress in my recovery but I still find it hard to talk about my attraction to violent sex. I feel so ashamed and like I am truly a worthless "slut." So when I read your article I was amazed at your courage to talk about it, to the whole world. I would've written a comment in reply but I didn't want to know what other people had commented, because I was afraid of the worst. But I wanted to tell you that you did an amazing thing in writing that piece. I don't know what I am going to do about my own stuff, but I feel better knowing that a few people are coming out and talking about what I have always thought was a dark and terrible secret. You made me feel less like a terrible person, and a little more human and deserving of compassion.

Thank you,
Nicole

To: Mac McClelland
Date: Mon, Jun 27, 2011 at 4:13 PM
Subject: Thank you. Re: PTSD

Hello Mac,

I feel so stupid writing this . . . I just happened across an article of your experiences with PTSD and I just started crying my eyes out.

I have life-long PTSD . . . I've known it for years, and I've been in various kinds of treatment, but I still have to live my everyday life, and thirty-one of my thirty-six years have been spent in an extremely high state of hyper-arousal. I've heard combat veterans, and now you, describe my daily life since childhood, the crying and the neck-snapping tension and the "odd" fantasies . . . and while talk therapy has helped many of my symptoms, I've always run into trouble specifically with anything like sexual healing.

I have no trusted friends that could possibly overpower me (I'm 6'1" and 280 lbs and all of my friends are women) . . . I've more or less given up hope of exploring what I feel I need to safely feel to heal (hopelessness, inability to do anything) . . . most of my therapists over the years, especially psychiatrists and medical doctors, have actually told me I'm abnormal for even thinking those thoughts . . . it's so good to read someone getting some healing out of choosing to try something that seems counterintuitive but also totally logical, and that there's a thera-pist not making light of it.

I think my current therapist would be so supportive, but I have never been able to bring anything like this up in session. I will try and do so.

I'm sorry you ever needed that or felt what I feel every day. It's so exhausting.

Thank you, again,

Michael

I was amazed that I was getting these e-mails, and that I wasn't getting hate mail. I was also amazed that these people who were legitimate victims didn't think that I had no right to traumatization. There was one e-mail that I wished all the people writing those sex-related e-mails could read. It was from a sex therapist in San Francisco, Dimitry Yakoushkin. His practice, which had a long wait list, specialized in erotic transference—no nudity or kissing between patient and practitioner, but plenty of intimate touching and role-play. He said one former, one potential, and two current clients had brought the essay to him. He and his colleagues, Celeste and Danielle, MA, MSW, PhD, treated men and women for all sorts of sexual concerns— dissociating during sex, asexuality, hypersexuality, not being able to climax, not being able to look sex partners in the eye. Invariably, he said, as clients worked toward the root of their issue—sometimes for years before finding or facing it—trauma came up. He simultaneously broke and warmed my heart when he told me he had a client who was formerly abused, seventy-six years old, and determined to have her first orgasm before she died. (After a year of working together, she was getting very close.) Anyway, the most frequent ac-tivity his female clients discovered they wanted or needed was safe explora-tion of fantasies—which more often than not included rough sexual role-play and/or rape scenarios. People came from multiple states, and countries, to work with them.

Not that all of the e-mails I was getting came from fellow sexual deviants. Plenty of the writers didn't talk about sex at all, but still related to my symp-toms. Some of them had been in a bad car accident. Some of them didn't say how they'd been traumatized, because they didn't feel like it, or because they never did ("My reasons are the kind I can't really talk to anyone about"). Some were women; some were men. Some didn't have PTSD but had loved ones who did ("I'm a journalist whose partner has severe complex PTSD fol-lowing a lifetime of trauma. . . . I know the blank stares and dismissals you often receive when the subject is brought up"). But they all shared one thing: their sense of isolation.

It made me sad that we didn't all know that our symptoms were so com-monplace. So commonplace they were practically boring. But here we were flipping out that we were raving and rare and gross. There were only a few people I heard from who knew that their symptoms were business-as-usual PTSD. Those people also knew better than to admit their symptoms to the non-traumatized public.

"Yeahhhhh," Brannan Vines, a thirty-one-year-old from Alabama drawled to me over the phone. "We don't really tell normal people *how* crazy we are."

Brannan was the founder and CEO of Family of a Vet, a nonprofit dedi-cated to helping military veterans' families cope with PTSD. Brannan was also a PTSD-veteran's wife whose life with her traumatized husband was so difficult that she herself had developed PTSD.

I'd got in touch with her first, before the essay came out. I found her in the same way that a lot of people would find me now, by Googling symptoms and sex and stumbling on something she'd written on her organization's site. I'd gone on that research quest (adding *veterans* to the search terms) for work more than personal reasons. I would have to pitch new story ideas soon, and it had occurred to me that if sexual dysfunction weren't limited to myself and other clients of Meredith's who had PTSD, some veterans would be experiencing it, too. Ten years after the invasion of Afghanistan, people were tired of reading about soldiers period, much less combined with the impossibly unsexy topic of mental illness. I was pretty proud of myself for thinking of an angle that might make an important topic compelling: their postwar sex lives.

I'd interviewed Brannan while I was in Ohio, gathering information for the potential pitch. After my personal essay came out, she became one of many allies from a corner that I never would have anticipated support or validation, had I anticipated support from strangers at all: the military.

"Fuck what everybody else has to say that's negative about you!" a marine named Chris wrote to me. He told me he'd had PTSD since his first tour in Iraq. He seemed sympathetic to the fact that the constant crying was freaking me out, even if he couldn't relate to it. "I CANNOT cry," he said. I obviously didn't have any such problem, and his trying to help me while he was having so much trouble himself moved me to tears—the good kind of tears, which had become unfamiliar to me.

So, at home in San Francisco, broken down and raw, I had, for the first time, a spontaneously assembled community trying to help me hold my pieces together. They bore some of the weight of my shame. And Nico still loved me, he assured me, despite having followed (and translated) the debate about my character, all the while unsuccessfully trying to teach me the French art of unlimited *blasé*.

"It's not important what other people say," he kept saying, looking at me over Skype like I was crazy for not getting this.

"You might be upset if you opened *Le Monde* and it said you were a whore and didn't care if you destroyed people's lives for your own fame," I said, quavering as always. "And if your grandma saw that."

And he would shrug.

He had been right, what he'd said when I tried to break up with him. I was incapable of severing contact. I couldn't imagine my future without him. Even when I'd still been closed up in Ohio, in my work and reality-TV bubble, I thought about him constantly.

When I'd stopped not having feelings about everything, I'd stopped not having feelings about Nico. My need for him intensified, and I missed him unbearably, though again, I'd never had him next to me long enough to get used to. It piled on top of my other physically painful emotions.

"I need you," I kept telling him, despite that not being a thing that I traditionally said to anyone.

He couldn't come.

He couldn't have helped me anyway.

Having feelings had its price. PTSD gets worse, all the way worse, before it gets better. "Healing does not always mean that we will feel better," world-renowned wellness guru Donald Epstein says in his book *Healing Myths, Healing Magic*. "We cannot heal what we cannot feel, and healing often requires us to feel things we don't like feeling."

I didn't have any assignments planned; the Haiti feature had long been published, the Congo piece was turned in, and the reporting was done for the Uganda and Ohio stories. All I had to do was write them. For the first time in fourteen months, I prepared to sit still. I hadn't seen Meredith since before the Hague-and-Africa assignment, three months earlier. I had collapsed into a mess, and away from drinking and the constant moving and traveling, even with my impromptu band of supportive e-mail strangers, I stayed a mess. The vise was back around my rib cage, and my awareness of it was at an all-time high.

One night, I went to a yoga class in my neighborhood in an attempt to undo the suffocation. I hadn't breathed, it seemed, in months. Halfway through, on a mat on the polished wood floor, I dropped into a forward fold, and a thought that I had never, ever even come close to having before suddenly presented itself. The moment it arrived, it rang and resonated through my whole body.

I didn't want to be alive anymore.

PART TWO

You do not have to be good.
You do not have to walk on your knees
for a hundred miles through the desert, repenting.
You only have to let the soft animal of your body
  love what it loves.

—MARY OLIVER

9.

Denise Benson, MFT, Master Somatic Coach, California Institute of Integrative Studies instructor, and prominent Bay Area psychotherapist, came highly recommended. Sometimes she was hired to run leadership seminars for executives of large organizations, but during her normal days, she saw clients one-on-one. And for that, her expertise was in trauma. Meredith spoke of her as if she was some kind of legend; she was seasoned but progressive, and supposedly very intense. With Meredith on maternity leave and my mental health what it was, I called her up when I returned from Ohio. A few days later, I arrived at her office in downtown San Francisco.

"How did it go with Denise?" Tana asked me after our highly anticipated session.

"OK," I responded. I added, to her and to anyone else who asked me how I was doing: "She says I'm dead inside."

She hadn't said that. Not exactly, in so many words. But that was how I'd interpreted what she'd not only told me, but shown me.

Denise's sessions weren't your standard sit-in-a-chair-and-talk appointments. As a somatic therapist, she, like Meredith, approached mental health issues not from the mind, but through the body. "[E]very person is a composite functioning of two simultaneous processes: the mental and the physical," it says in the foreword to *The Anatomy of Change*, a book by Richard Strozzi-Heckler, a pioneer of somatics who founded an institute in California and, as it happens, trained Denise. His clients have included everyone from the Special Forces to professional athletes. I'd lucked into somatics when I got the recommendation to see Meredith years ago, but now, I chose a somatic therapist deliberately. There was no denying that my bodily symptoms were real, even if they didn't make sense. My symptoms were in my body; my fears were for my body; somatic therapy seemed smarter than ever. I'd had to accept that I wasn't going to be able to rationalize my way out of this. Believe me. I'd tried.

However West Coast it sounded, the body had feelings—emotion was intricately tangled with physical feelings. Whether people liked it or not. As the sensations couldn't and shouldn't be avoided, the theory of somatics went, they were a source of guidance and information. Learning to use that source led to wholeness, and I needed wholeness to take on something as serious as PTSD. Plenty of animals living happier lives than I had survived without rationality for millennia, I supposed, and to get through this, I had to give up my total faith in it, too.

The Establishment wasn't ready to do that. Accordingly, somatic therapy was far from the norm. Though it was plentiful and easily accessible where I lived, for a long time, it had been marginalized in a field built upon talking. In 1997, Peter Levine helped bring attention to it with his best seller *Waking the Tiger: Healing Trauma*, an explanation of his Somatic Experiencing therapy, which focused on invoking and fully experiencing uncomfortable bodily reactions. And before that, Bessel van der Kolk, who was the director of the Trauma Center of the Justice Resource Institute in Massachusetts (which he remains) and a principal investigator of the *DSM IV*'s field trials for PTSD, came to the conclusion that somatics was an effective treatment for trauma when he met a woman who'd developed debilitating PTSD after a car accident. Van der Kolk's training was old-school, but he discovered that the woman responded to EMDR, a then relatively new modality. Eye-movement desensitization and reprocessing therapy involves keeping traumatic events in mind while receiving visual, tactile, and auditory stimuli. These help the brain process and file the memories so that they won't pop up as if they were real anymore. Parts of the brain, Van der Kolk realized, went off-line when people remembered traumatic events normally. This would shape the rest of his career, and was his gateway to realizing that in order for him to help traumatized patients to process their distress, he first had to bypass the verbal system and get their body to feel safe. Trauma couldn't be resolved just by talking about it. It was practically blasphemy. But he started training legions of practitioners to treat traumatic stress through the body.

Denise practiced "direct experience" somatics. "If we know that what's locked up in the body is a deep contraction that came from fear, it's unethical to not touch" was her philosophy. So if there was a way she could help her clients release and feel safe by touching or manipulating their bodies like an acupuncturist or massage therapist, she did.

You wouldn't necessarily guess she was the type. She didn't seem touchy-feely; a tough, compact dyke in her sixties with short dark hair and ageless olive skin, she wore no-nonsense button-downs, as no-nonsense as the desk and couple pieces of furniture in her office. She was sharp and serious. She smiled, but not gratuitously, and looked like she didn't take any shit. I wasn't planning on giving her any, but felt nervous around her just the same.

That first session, we sat in chairs across from each other while I (crying) gave her some background, like at any other intake. We talked about somatics some. One simple way to demonstrate how impacted and involved the body was in everything, she said, was just to say "No! No! No!," and feel how the body contracted; feel the difference between saying that and saying "Yes. Yes. Yes."

Soon—after she was sure I felt safe in the environment she created, and safe with her—she had me do something a typical therapist wouldn't: lie on a massage table.

I would end up like this for most of our sessions. Lying faceup, breathing. Answering her questions about what I noticed. How I felt. She would stand next to the table, near me, while we talked. During our first table session, she at some point happened to pass her hand near my face. And she realized something.

She stopped, and put her hand in front of my face again. Then she drew it back and thrust it toward my face, stopping just shy of hitting me. She repeated that several times.

"You don't flinch, or even blink, when I put my hand in your face," she said.

I thought about this for a second. "Maybe it's because you're my therapist and I trust you," I ventured.

"Um . . ." she said, trying to let me down easy. "It's a reflex. It should work no matter what."

She wouldn't tell me another thing she noticed until later, because she didn't want to freak me out, but when she picked up my hands, they felt lifeless and empty.

Like a corpse's. But with less substance.

I didn't think it was fair that I could be barely inhabiting my stupid body but doing so much crying and suffering anyhow. I didn't understand that. But I did understand that there really was no place I less wanted to be than inside my own skin. My body was unpredictable. It was agonizingly painful. And when my symptoms took over, it was terrifying.

"Trust your gut," people say, in a demonstration of the small collective understanding we do have of body knowledge. (Ditto "My shoulders are so tight because I'm so stressed out!") But my guts were misfiring.

Say I was sitting in bed watching TV, since I still used mass amounts of it to try to numb myself. Having run out of every episode of *Grey's Anatomy* ever made, I took on the six-season catalogue of *Criminal Minds* and two of the three *CSI* franchises. Or say I was watching *The Daily Show*, and suddenly fear exploded in my stomach. It said: I'm going to be attacked.

This feeling, however untrue, wouldn't go away just because I recognized it as untrue. *I'm going to be attacked I'm going to be attacked I'm going to be attacked*, everything in my body said. *No you aren't*, something else in me tried to tell it, but to no avail; I became so tightly wound against the attack that my whole system boiled. Generally at this point I would take out a bottle of Ativan, which my alarmed GP had recently prescribed for emergencies, and clutch it hard or stare at it, pacing my apartment, trying to stomp the crazy out through my feet, prepared to medicate if I couldn't calm down soon because sometimes, the stress and exhaustion of the terror would lead me to the thought that I couldn't stand to be alive anymore.

"Yeah, that's PTSD stuff," Denise said, shrugging or waving a hand when I came to therapy and recounted these episodes, or how I'd lost all emotional sensation in Paris. She was almost dismissive. But to me, even after almost a year of alternating between being totally numb and an all-feeling uncooked mess ("Yeah, that's normal," she said of that, too), every symptom was somehow still a terrible surprise. In the way that Brannan Vines, the Family of a Vet founder, was an old hand at PTSD, Denise also was used to it—having treated sisters who'd been serially molested and sons and daughters who'd been unspeakably abused and even single-episode-trauma-havers, such as car-accident victims. Someday, the tone both Denise and Brannan took suggested, I would be used to PTSD symptoms, and to their oscillating extremes.

In the service of that goal—increasing my threshold, Denise called it—she and I started with the simple but surprisingly big task of trying to get me to inhabit my body. I would lie on the table, and she would prompt me to notice how I felt. What I felt. What body parts I could feel the most and the least, and what felt like it wasn't connected to me, or didn't exist at all.

I hated it. I was so afraid of it. And I didn't really want to know how much of my body I had dissociated from. But as scary as the idea of experiencing all the feelings in my body was, scarier was the prospect of being so disconnected from it that I didn't have reflexes anymore.

Denise encouraged me to try not being scared of and mad at my body. My guts were misfiring for good reason. My symptoms were not a dysfunction, but an adaptation to some very dysfunctional situations, situations I hadn't fully processed. Trauma had been perpetrated upon my body, and lived in my body. It was my body that was reacting to trauma. It was my body that was trying to, and going to have to, work through it.

It wasn't like I hadn't noticed that I couldn't count on my mind. Not only could it not intellectualize my symptoms away, it sometimes seemed like the bigger traitor here. It had been through so much learning and socialization and corruption; a mind could tell a dangerously underweight anorexic that he was fat, or a genius that she was an idiot, and it certainly was telling me, when my symptoms or an episode flared, that I was a fucking loser, which eventually led me to think that I was ruined and would suffer like this forever, which could quickly, ultimately lead me to the thought that it would be better if I was dead.

Every time I got on the table, I was prompted to feel. It started with breathing. Increasing my breathing, or doing different kinds of breathing. Lying still to give time and space to any feelings that felt like emerging. Sometimes Denise would put her hand on my chest and press. Sometimes she would cup her hands around my rib cage and apply light pressure, replicating the tension there from the outside so it might feel safe enough to give a little from the inside. Sometimes she would bind me tight in a sheet. But as I had after Haiti Part I, the moment I started relaxing, I started panicking, crying, and pulling back. I didn't want to do this anymore.

"OK," Denise would say. "What's going to happen?"

"I'll die," I would say, and saying that would make me cry harder, because I knew it wasn't true, but there it was: my body's truth. And I meant it literally. I didn't have to specify that to Denise. She knew.

"Got it," she would say.

We progressed to mixing in centering exercises. The more centered and grounded I was—that is, the more in my body, not in denial or dissociation or just in my head, since memory and fantasy and rationalization weren't concerned with the actual experience of being alive—the more fully I could stay with and enter into any experience. And the more I practiced centering, dropping down into my body, fully experiential, connected to reality and to who I was—the easier it would be to get back when I was thrown off.

"Just because our feet and legs are on the ground does not mean that we are grounded," Strozzi-Heckler writes in *The Anatomy of Change*. "We establish our contact with ground by allowing our energetic presence to move as a living charge through our legs and feet into the ground."

In the simplest centering exercises, Denise and I would stand up and face each other, and I would ground the best I could. I concentrated on my feet's connection to the floor. I dropped my weight into my hips rather than supporting it up top with scrunched shoulders, lowering my center of gravity to where my guts were, focusing on what was in there, what I was really made of. Denise had directed me to store what was important to me an inch or two below my navel. I'd picked my convictions, my friends, my work. My relationship with Nico. Letting my weight and attention gather there, I would breathe deep into my chest and belly. And then Denise would lunge and grab my arm.

She'd told me she was going to do it, of course—she'd asked me if I was ready several times. And she told me why she was doing it: The grab exercise was like life, where you're going along, fine, and then something happens, and you're not. The purpose was to help me learn what happened in my body and work back toward normal. But even though I knew Denise's grab was coming, I flinched and jumped every time.

"Notice the sensations," she would say, still holding on, the way an episode—or a predator—would. "Feel the uncomfortable sensations. Notice how it shapes you." When I did, she'd tell me to reclaim my shape. "Get it back," she would say. Try to feel relaxed *and* grabbed. With my arm extended, her hand gripped around it, I tried to get back to the place from where I'd just been startled. Not to force it, or to trick it, but to acknowledge the agitation, let it be there, and transition into the next phase, back to grounded. "Take your time," she said as I shifted around her, still not letting me go. "Reclaim your personal space," she said. "Find your center."

I felt like I was in kindergarten for aspiring ninjas.

In the remedial class.

We practiced other tools for dealing with episodes—breathing practices, acquainting-myself-with-reality practices, mantras and attempts to let the sensations be. It was crucial that I felt empowered to help myself and that I helped myself not suffer. It would help me feel like I wasn't a victim of my own system. We had many conversations about compassion, which Denise kept telling me I needed, to accept and not fight against my episodes or make them worse with fear or shame. Trying to steel myself against my crazy, both with physical contractions and emotionally, didn't help, and just made me more vulnerable. It was like a building that hadn't been retrofitted. When the earthquake came, it remained rigid, and unable to sway with the shock, it cracked and crumbled to pieces.

"Be nice to your crazy," Denise said, sometimes adopting my language for it in solidarity, though she didn't support it. "You don't have to like it, but you can be welcoming of it." The somatic principles of using the flow of an obstacle—to go with it, not against it, of welcoming and integrating—weren't unlike some principles of martial arts. They were the same principles that made up key tenets of Buddhism.

"Hatred never ceases by hatred, but by love alone is healed" goes one of the Buddha's most central and famous teachings. "This is an ancient and eternal law."

But I had gone to Catholic school. Self-compassion wasn't exactly in my skill set. I definitely hadn't learned self-acceptance from teachers who taught me as a child that if I masturbated, my dead relatives would watch me from heaven as I did it, Aunt Karen and Uncle Timmy gazing upon me in sad, repulsed horror.

So at the age of thirty-one, I was now trying for the first time to be welcoming to natural feelings I couldn't control. There I would be, sweeping my apartment, standing in the middle of my floor with a broom in my hand, when my system would erupt into turmoil.

Danger, it would say, all my senses hyperaware.

Dangerdangerdanger. Somebody will attack you. Soon.

Hypervigilance was like having a murderer in your house. It was how you would feel if it was dark outside, and the power was out, and you couldn't see him—the way your stress responses would spike, readying you as you felt your way along the walls, the sensitivity of your straining ears, the tautness in your muscles. Alertness shooting around inside your skull.

First, I panicked. First, second, third, and fourth, actually. But sometimes, eventually, I remembered to employ my practices.

I started with the simplest breath exercise, three slow in, three slow out. But I couldn't even get through it. Halfway through the first inhale, futility overwhelmed me, and I was too agitated to even fill up my lungs once, much less for three cycles, and it would not bring a solid feeling back to my middle when I was this far gone.

It's OK, I told myself, attempting compassion next. *This is not a dysfunction. It's an adaptation to dysfunctional situations, and you haven't fully processed them yet.* But I couldn't hear it, triggered like that. It sounded meaningless. *These*, my mind countered to its own counsel, *are the sorts of bullshit excuses you make for yourself when in fact You. Are. THE WORST.*

There was another grounding exercise, too, called GRACE, in which I was supposed to feel the Ground, Relax, become Aware, Center, and Energize, but I didn't endeavor to try that, either. By then, my spiral of symptoms and agony and shame was so strong that I was convinced the only way to stop it was to distract it with physical trauma, such as throwing myself into the double-paned window looking out onto my backyard.

There were two reasons not to do this. One was the obvious one, that it's not the sort of thing one should do. The more important one was that wounding myself was another form of dissociating—sure as my leaving my body, or alcoholism—and dissociating is the opposite of processing. One theory for why dissociating during a traumatic event the way I did in Haiti led to long-term PTSD is that the trauma was never fully experienced in the first place. During trauma, parts of the brain—as Van der Kolk, among others, had determined—become overwhelmed by the sensory information coming in about the event and start to shut down. Unprocessed, the sensory information, which meanwhile continued coming in, remains doomed to revisit itself on a person again and again until it is processed.

Avoiding avoidance in general was an important part of my treatment plan. I did still drink decent amounts and watch a lot of TV. I tried to engage in the latter more than the former, but I had to do *something* sometimes; I could not bear dealing with myself for the full number of waking hours in a day. I was trying my hardest, though, to let full-blown episodes run their course when they emerged.

So it was better on multiple counts to not hurl myself into my window. *Stick with it*, I instructed myself. *Try to weather it. Ride it out.* The only tool that was left was to go get the bottle of Ativan and clutch it for comfort. I very rarely took it. But waiting for the excruciation to subside, I coaxed myself away from self-destruction with the promise of pharmaceutically induced relief. *You will be fine*, I said reassuringly. *You don't have to hurt yourself. Because if it doesn't end soon, you can drug your way out.*

My therapy experience was not at all the kind of therapy experience my new buddy Chris the marine, who'd e-mailed me after my essay came out, was having.

Despite variance in causes and severities, the symptoms of different PTSD sufferers are similar. There are different types of trauma, different degrees. One terrible event—a mugging, a rape—might leave you with "simple" PTSD. A pattern of traumas—domestic abuse, war—can lead to severe or complex PTSD, trauma upon traumas compounding themselves to make worse trauma. Having one trauma doesn't always mean you end up with only simple PTSD—it can activate or exacerbate complicating issues such as attachment difficulties or personality disorders—and having simple PTSD doesn't mean your symptoms necessarily go away faster. Obviously, categorizations of something such as trauma aren't so strict or easy.

But in general, for everyone on the PTSD continuum, traumatic events are improperly encoded and keep intruding as if they were reality. Having not been filed in the brain as memories, they are not really memories at all, but occur in consciousness just as they did the first time. I knew that my experience couldn't compare with what Chris had been through in Iraq. Yet he, like every other traumatized person I'd ever encounter, didn't think getting sympathy for PTSD was a question of severity or credentials. As far as he was concerned, we were both suffering. Certainly he knew that some people thought he didn't have the right to trauma as a perpetrator of the war (and a heavily armed white male one). But in the moments he'd been terrified, that context was irrelevant. Trauma was something of an equalizer that way; in a moment of pure trauma, a man was a woman was a body afraid for its life.

He wasn't interested in saying to me "What happened to you is not that big of a deal" any more than a penetration-rape victim would say that to a child who'd only been groped. Any more than Chris would say to an earthquake survivor, "You know what's really awful? War." Any more than anyone would say to someone in a war that if they thought regular war was tough, they should try surviving a genocide. Although, then, many genocide survivors would need to be reminded that they were lucky to have been spared the longer-lasting and wider-spread horror of the Holocaust.

This atrocity hierarchy, which one's nervous system is unfortunately unaware of, is imposed on traumatized people by nontraumatized people, and by themselves (consider the e-mail from the gal who said she'd never experienced anything as extreme as I had—only that her guerrilla-fighter father abused her from the age of two to nineteen). I've never heard it brought up from one traumatized person to belittle another. In the world of the traumatized, the line of sympathy is drawn between those who have PTSD and those who do not.

Regular people, whether they realize it or not, walk around believing, as you cannot make your way in the world without believing, that the universe is holding them.

Well, the people on our side of the line thought, *the fuck it does*.

After our first e-mail exchange, Chris and I continued writing each other, united by our total distrust of the world and ourselves. Whatever our backstories, we still had a lot in common. Flashbacks. (Flashbacks! Not just for veterans!) Crippling numbness, while alternately, or at the same time, our physiologies had a new baseline: hyperawareness and hyperarousal. Adrenaline-sharp quick-scanning for danger and triggers. For PTSD sufferers, this incessant alertness persists even in sleep, and people with PTSD can have nightmares and twitch during sleep stages in which regular people don't move at all, waking up as if from torture, physically exhausted and sore. Like me, Chris moved through life both uninterested in and cowed by it. And like me, he was in therapy to help him adapt to it.

Chris's therapy was talk-based. The Department of Veterans Affairs, which was responsible for his treatment, most commonly used cognitive-behavioral therapy and exposure therapy, in which you talk and talk about the traumatic things that have happened to you until they eventually, theoretically, lose their traumatizing power. Often at the VA, this was done in groups. But often, talking about being traumatized was not something marines were particularly interested in doing, never mind in front of other marines.

"We just suck it up!" Chris wrote me one day. "What we have is our training that keeps us focused on the mission 100%. We don't have time to think about our 'FEELINGS' because the Marine next [to] you depends on you doing your job at 100%." Now that he was home, he was finding it impossible to adjust. "I get very reclusive and don't want to be around anybody. I don't like going to the store, mall or movies. I feel like people are watching me. I only drive on the far left side of the road because of IED's. Been hit by 2 and near numerous others. I get irritable easy. Have medication that makes me sleep because I can't on my own. And to get personal, I don't even like sex anymore. I can't get that personal with anyone."

Some of what Chris was experiencing was applicable to traumatized civilians. Not the IED (improvised explosive device) paranoia, but the irritability, the intimacy and avoidance issues, are classic post-trauma symptoms that can last long after intrusive craziness has worn off, even a lifetime. Other people will say about these people, like people say about alcoholics, "His childhood was super messed up." Or "He has *issues*." And then shrug. Ruined person. Fact of life. End of story. What they are often talking about, though less obviously than in a combat veteran's case, is unresolved trauma. And there are lots of treatments for unresolved trauma.

I was doing more research for the story about veterans' sex lives, which I'd conceived before my PTSD essay had been published. But now that e-mails such as Chris's were coming into my life, I was obsessed with the topic, and I did have to go to work anyway. My bosses had asked me, after the essay's publication, if I thought I still had PTSD, and I told them it was Denise and my GP's opinion that I did; they knew I was in treatment, and that was the end of that conversation. I didn't know how long I could keep it all up, but I forced myself through a demanding schedule of appointments and interviews and meetings that—with the help of getting drunk a couple of times a week—made me numb enough to function for long hours at a time when I wasn't at home or with Denise sobbing hysterically. When the sobbing distress and distaste for life broke through at the office, I took it into the bathroom or the stairwell. I wasn't functional enough to write, having to request multiple deadline extensions for the magazine feature about Ohio because every time I sat down to do it I found myself unfocused and without the energy or ability to make my brain create anything. But research I could mostly handle.

As I dug into it, I was learning that there were nearly as many treatments for PTSD as there were causes. We'd come a long way from the World War I–era method of trying to electrically shock and emotionally abuse PTSD out of soldiers. The VA was funding more than a hundred treatment studies, given its care of more than a quarter of a million Iraq and Afghanistan vets with PTSD. Their methods ranged from the ultra-Western, such as giving patients hypertension drugs to mitigate intrusive symptoms, to quantifying the effectiveness of meditation therapy. Brannan Vines would call to tell me about one wife on her unpaid Family of a Vet staff whose veteran husband had enrolled in a private clinical trial in which a needleful of anesthetic had been injected into a bundle of nerves at the top of his collarbone. Within minutes, he was a completely different, calmed person—though it eventually wore off.

Advanced treatments weren't just for soldiers anymore. Between government funding and the private sector, veterans and civilians, there were trials in which people took Ecstasy while talking about trauma to promote positive associations with the events. Acupuncture as treatment, meditation as treatment: These methods played to the same principle as somatic therapy, namely getting the body to feel safe. But there were all sorts of innovations now. There was a study looking at whether eating synthetic pot extinguished fearful memory recovery. There were trials in which rats were lightly tortured and then injected with a peptide that stopped enzymes in their brains from being able to form memories of it. And long-established centers existed that were dedicated to teaching yoga for traumatized people. All of the above had got great results, but so did the more standard, older guard of existing therapies. Practitioners of cognitive behavioral therapy and exposure therapy, such as the methods the VA used, reported vast improvements in their patients. Much of the treatment community, including the VA, endorsed EMDR; the VA evidently didn't accept some experts' feelings that it was primarily effective in cases of single-trauma events. Many practitioners didn't subscribe to just one or another of these methods, mixing and matching as they saw fit. Medications were almost always prescribed by conventional therapists, but they needed to be accompanied by other interventions. There was no evidence that you could cure PTSD with pills alone.

If only the science of treating PTSD were as precise as baking a cake. It was erratic and imperfect. But it still helped a lot of people get better. The available treatments still saved lives.

Chris didn't say how long he'd been in his therapy. But unfortunately, he didn't think it was working. "Marines are a rare breed," he wrote me. "We don't ask for help when we need it. That's why I have lost 6 of my buddies to suicide after we got back to the States. Including myself. I think about it allot. I wish sometimes that I was with my buddies so they know they are not alone. I don't know what keeps me from suicide. I don't do drugs and I'm not an alcoholic. I don't know what keeps me sane anymore."

"I have not spoken to anybody about allot [of] personal stuff," he wrote in another e-mail. "I have a huge (China) wall up is what the VA Docs say. But, I would love to try and talk to you. Maybe it's what I need."

We agreed to talk on the phone. On my end, I told him, I wanted to talk because our experiences were important, because I wanted to talk to someone else who understood—and because I wanted to thank him more personally for being so supportive. If validation was crucial to healing, Chris was my first big leg up in accepting my trauma as valid. *His* trauma was valid, I was sure, so if he believed in mine, maybe I could, too. I wasn't sure if I had much to offer him. He was additionally suffering from traumatic brain injury—long-term damage from multiple concussions—and I was learning from research that that could make it harder to treat PTSD.

But if he was willing to explore our usefulness to each other, so was I.

One thing Denise shared in common with the VA was EMDR. She used the process in her sessions sometimes. But not with me. Not yet, because she didn't think I was ready to handle it.

In the meantime, we plugged away at keeping me from wanting to die. I had told Denise, though I was hardly broadcasting it otherwise, how the feeling had come over me a few times. We did more grounding exercises, practiced centering. It was important to practice when I wasn't triggered, because the more my body experienced centeredness, the easier it would be to find it even when I was triggered. Denise almost never talked about Haiti without mentioning that it had come right after Deepwater Horizon and Oklahoma; she thought that my being so tired and long-displaced—big contributors to being off center—when I arrived there likely helped make the difference between a tough trip to Haiti and the beginning of a long bout with mental illness.

In Denise's experience, there were three things that made a person more likely to develop PTSD. She jokingly once referred to them as a trifecta of doom. The first thing, obviously, was experiencing trauma. The second was being bright—bright enough to see what's going on around you and to see the big picture. The third was sensitivity. And in addition to having been off center, having arrived a bit discombobulated in Haiti, I had all the elements of the trifecta.

First: trauma. As an expert, Denise measured trauma according to how it impacted someone, not by whether the trauma won the pissing contest of whose was worse or bad enough. Regardless, she would brook no arguments that mine wasn't that bad to begin with.

Second: big-picture brightness. Take the events of a day, when we were kids, that my mom brought us to the mall. We were waiting outside for her in a side lot I think behind Sears, and I was walking atop a short stack of two-by-fours as if they were a tightrope, my arms out for balance, when I noticed the exhaust pipe of a semitruck parked nearby. Sticking vertically out of the top of the cab, the whole top half of the silver cone was crusted with black. This would've been long before the big panic about global warming, but when I looked at the pipe, all I could think about was how much black smoke had had to come out of that one pipe, and how many identical pipes there were spewing black smoke out of all the trucks on all the roads in the world. I was awed by the scale of human pollution. I couldn't have been older than nine.

Third. Consider my response to the scene in the Disney cartoon *The Sword in the Stone*, which my siblings and I watched dozens of times, where the human protagonist is briefly turned into a squirrel. In that short time he manages to attract the affections of a girl squirrel who clearly thinks they will have a future together. Then he is turned back into a human, right in front of her, and she starts crying.

I remember looking to my siblings for a reaction about this, but finding none on their faces.

I was sick with grief for her.

My sense of empathy was overdeveloped. There was such a thing as too much. "You could see how a kid like that," Denise said, "might end up struggling with this severity of PTSD, with the things you've seen."

Yeah. I guessed. Although "the things I'd seen" may have got to me even if I hadn't been a kid like that. Chris probably never cried over Disney characters, and look how he'd ended up.

Anyway, here I was with a disorder that can make people who aren't sensitive in the first place oversensitive enough to kill themselves. The first stage of treatment, with many trauma-sensitive practitioners, was producing safety and stabilization. I was in a safe environment, which was crucial, but the matter of *feeling* safe could take years, and could continue to need to be reestablished in tandem with moving into the next two stages. These, Denise often illustrated as twin foundations for healing. She held both of her hands out, palms up, when she talked about them. On the left, there was validating, naming, and working on the trauma itself, moving into the uncomfortable feelings it produced and processing them. On the right, there was choosing to go forward, restoring relationships, pursuing the kind of life you wanted now. With her holding her hands out like that, I couldn't forget: I needed them both.

We were very much still in the validating and processing phase, where we would remain for a long time. But Denise had still asked me, on our first day together, what it was that I wanted in the long run. What was my goal, in the end? What did I want her to help me with?

"I want to be able to feel myself in the world," I said (sobbing, because I was already sobbing, always sobbing then). I was simply pointing to the basic functionalities I'd lost. "And to be able to deal with the feelings I do have." I don't remember having said it, because I was deeply episodic, and there was often a strange amnesia around episodes. I wouldn't remember what happened for very long after they were over unless I wrote it down. If I didn't write down the specifics, I remembered only the pain.

But Denise wrote it down that time, and would recite it back to me throughout our work together. She would say it to me when we were working on being present in my body and I could feel how awful I felt, scared and depressed and disgusted and anxious and resigned. When my despair overwhelmed everything else, she would quote me to remind me why I was enduring the torture: "I want to feel myself in the world."

No, I didn't. Not now that I was actually doing it. Not when all my feelings were like this.

Even TV, my last sanctuary, was turning against me. A commercial with guinea pigs in it reminded me of my sister Jessica's guinea pig, which cried incessantly in its basement cage. Not like a puppy's cry, which is sad and whiny and makes you feel bad that you're not giving it what it wants; a guinea pig screeches as if it's being stabbed in the face. *Wheep! Wheep! Wheep!* it screams, like the violins in *Psycho*, as if its tiny frame can't bear the torment. I think it was thirsty. Maybe it was lonely. *Why didn't I take better care of that guinea pig?* I demanded of myself while its cries echoed around in my head, and now I was watching Hulu with my eyes scrunched tight and my hands clamped over my ears against a sound that wasn't happening. In one *Criminal Minds* episode, FBI special agent JJ got a black eye, and though it was a tidy, sexy-tough one, when I looked at her face I could see only my ex-girlfriend, who got two black eyes when she was traveling for work and someone assaulted her at her hotel and she ended up knocked out, waking up on the floor with the guy's blood on her and no memory of the fight, retaining the big black swollen eye sockets for weeks.

Experts and clinicians know that trauma patients have to deal not only with whatever event brought them into therapy, but with every mini-trauma that had been abruptly knocked loose from wherever it had been stored before they got PTSD. Like they didn't have enough to do already. I found myself suddenly assaulted by visions and emotions around all manner of historical ugliness large and small come to slap me as intrusively traumatic now. I started to conceptualize the remnants of any bad stuff that had ever happened, which had fossilized and been packaged safely away, as having forged a little trauma asteroid that floated around harmlessly inside my body. I pictured my first weekend in Port-au-Prince as if it were a force, a shockwave that radiated outward from an explosion in a movie, a barely visible but deadly tremor that slammed into my system, wreaking its own devastation while shattering the asteroid, the shrapnel puncturing my organs. The wounds were infected, inflamed. If I was going to regain function, Denise and I were going to have to find the abscesses and acknowledge them, drain them and dress them, one by one.

In his day, Freud speculated about the connection between old trauma and new. An incident that triggered hysteria, even one that was nasty in its own right, he argued, could trigger psychological damage from an older incident, which he thought was often the true cause of the symptoms.

More than a century later, the importance of old trauma was reasserted when researchers started screening soldiers and cops before and after deployment in their quest to answer: Who gets PTSD?

According to the contemporary studies, having parents with mental health issues, including depression, is on the list of risk factors that make a person who experiences trauma more likely to develop PTSD. A history of child abuse or neglect is on the list, as are having other mental health problems, and having no good family/friend support system. So is "being female," which suggests that the female body is constitutionally unsound, lacking the integrity to withstand trauma when all other things are equal, when in fact it's on the list because being female means being subject to far more threats and violations to boundaries and sexual and physical safety. Which means being exposed to more trauma, not a predisposition for not being able to handle it, and therefore it should not be on the list at all.

And then, in addition to childhood abuse, there's the more general "previous trauma." Whether it had made me more susceptible to PTSD or was just creating more work now that I had it, Denise wasn't surprised to see it coming up. But as this was a work injury, she wasn't the only one who would be interested in my past.

I was paying Denise out of my savings, some $600 a month. Later, when I started seeing her more often, it was more than a thousand. I had health insurance through my job, and it did cover therapy, but only group therapy, they told me when I called to inquire. It hardly compared to the intuitive, specialized care I was getting from Denise (and some experts considered group inappropriate during intrusive symptoms and inadequate for recovery), so I kept seeing her, as a matter of survival, while my employer's insurance company buried me in workers' compensation paperwork and requirements to get her individual sessions covered. I had to prove that I had PTSD—and that if I did, that I hadn't secretly had PTSD before, from something else. They couldn't take Denise's word for it. I had to see a State of California Division of Workers' Compensation Qualified Medical Evaluator.

Dr. Aaminah Shere's job was to determine whether my initial onset of PTSD was strictly due to work-related activities. Before the insurance company would pay for any of my treatment, I had to go see her for an evaluation in a bland room in a bland office building. I was my usual self—which, at that time, meant crying and shaking a lot—while she assessed and grilled me for two hours, looking for something non-job-related that could be blamed. And she couldn't do that without asking me a lot of questions about every bad thing I'd ever gone through before.

Sigh.

OK.

Number one.

A few months before I graduated from college, in 2002, my parents came from Cleveland to visit me at my apartment at Ohio State. My father sat on a couch across the living room from me, and my mother, in a chair to his right. Calmly, my father said, "I've been seeing someone else."

I didn't believe him. Though I also couldn't think of why he'd make something like that up. When I looked over toward my mother, she was suddenly on the floor, halfway across the distance we'd been sitting from each other, crawling to me on her hands and knees.

What a superweird joke they were playing! My parents were the couple that my friends and other married couples wanted to be, the way they were always going on dates and sexy tropical vacations and singing songs together while my dad played guitar. Plus there was no way he could have a girlfriend without my knowing it because we were best friends. The first time I remember seeing my father cry was when I told him that I filled out his name next to "Who is your best friend?" on a survey for a high school religion class, which, given the strength of my friendship with Stacy Morabito, was quite a statement. I had built large parts of my identity on the foundation of our father-daughter ties. The fact that he had, too, was evident in my mother's saying to me that day in my college apartment, the two of them on either side of me on the couch now, "Tell him you'll never speak to him again if he leaves."

Instead, I said, "I can't believe what a dick you are." Before they left, my mom gave me a cherry-cobbler pie from Bob Evans and a bottle of Percocet, while my dad kept apologizing for "rocking my world."

My father's mistress, who was of course about my sister Jessica's age, turned out to be one of two mistresses. He needed more sexual freedom and adventure, he told me in a fancy restaurant several weeks later. It was a long life. He couldn't be expected to stay cooped up with my mother for the rest of it.

But then he decided to come back and heed my mother's pleas to stay together. But within weeks he had left her again. When I drove up to the house my parents once shared and found my father's Cadillac in the driveway shortly after I graduated, I wondered if they'd got back together again, again. Or if somebody had died.

Rocking in an expensive patio chair on the back deck, my father confirmed that they were talking about getting back together—but that, more pressingly in that day's news, over the course of much of my life, he'd embezzled millions of dollars from his company and had finally been caught.

He was cutting deals to avoid prosecution. But all of *this*, my father said, gesturing vaguely around us, encompassing the house and all of our belongings, was "going to go away." My mother didn't look at me. She seemed to have become catatonic.

For the previous few years, I had noticed that my father was spending money as if he were famous, or delirious. There'd been a lot of extravagant dinners and hundred-dollar bottles of wine. More vacations than seemed reasonable. We were poor when I was born, then middle class as I got older, and my dad had kept working harder and working his way up until, when I was a teenager, we seemed solidly upper middle class. From that point on, my father always reminded us that there was no sense in saving because we only lived once.

He said that his crimes had started a few years after Uncle Timmy died in the car accident and we'd adopted my cousins. The court-mandated family therapist said my parents needed to give the grieving youths their own bedrooms, so we'd moved quickly from a small house to a doubly large one. My father, who was solely responsible for our finances, never discussing them with my mother, underestimated the costs of that mortgage plus the higher utility bills—we had a rule after we moved that if we left the lights on in an unoccupied room we were grounded that night. Plus there was the cost of the new van he bought to fit the whole family, and the extra groceries, and the therapy and the custody-lawyer's fees. He'd started paying our gas, electric, and phone bills along with the company bills, with company money. It'd devolved into a consumption addiction, living up to our big house and new cars and then to his new, fancier colleagues as he'd worked his way up in the company, eventually buying it, along with car phones and new tailored suits and nicer cars and an even bigger house filled with custom furniture and art.

He said he'd survived the guilt of the stealing and the inevitability of getting caught by going numb. That while we were all having parties and vacations together, he hadn't felt anything. While we all thought everyone was having a blast, for some fifteen years, he had faked his laughter, and enjoyed nothing.

Now, despite the amount of money he'd stolen, he had only a few hundred dollars in his checking account. Everything we had was leased and mortgaged; the house and the cars would all have to be relinquished. My own new car was a weeks-old graduation "present" that, my father explained now, he had leased in my name with no money down. He'd also taken out tens of thousands of dollars of extra college loans I didn't need that I was going to have to repay. I remembered signing the papers he'd handed me, saying that though my name was on them, he'd pay it all back himself, and that there was no reason not to take it in addition to the maximum loans he'd taken in his own name because with the low interest rates it was "free money." I'd turned large amounts of it over to him after it was deposited in my bank account so he could go to Mexico or a dinner club or Palm Springs.

Having just graduated and not found a real job, I was working at a moving company, the same manual labor I'd been doing during summers at home throughout college, but it wasn't going to cover the sizeable debts I now apparently owed. The morning after The Fall, as my mother came to call this culmination of their marital and financial ruin, I sat in the family room trying to figure out a game plan. My father swirled around me, gathering valuable things out of our house, while my mom shuffled around, heavily medicated, like a hospital patient. He hocked his dead brother's guitar. And his golf clubs.

I went back to Columbus and got a waitressing job. And a housecleaning job. And a job in the admissions department at a vocational school, working maniacally to pay the monthly dues on my surprise deficit. I worked overtime to hoard money for a trip. I was an accomplished traveler already, and over the next year and a half, while I waited for my boyfriend, a college senior, to graduate, I saved enough for us both to travel for the six months between his commencement and the start date of whichever grad school would give us both free rides. While planning the vacation, I realized our stop in Fiji would be a perfect place to get married. "Someone needs to do something to bring family together and have some good news," my mother said approvingly of the idea; "Don't you think you're as ready as you'll ever be?" my best friend asked when I expressed last-minute doubts. Though the correct answer was definitely *No*, for having gone into something as serious as a marriage with the wisdom of a recently rattled twentysomething, I got married to an amazing guy, the smartest and most reliable, the funniest and most supportive man in the Midwest, on Taveuni Island, under a waterfall, in 2004.

When the trip was over, my father-in-law picked us up at the airport. It was an abrupt return to reality in my home country when he said he wouldn't take us back to his house because long-term guests hadn't been cleared with my mother-in-law, and we couldn't go to my parents' houses, either, because both of them were homeless, living with friends.

After The Fall, my parents' lives unraveled personally and materially, their divorce impending as my father left again. They had both called me constantly. And I'd had little sympathy for them. That I kept wishing my father, who started making mild threats of suicide, would please suck it up, dismissively reminding him that he still had his health and his looks and his intelligence, is less surprising, since he'd done what he did to himself. But my frustration with my mother, too, was considerable.

Have I ever mentioned how much *I* hate victims?

Yes, I acknowledged, something horrendous had happened to her, and it was undoubtedly tragic. But there was no time for sitting around moaning about it. She hadn't supported herself since the seventies, and the possibility of living off my father or alimony forever was over now. Neither of my parents had gone to college. She needed a strategy. She needed to get her shit together and move forward. My irritation overwhelmed my feeling bad for her as she stayed holed up and helpless, her husband having left her three times, growing more despondent and poor, waiting for the bank to repossess the house while the gas company shut the utilities off around her.

My own handling of the crisis may not have been perfect. The workaholism and the marriage and the trip—which had, in addition to motivations of genuine curiosity and adventure, a ring of escapism to it. But I did exhibit the normal range of human emotions under the circumstances, sadness and anger and disappointment, but also excitement and joy and intimacy, and continued making goals for myself and meeting them, plans for my future and executing them, for that trip and beyond. I maintained relationships with my parents, who dropped all pretense of acting like parents. My family turned out to not be everything I had thought it was, but I continued to believe, even if I'd based much of my worth on my dad's word, and many of his words were lies, that that didn't have to change the better things that had always been true about me. Though I did worry about it sometimes. It wasn't the charmed kind of wifely exasperation my mom used anymore when, if she disapproved of something I was doing, she told me I was just like my father.

Number two.

The other divorce. My divorce.

My marriage was probably over several months before it started. It perhaps was obvious, the way we'd slept together five times on the six-month trip—the week in the enchanting Fijian honeymoon cottage included—that we were mostly friends. Before Fiji, in Borneo, I had become infatuated with the thirty-two-year-old Malaysian who guided us deep into the jungle, though he drank too much and admitted heavy patronization of $8 Chinese prostitutes. One night, after a long evening of drinking homemade rice wine in a village, I got up at two in the morning from the floor of our stilted longhouse to find him awake and still drinking by candlelight at the table in the adjacent room. I considered, when he asked me why I wasn't asleep, slowly walking to him and sitting on his lap. My wanting to lead him past my sleeping future husband and into the hall to press him to a wall and to ask him, while he watched me with his wide mahogany eyes, if he wanted me, and to tell him he could touch me anywhere he liked, I chalked up to extramarital fantasies being the nature of desire. Not to a sign that desire was lacking in my relationship. Later in the trip, scuba diving just a week before our wedding, I wanted a British dive master who was neither smart nor good-looking, and I took it as further confirmation that people who are responsible—who get steady jobs and husbands and move on from a life of wanderings and making out with backpacking Italians in Spain—still fantasize madly about strangers, but rise above by not acting on it. My feelings were indicative of nothing more than the grown-up truth, I reasoned, that all married people must just always want to fuck everyone they meet out of town.

My brand-new husband and I returned to Ohio two months before the school that gave us both the biggest stipends—the University of New Orleans— began. If I hadn't noticed my marriage was in trouble yet, it might've struck me the day we were getting ready for bed under the soaring ceilings of our just-moved-into Crescent City apartment and I said, "I think we should be allowed to make out with other people."

Just because it was true that my marriage was not going to make it didn't mean I was ready to accept it. I did not like failing. I did not like hurting people. I never made promises I couldn't keep. For a year after we'd made the agreement, neither one of us used our right to extramarital relations, and we continued on as usual, the world's most amicable grocery-shopping team, me uncharacteristically developing crushes on unlikely friends, starved for a certain kind of connection. In retrospect—naturally—it seems we were missing more than one kind. He didn't understand why I had such strong feelings about things, and I couldn't relate to his too-even keel. During our four-month Katrina evacuation I took up with an ex-girlfriend. My husband and I had a hundred tearful conversations about how we could make it work and salvage our elaborate plans to build our life together; my ex-girlfriend/now girlfriend and I tormented each other, she inconsolable that I wouldn't leave my husband for her, me starting fights as an outlet for the stress and doomed affections and guilt. A year and a half and yet another mistress later, I moved to San Francisco, pointing to my career rather than our marital death. It took us several more months to admit that it was both, and untwine our futures, and our bank accounts, and finally file for divorce.

* * *

But what all should be counted as *trauma*? Any tear-soaked event that, as my dad put it, rocked my world? Or the world of those around me, since by definition trauma includes witnessing threats or injuries to others? I think I barely mentioned to Dr. Shere, my psychiatric assessor, what, considering the size of its disruption, would probably be number three: the adoption. Though it was a big deal when it happened, I'd never felt that it had long-term ramifications for me personally.

From the moment my parents told me that my newly parentless, out-of-state cousins, whom I'd met only once, were going to be my new brother and sister, my excitement was uncontainable. My parents had to keep telling me to stop, for Chrissake, bouncing up and down around the house or dragging my new little sister about, with her blond hair and dimples and wild Southern accent. But my lightheartedness wasn't shared. My excitement aside, my adopted siblings were in fact two recent and uprooted orphans, and my parents, two young married people trying to negotiate the financial and emotional shocks of burying my dad's brother and doubling their child load. And then going to court to keep it, as my cousins' maternal grandparents fought to have my parents' custody revoked and given to them. I must have been more susceptible to my household stress than I realized, because at Christmas a couple years later, the post-adoption therapist presented me with a miniature calendar featuring teddy bears in various poses, and I threw it at her.

It was the most disrespectful thing I'd ever done. It probably still resides on my list of top five. I was a behaver. A laugher. I was pretty demanding and tended to get my way, but I did what I was told. A chores-doer. A rule-follower. Not a Christmas-present-thrower. My mother was stupefied. Had the perpetrator been one of the other kids, this might have been dismissed with a routine grounding, but in my case, it called for a full-on all-parent conference when my dad got home from work. The three of us locked ourselves in my parents' bedroom that night, my mother pacing worriedly, my father saying softly, "I don't understand. I don't understand," sitting on the edge of the bed while I cried, my wailing face pressed into their comforter, which I'd never done like that before.

Because I didn't understand, either. I *had* told Julia the therapist that I was in a bad mood, and I *didn't* feel like she was listening when her response was to give me a teddy bear calendar, even if I wanted it. I remember having a sense that those teddy bears were an insult to, not an acknowledgement of, my pain, which I hadn't recognized myself but was suddenly drowning in now that I was aware of it on my parents' bed. It still didn't really seem like it called for throwing Christmas presents at a therapist. Over and over, I just repeated to my parents the only thing that felt true, wrenching its way all through my sick guts.

"I'm just having a really bad year," I said.

It had passed. I had cried it out, and afterward, gone back to being a generally effervescent child.

But the stress among the rest of my family, even if I didn't feel that involved in it, continued. Four years after the adoption, my thirteen-year-old brother moved back out of our house. He had behavior problems—always had, even with his own parents—and my parents thought it would be better for him and the whole family if he lived with the maternal grandparents who'd been fighting for custody of him, and with whom he'd been screaming he wanted to live, since his parents died. His sister, my adopted little sister, stayed with us until I was fourteen, when she went to visit her brother and grandparents in Florida, as she did a couple times a year, and never came back. While my parents were trying to figure out what the hell had happened, an official came to our house. I couldn't help thinking of the episode of *Full House* that my little sister and I had recently watched—in which Stephanie's new friend is taken away from his abusive father—when the official on our doorstep delivered papers alleging, out of nowhere, that my parents had abused and dangerously neglected her. My little sister had gone with her grandparents to the police in Florida and given this testimony formally. My older sister, Jessica, and I read through it, shocked. A social worker came to make sure we weren't battered and were clothed and fed. My parents could go to Florida, possibly face criminal allegations, have to prove they weren't true, and go through another custody battle, or let my little sister stay in Florida. It was evidently where she wanted to be. So, after a lot of fretting and legal consultations and, ultimately, resignation, the number of children in my house—some ten years after it had suddenly doubled—was, with the serving of some court papers, just as abruptly back down to two.

Hurricane Katrina. Number four.

Because my husband had made me leave, I was well out of the city by the time the floodwaters poured in. Making our way east with my best friend and neighbor, Lauren, we'd left the frazzled mothers in the lobby of the Holiday Inn Express in Jackson, Mississippi, who were nearly in tears about paying $85 for a smelly smoking room. They consented because it was better than returning to the car at 1 A.M. to tell their children they had to keep going. We'd continued on and found an interstate-exit dive twenty miles beyond Jackson whose $50 nightly rate was more in our price range and, we discovered, included unlimited free porn. When we woke up the next morning to see on the Weather Channel that the storm had strengthened, it looked as if we might not be going back to New Orleans anytime soon. And as if the storm would hit Jackson, too. Our resources were going to run out quickly. Lauren was from Iowa, and my husband and I from Ohio, so the closest that anyone could put us up was in the Midwest. Since my parents were homeless, house-crashing interlopers themselves, we headed for my in-laws', who lived not far from where my family had recently fallen apart. We were in Greater Cleveland by the time the winds had even kicked all the way up in the South.

The ripples of the flood's devastation easily reached us there. The CNN coverage we watched for weeks didn't tell us whether our neighborhood had flooded, or our school, and certainly couldn't tell us if our university jobs or graduation plans for the following spring were still valid. FEMA's hotline was answered by an automated overload message that told callers to try back another time and then hung up on them; when I did finally file an application, by staying up until the middle of the night to get through, we were ultimately denied assistance because, I realized after several weeks and two dozen additional phone calls, we'd answered a question wrong and that answer couldn't be changed. The lady on the phone suggested we go to the Red Cross.

We had done this already, one day after putting Lauren on a train to Des Moines, realizing that it was probably time to get ourselves some help. After half an hour of filling out paperwork at the local Red Cross branch, we had reached the question requesting directions to our apartment in New Orleans.

"Like, directions from here?" I asked a worker.

"What should I put here?" that worker asked a female coworker, pointing to the "Directions" spot on the application. "I mean, it's not like we're going to go *there*," he said. The city was still flooded.

The coworker shook her head. "No." She looked at the man, and he smiled. "No, I guess we're not." She laughed, and he laughed, while my husband and I stared at them. They gave us a $75 grocery voucher, a $260 clothes voucher valid at Super K-Mart, and two tiny plastic bags containing mini toiletries.

Anyway, I told the FEMA lady, not only had we been to the Red Cross once, but when we'd called them again later and asked for more help, they'd said that they had already given us a grocery voucher, and when I replied that between the two of us, we ate more than $75 of groceries a month, they cut us a check for a couple hundred more and told us never to call them again. When I went to Walgreens the next day and the checkout kid asked me if I wanted to donate money to the Red Cross for Hurricane Katrina victims, I swore at him.

It was four months before we could go back. Though all our belongings were intact when we finally returned to New Orleans in December, not so our neighborhood, or city. Or us. In four months of living with my none-too-thrilled in-laws, regularly visiting my post-Fall parents where they squatted, in the *last* city my world had been destroyed in, I'd felt keyed up, unsettled about our uncertain future. My husband and I barely even tried to pretend as if we were interested in having sex anymore. Determined to continue doing the right thing, I'd told Lauren when she came back to Ohio from Iowa for Evacuation Thanksgiving that if I had to give up sex in order to have a husband as wonderful as mine, I was prepared to do it. But no matter how I wanted that to be true, I wasn't. It wouldn't be long before I would get into a pattern of get-togethers with my ex-girlfriend that involved alcohol and very heavy petting.

Finding our personal and collective grounding wasn't any easier once we got back to Louisiana. Lauren went from crashing at our in-laws' to crashing with her own parents to crashing with us in our New Orleans apartment, since she'd lost her own apartment and everything in it, just a few blocks away. The state of my marriage didn't help uplift me from the conditions of the rest of my surroundings. But I avoided the pit of alcoholic despair everyone else seemed to fall into. Unlike a lot of people—who probably had PTSD, if you're looking at the diagnostic checklist—I didn't have to drive around way out of my way to avoid seeing certain neighborhoods, or have a nervous breakdown when I did see them. I did my job teaching English composition at the university, though it was still full of broken glass and mold, and finished my master's thesis. My self-preservation instincts survived. I broke off my turbulent affair. It took a couple times. But I persevered, and it did eventually stick.

Years later, in San Francisco, my disaster mentality persisted in the form of my having no real furniture or valuable belongings. Everything but my clothes was something someone else had junked. I didn't count on nature, and the future, under even normal circumstances anymore, and according to the United States Geological Survey, the Bay Area's next big earthquake would happen by 2020. My way of coping was accepting from the outset that everything I owned would be destroyed, and therefore owning nothing I was attached to.

But unlike a staggering number of New Orleanians, if the research was accurate, I didn't want to die. I was taking steps to live, to live healthier, moving out of the city before the next hurricane season because I had the resources and because I knew I didn't want the stress. I took the initiative, moved on from my marriage, staked and built my life in another city perched on the edge of certain geological doom, sleeping on a possibly gross bed I bought for $30 from a transient lesbian but sleeping well, never staying awake all night waiting for the building on top of me to collapse in the great impending quake, even on the nights when smaller, sneak-preview quakes would rouse me, but only briefly, before I went back to sleep.

Number five.

The rocket scientist. One can't very well go crazy following a couple of rape-related incidents of various sorts and not have to consider, at some point, the rocket scientist.

I suppose the most succinct way to explain what happened with the rocket scientist is the way I opened a journal entry dated early December 1998. I was not a regular journaler; this was a note to myself on a special occasion. I was eighteen years old, a freshman in college. "The day before yesterday I had sex with some boy I did not know," the entry says. "I told him probably about ten times to stop and go to sleep but he kept trying. 'Attacking me,' he called it."

The rocket scientist was a friend of a hometown friend's. An aeronautical engineer—an actual rocket scientist—he offered to give me a ride back to Ohio State after Thanksgiving break on his way to his own, prestigious university. I'd met him in Cleveland the Saturday night before we had to return to classes; my parents were relieved not to have to make the drive themselves. Because of the traffic that post-holiday Sunday, the usual two and a half hours to Columbus took five, and he had at least that many more to go after dropping me off, so when he asked to spend the night in our dorm, my roommate and I said fine. We talked about math. He was cute and supersmart. When it was time to go to bed, I wasn't sorry we had to cram close on my twin mattress. Then, according to my journal, "[h]e kissed me and I hated the way he kissed, and I told him to go to sleep." Then "a couple times he started kissing me again and I kept telling him to stop. I told him we shouldn't have sex."

But we did, after some more arguing back and forth and this terrible sentence: "At that point, I stopped protesting."

That night, when he fell asleep, when he had finally finished to my great relief, I got up and got away from him. I took a long, burning shower in the abandoned communal bathroom. I grabbed my French book and sat on the floor outside my room in the hallway and stared at verb conjugations for several hours. When it was barely dawn, I woke him up and told him he had to leave. He whined, saying he wasn't ready, saying come on, let him sleep, protesting some more, until finally I started yelling at him and he went back to his car.

A day and a half later—in an intro-to-women's-studies class, of all places—I started crying, and could not stop.

Back at the dorm, I wandered down the hall to the room of the best friends I'd made in the short months I'd been at school. Unfortunately, they were eighteen-year-old men. More unfortunately, the most outspoken of them held some views that were, though I wouldn't learn to recognize such things for years, deeply misogynist. This was an honors floor, and so I sat there, supposedly precocious, debating the ethics of what had happened with other ostensibly gifted students, all of us chain-smoking and using logic and rational language, though I continued crying for the entirety of the discussion. Yes, I had flirted with him, I admitted from the onset, had even said during our drive that I could be interested in having sex with him, but I had changed my mind, and I had said no. My argument for being upset was that I had said no, no, no, so many times. The outspoken philosophy major countered that, culturally—or maybe it was biologically, or evolutionarily, or all three, I forget—it was my job to say no, just as it was the rocket scientist's job to talk me into it, overcome my professed resistance and other obstacles of the hunt, pursue me until I was disarmed and he got what he and probably we both wanted. That I had allowed him into my bed to begin with had been my green light to engage in this game. That I had said "No" multiple times but failed to start yelling, kicking, or trying to run demonstrated my willingness to continue playing it.

This philosophy major wasn't saying anything I could disagree with: All the representations of relations between the sexes that I knew positioned man as pursuer and conqueror and woman as resister to be won over—or finally admit that she'd wanted it but was just pretending she didn't all along. Everyone knew that. Everyone in the dorm room agreed, myself included, that I was the kind of girl who could stand up for herself. Self-confident and queer, strong in debates, I was, we extrapolated, perfectly capable of fighting off unwanted advances, vehemently if need be. If any of us had to guess, we'd guess I would start a fight if I really had a problem with something. Again, since it was my job to automatically say "No" no matter what I meant, it was also my job to show that I really *meant* no by screaming or fighting.

This all sounded reasonable to me.

I returned to my dorm room. Still unsettled, I wrote the journal entry. I spent most of the rest of the eight pages trying to figure out how I let it all happen. "I didn't want to fuck him," I wrote. "So why did I? Why do I let myself wear down like that?" Some of my speculations are frenetic and nonsensical. "Because I was taught that sex was so important and sacred that I wanted it to be such a great experience with me? That really doesn't sound right. My dad always says I'm the best. Do I feel like I have to be the best at this? Why? Because it's so personal and the competition is so unknown and fierce?" Did I want to pacify him, "despite the fact that it was against what I wanted?" Did I not want to make him mad? And if so, "why not? What the fuck do I care what some stranger thinks?" Did I just want to be "something cool, something sexy"? Did I "have some sort of void" in me? "I really do have a lot of self-respect," I wrote, but "maybe my sense of self-respect comes from others thinking well about me"? "Maybe I needed to make him happy because that makes him like me and maybe that's supposed to make me like me too"? Maybe I just "wanted to be a beautiful girl who put out." Maybe I was "showing off." It hadn't been the way I usually made decisions, but maybe I just felt like I had "to prove something."

Though I had clearly decided this before I even picked up the pen, I went on to "conclude" that the events were my fault. "I can't say it's his fault, I didn't tell him enough times how I felt. Not that I should <u>have</u> to, but I know from experience what's necessary." I'd had sex with two other men before, and made out with several others. After I stopped protesting—"I saw sleeping with him as the only option and I wanted to get it over with"—I wrote that after penetration started, "I hated it. I wanted to ask him to stop a lot more times" but didn't bother anymore, giving in, the whole time "thinking I just wanted him to get off, really fast, and be done. I hated it." I name myself as the one responsible for "perpetrating" it, and being "disgusted and disgusting." "I said no, but not enough. I fully consented to sex I absolutely by my will did not want to have. Consented by default. Because I didn't want to fight."

Looking back over these sentences as an enlightened adult, I feel sad for this girl, of course. Not just because her socialization has blinded her to the glaring contradiction between "I said no" and "I fully consented," but because she doesn't know that "didn't want to fight" was really "couldn't fight." Because her lack of information and education about certain innate responses to threats, responses that were common to lots of other people and that she would experience again, leads her to blame herself. Just like she would again twelve years later, when she is diagnosed with PTSD.

"Why don't I want to fight?" I asked myself several times, frantically, in the journal pages. In the day-to-day, my self-protection practices were on point, especially for a teenager. I didn't fuck assholes. I didn't get in cars with anyone who'd been drinking at all, ever. I can understand why I was so confused about why those systems had failed at a crucial moment. "I think probably the only way he would have stopped was if I yelled really loudly or left," I wrote. "I honestly didn't even think of either. So I let him do whatever he wanted."

And there you had it. My first fateful freeze.

A month later, I had sex with him willingly. My female friends, also eighteen, also knowing nothing—and who among them could say it hadn't happened to them, that one time they'd said no at first, or second or third or fifth or eighteenth?—agreed with the misogynists down the hall that it seemed like a reasonable misunderstanding. Convinced I hadn't been wronged, I started taking his phone calls and constant online-chat messages, dismissing my profound anger and resentment. Anyway, if we were having long-distance phone-fun, talking about classes and our families and joking around, then he must not be a monster, and what happened must not have been bad. Both back in Cleveland for Christmas, we saw each other again, and I consented to sex this time, after we'd hung out all night and early morning was starting to break.

I consented to sex, but I still felt strongly that I did not want him to come inside me—as he had done the first time without asking. (Let's not talk about the idiocy of my having not used condoms when I was on the pill at this age.)

I told him to pull out. I told him more than once.

He refused.

I didn't cry this time. But I wouldn't make the same mistake again. As I had done in my past, I would make certain for the rest of my future not to sleep with anyone until I was sure he or she respected me.

What about that time when I got lost on the beach in North Carolina? When I wandered away from my parents near the water because I was composing a story in my head, and couldn't find my way back to them and I really thought I'd never see my family again? "You just walked up to me being so cool," my mom always said when she recounted our reunion that day, "but I dropped to my knees and put my arms around you and your heart was pounding so hard. You were so cool about it," she said, "but you must have been petrified."

Or the night some guy who turned out to be my dad's friend was skulking around our house when I was home alone in fifth grade and I called the police because I thought he was going to break in and murder me? Or when I was sixteen and I got caught having sex with my girlfriend? My parents came around and became accepting after a while, but that first night, my father pulled me downstairs, ambushing me for hours with how twisted I was, repeating that I was so fucked up as my mother stared unhappily into space and I cried, enraged by their narrow-minded condemnation.

Under the right circumstances, any of those might evoke the feelings of extreme fear or helplessness or threat that could be the T in PTSD. Anyone who was asked to make a list of bad things that had happened to them could have something on it that has given someone PTSD at some point: a death, a mugging, a car crash. At least 25 percent of Americans have experienced a trauma by the time they reach adulthood, and by the age of forty-five, almost all of them have. Child abuse, domestic abuse, parental neglect. Cancer. A break-in, a fire, a natural disaster. Rape, assault, terrorist attack, war, torture, childbirth. Getting divorced or going to prison. Civil conflict. Watching too much terrorist-attack footage on the news! The normative human response to trauma is recovery, and if I had recovered from all the previous "traumas" in my life, who could know how traumatizing they'd been, or if it was their existence that made trauma in Haiti one trauma too many? Or if it had been just too many work traumas too close together (long assignments being an additional risk factor for journalists)? Or just one trauma that was *just* the right amount of traumatic?

Attempts to answer these questions definitively seemed to require impos-
ing sense and blame on a phenomenon that was accountable to neither.

Other contemporary studies had found that personal characteristics didn't
matter, and that the *trauma*'s character was the deciding factor in a person's
resultant psychological condition. And while some research suggested that
previous trauma might be a statistically significant risk factor for developing
PTSD, it was certainly no guarantee.

Nico was evidence of this. During our first night together, he had told me
about his father's suicide, when he was seventeen. It wasn't until we'd spent
more time together that I realized that that story was even worse than it'd
sounded. That he and his father had had a long heart-to-heart the day before.
That they'd all had Easter dinner the day of the incident, everyone in the
family eating together and drinking some wine—but not too much for Nico,
who'd got the *Don't you dare* face from his father when he picked up the
bottle to pour himself a second glass. After dinner, Nico took a shower; his
dad caught him in the hall to say that he would go running with him tomorrow. Nico went to join his mother in front of the TV. His dad didn't come. His
dad took the leash to walk the dogs, but no one ever used the leashes because
they lived on a farm. His dad arrived in the living room, drank a cup of coffee, and a glass of cognac, and left out the back door.

Thinking he'd been acting weird, Nico gave him ten minutes. Something
felt wrong, but maybe his dad just needed time alone. When he didn't reappear, Nico went to look for him. He checked the kitchen and the bathroom.
The garage light was on, but the door from the kitchen was locked. Not wanting to alarm his mother, he asked, "Is it nice outside?" before walking out the
front door and around to the big garage door. He pushed it up. No one was
in there. He walked past the motorcycle several times, not seeing the letter on
the seat. He went back outside. Walking back toward the house to get the car
keys so he could canvass the surrounding streets, he looked to the outbuild-
ings and noticed a light on in one, shining through the bottom of the half-
closed roll-up door.

He was too late. He tried to scream but nothing came out of his mouth.
He jumped up to unclip the leash his father had strung over the rafter, and
fell to the ground under his weight. He tried to pry off the noose, but it was
too tight, as if it'd become part of his neck. Having run back to the house, he
couldn't figure out what to say to his mother.

Hey, can you help me with something? No. That didn't seem appropriate.

What was he supposed to say? He had to tell her what happened two or three times before she comprehended it. He told her he couldn't get the rope off. They went back together with scissors. They still couldn't get it, and didn't want to be aggressive because they didn't want to hurt him, though he was already dead. They called the fire department. They waited, and had to call again. It came, and then the police. The doctor filling out the death certificate had drugged his mom, so Nico identified the body. If he wanted to cry, he should, the doctor told him. He didn't want to, no—he thought he should, too, but couldn't. He slept for an hour, but his mom's screaming woke him up. So he went to the police station and gave his statement, then took his parents' address book, and started making the phone calls.

Then, five months later, Nico's best friend came over to his house, asked him for help with tying his necktie, went out to a fancy dinner, drove to the woods, and hung himself from a tree.

Somehow, Nico finished the year of high school he had left. Then he started at the University of Strasbourg, an hour away. But within three months of medical school, broke and feeling adrift, he dropped out and started working odd jobs before signing up for a career as a gendarme. *Gens d'armes*: men at arms—there is no equivalent American service, but their duties most roughly resemble the National Guard's. He specialized in SWAT operations at home and abroad, getting up in the middle of the night to stand outside doors, waiting, before storming into drug dealers' houses; chasing them, first in formation and carrying a ballistics shield, when they ran; stalking immigrant gold pirates through the jungle of French Guiana, one of several territories his government never returned to independence; acting as riot police in Paris; lent as peacekeepers in Haiti, where, like the displaced, the gendarmes slept in flimsy, leaking tents, listening as they lay in cots to the gunfights echoing across the valley, hoping a stray bullet wouldn't land them on the list of the night's murders posted on the bulletin board before breakfast: *1 person found stabbed at the edge of the road, 2 people shot*, etc.

If none of that was enough to trigger his old trauma and reduce him to a quivering mound of post-traumatic stress, backing up local police forces could have been, particularly when it involved recovering dead bodies, like dragging the body of a woman out of a river in New Caledonia one night alone.

Previous trauma wasn't the last match Nico had on the list of risk factors. He also—evidently—had a parent with "mental health issues, including depression." And Nico's sense of safety as a developing child was threatened way more often than mine; while his father had a terrifying hair-trigger temper, mine was a bucket of hugs. Both of us were clear of the rest of risks. He did have me bested on most of the "resilience factors," though. Those were elements and activities thought to reduce the risk of developing PTSD. Did Nico feel good about his own actions after he faced danger? Yes. Was he capable of overcoming fear to react and respond effectively in those situations? Sure, by precisely that kind of training. His test to join his unit involved a long and exhausting obstacle course in which he had to complete complicated tasks both before, and then after, being assaulted by a guy whose job it was to assault recruits. The vessels in Nico's nose burst when the guy punched him in the face. Blood poured down his mouth and shirt for the rest of the exam. Once, I asked him on Skype, "What did you do today?" and what he did that day was get punched in the face some more; he had regular training days that involved face-punching, so nobody would forget what it was like, how to move past the shock of it and get on with their duties. And did Nico have coping strategies for the negative events he encountered? Yes, he did. He pointed out to me once that when *he* had had a violent or upsetting afternoon at work, he did his daily 400 push-ups (half with his feet on the ground, half with his feet elevated on a chair), ran between five and fourteen miles, and talked it over with his unit buddies.

I, you know, got drunk by myself.

But by these measures, I did do some things right. I reached out to friends and family. I took up therapy or a support group. Resilience factors aren't guarantees, either. And like the risk factors, they can sound a little victim-blamey. As if certain people should never leave their houses, and that if they do and something bad happens, they had PTSD coming. And as if certain other people should've better employed great reserves of coping skills and self-care knowledge—which, if they were raised in most modern cultures, they never would have learned. And as if those same people should have accessed and practiced these tools in a society that was hostile both to mental illness and to victims. Forget risk factors and resilience factors. The National Institute of Mental Health puts it best when it says, "Anyone can get PTSD at any age." Or as the Mayo Clinic explains simply, "Doctors aren't sure why some people get PTSD." It was impossible to know if I could've somehow prevented my own post-traumatic condition. It was impossible to know why one moment in Haiti had kicked off a disorder that would change my physiology and my future. And at this point, who cared?

Well, my insurance company did. Dr. Shere concluded that for whatever else had happened to me in history, it was indeed my rolling into Haiti on an atrocious day of that atrocious earthquake year and working on an atrocious story that had been the "sole cause" of my emotional destruction, according to her official report. Given the strength of my dissociation in Haiti, I'd been a likely candidate for long-lasting PTSD. Given the strength of my symptoms, I'd been in need of a lot more therapy before doing anything else. In Dr. Shere's opinion, I had continued to be, as I embarked on new assignments in Haiti II and Europe and Africa and Ohio, "severely impaired." Drastically more impaired than I was giving myself credit for, she told me in her office.

"PTSD is like a football injury," she said, chiding me. She'd stared at me in wonderment—and, I felt, judgment—as I recounted the progression of events and assignments. "Once you incur an injury," she said, "you need to stay on the bench until it's a hundred percent healed." With veterans, the incidence of PTSD increases with the tours and amount of combat experienced, and the longer and harder they serve, the more vulnerable they are.

Dr. Shere's professional speculation was that by not going on indefinite leave the moment I'd got back from Haiti the first time, given the severity of my symptoms, I'd exacerbated my disorder. In Dr. Shere's opinion, rather than submerging myself in more atrocities, I should have been trying to get on disability and letting myself get better. Repeated exposures to trauma can affect how difficult it is to recover as they accumulate. And Haiti Part I had arguably been multiple traumas, already. "Though I understand you may not have the resources to stop working," she conceded.

Maybe working in the field had made the initial condition worse. Maybe not. PTSD sufferers often move between intrusive symptoms (the berserk ones) and constriction (the numbing stuff). My periods of calm post-Haiti Part I could have been that containment that naturally sets in, when trauma turns sneaky because you think you're OK now that the screaming and sobbing is over. When you're fine, if a little empty, or just prone to more pedestrian symptoms such as outbursts of anger, fear-fueled jealousy or intimacy issues, self-harm or nagging malcontentedness. When you wouldn't present as PTSD symptomatic in a way that would make you go to the hospital but just in little life-ruining ways, persisting for so long after the incident that you might get misdiagnosed as depressed or anxious, but probably you'd never bother going to get diagnosed at all. You might move back into intrusive symptoms sometimes. On traumatic anniversaries, or because of particular triggers. Or because of nothing.

Anyway, Dr. Shere diagnosed me as alcoholic and suicidal. She diagnosed me with comorbid major depression as well as PTSD. She strongly advised full-time medication. Hers was consistent with Denise's assessment: Though I'd had some pretty good shakeups in the past, I was fine and functioning before Haiti I, and I might have otherwise stayed that way.

Officially, my previous trauma was cleared of culpability. I had strong previous trauma recovery and a stellar track record at life. I was clearly, visibly, and only disturbed, Dr. Shere's notes said, when she made me talk about Haiti, as opposed to anything else in my history. Still, regardless of whether it disturbed me daily—whether I "needed" previous trauma to have reached this traumatized state, whether anything was previous trauma's "fault," whether any of those events had been traumatic enough to qualify as trauma at all—all that stuff *had* happened.

And now it was coming back up.

"A secure sense of connection with caring people is the foundation of personality development," Judith Lewis Herman writes. "When this connection is shattered, the traumatized person loses her basic sense of self. Developmental conflicts of childhood and adolescence, long since resolved, are suddenly reopened. Trauma forces the survivor to relive all her earlier struggles over autonomy, initiative, competence, identity, and intimacy."

Suddenly, ten years after my parents' divorce, Denise and I were talking about it. We talked about it, and then we were done with it, or thought we were, and then we needed to talk about it some more. I'd done heavy crying about it when it happened, and had some rough days then, but I'd recovered. My relationship with my father had recovered. And I'd even covered it again, just to be thorough, with Meredith when we were talking about my own divorce. Now here I was crying about it all over on Denise's table, and harder than ever.

If I'd known that was going to happen, I'm not sure if I'd have been better prepared, or if I would have quit before I started. "How are we still *talking* about this!" I yelled at Denise as I started sobbing about my dad, or my divorce, or other old, already handled news. "Seriously, Hurricane *Ka-TRINA*?"

It was one thing, then another thing. My sister's screechy guinea pig? Come on. It was like we were playing Whac-A-Mole.

My obstacles to mental health had seemed formidable enough. The more I learned, and the deeper we went, the more impossible my task seemed. I sunk into a parallel depression of dauntedness. Where I used to look nice for my hours-long Skype dates with Nico, checking myself in the mirror and perching myself in a broken street chair at my crappy donated kitchen table, I now took them in my bed, propped on pillows like an invalid, laptop in my lap, lacking the energy to sit up. The only times he saw me dressed and vertical were when our schedules aligned such that I had to talk to him while I was at the office.

"Hi, gorgeous," I would say, my voice soft with exhaustion and affection, still enunciating very carefully. "How—was—your—day?"

"Hey, my baby," he'd say. "My day was good."

"What did you do at work today?" I would ask, slower and more deliberately than to a child.

And he would tell me about his deployment guarding the American embassy in Paris. Or evacuating the Eiffel Tower for a bomb threat. Or doing security at the G8 summit. Lately, he was on a long mission again, in Montpellier, supporting local police with the extra crime that came with the summer tourist season. He talked to me from stark dorms that housed his unit, trying to find moments away from his bunkmates. I attempted to talk to him about what I was going through, sometimes. A particularly frequent bout of Oklahoma flashbacks one week was an opportunity to give him details about the things that had scared me there. But I was shy. I was lying down and wearing pajamas most of the time, yes, but I still tried to give him the impression that I had some semblance of stability.

"What's going on?" he asked, searching my cheerless eyes.

I hesitated. "I don't want you to think I'm stupid."

"I need to know what happened to my girlfriend."

I felt like such an idiot when I started crying. But he was patient, and listened quietly when I whimpered, "They could've broken every bone in my face."

I missed him.

Again. Still. Always.

The thing about being disconnected from yourself is that it accommodates great amounts of denial. All kinds of denial. That, for example, missing half your human feelings is not actually a good or cool trick. And you only have to disconnect a little, just stop listening, to ignore the things your bones are telling you: That your marriage is over. That your father was spending more money than he made, despite his having denied it when you asked him once whether someone might come to repossess the furniture. That you are a person who is vulnerable. To the world, and to a particular Frenchman, who is your touchstone, the pebble that you placed deep in your belly to grab onto when you got swept away, though he was far away from, and had never been, your home. That your love is oversize enough to threaten heart explosion—threaten everything—and that with all the tortures you are currently acquainting yourself with, equal to any of them is the distance between you, and that to reduce that distance permanently, everything in your life will have to change. Starting with you.

10.

"*J'aime bien mieux etre malheureux en t'aimant, que de ne t'avoir jamais vu,*"
Nico wrote on a card he gave me in Montpellier when I arrived to meet him
there, quoting a seventeenth-century French writer. It was our third meeting
after Haiti, nearly a year after we'd met. We hadn't seen each other in person
since Paris, three months earlier. He was talking about how hard it was to be
apart all the time.

I would rather be unhappy loving you, he was saying, *than never having
seen you.*

Well. He had no idea.

I was in Montpellier because everyone was in agreement—my dad, my
friends, Denise—that I needed a vacation. I had been barely holding it together. I had arguably been not holding it together. I'd asked Nico during a
Skype chat if I could join him in Montpellier.

"Of course," he said. "You're welcome, my beauty."

The flight between San Francisco and France encountered rowdy turbu-
lence. People clutched and gasped around me. I sat patiently, realizing that I
would be more relieved than disappointed if we went down. That made me
sad. The only reason I cared if we pulled out of it was that I would've liked to
kiss Nico's face another time—it'd been so few times—before never doing
anything again. But other than that, I was 90-some percent resigned to our
imminent death. When it became clear that we were going to make it, I was
left with the sorrow of that peace.

On the ground, my symptoms stayed fairly well behaved. Conveniently, during that week, we were drunk all the time. Not in the PTSD way, but in the cocktail-before-dinner, then split-a-bottle-of-wine-because-it's-August-on-the-Riviera way, which, however different the motives, produced the same results. It kept me loose and open, so that I was touched deeply by the sex we were having, but the steady stream of booze assisted a light dissociation that kept my rawness to below-freak-show levels. Only small amounts of it seeped through. One night when Nico was inside me, I clutched him and begged, "Please don't ever leave me." A sentiment I'd never felt for anyone, even the man I'd married, uttered to a guy with whom I'd spent a total of eight days. Another night, next to his warmth, buried under blankets despite the humidity outside, I wilted, losing the rigidity that kept me put together, and cried. But Nico had just been telling me that when he pictured his father's face, he could often recall only how he looked hanging dead from a rope, so crying after a conversation like that gave me the appearance of a still possibly normal person.

Ditto my behavior when he came to visit me two weeks after I left Montpellier, in San Francisco. His deployment was over. He had some time off. He'd never been to America, and I'd been urging him to come since our first e-mail. Finally, almost exactly a year after we'd met, he arrived. I kept myself moving and kept myself busy with the task of impressing him with California's majesty.

"This cheese is made here," I said of the artisanal varietal I set out in front of him when he arrived. "And this wine. And these figs were grown here."

In our first couple of days, I fell into a dark, hopeless hole. But it was shallow. I looked sad but calm, not having raving, committable-type symptoms. Nico lay down on the floor with me that day, wrapping me up and saying, "If you can't be happy with me, you can't be happy with anyone." Pretty quickly, I got it together. I drove him to Marin County, north over the Golden Gate Bridge, past redwoods to a rented house in a small town with sea-salt-and-eucalyptus-tinged air. I fed him Mission burritos and world-famous chocolate tarts. I turned crazy and started yelling at him bitterly, over an indiscernible trigger, in an Indian restaurant that I'd hoped would astound him. But because his self-defensive mechanism to his girlfriend's becoming a quick bitch, like many people's, was to shut down and become an asshole, our yelling ended up looking like both our faults, a couple's misunderstanding, not something I had started with no cause.

On his birthday, which fell toward the end of his two-week trip, I rented him a motorcycle more powerful than the one he rode at home—with more horsepower than was allowed by French law—and climbed onto the back of it, giving him directions to Big Sur via California Highway 1.

I liked my guests to have a good time. But this time I also had ulterior motives.

Nico had sensed this from day two or three. Finally, a week in, he brought up his suspicions. "You just want I like California in case you want me later," he said at my apartment. He meant that I was trying to convince him that California was great in the event that I later decided I wanted him to move in with me. Meaning I hadn't decided that yet.

I got up from the table, where I'd opened an exorbitantly expensive bloomy-rinded California goat cheese with a line of ash through its center. I walked to the kitchen, opened a drawer, and came back with a jewelry box. I placed it in front of him on the table.

"What is it?" he asked.

"Open it," I said.

It continued like this for a while, until he did. The box had a copy of my house keys inside it. My friends would mock me for this move later, but Nico's eyes filled with tears.

"Excuse me," he said.

It was the same thing he'd said the first time I'd seen him cry in person, which had been the day I'd brought him back from the airport. It was late, and after he'd eaten and showered, we lay down in bed. I was propped up on one elbow, looking at him, then pressed my face to his chest to breathe him in, and kiss his skin, and he'd welled up.

"Excuse me," he'd said.

But emotionally overwhelming as my key-proposition was, it wasn't an easy question. He didn't answer me. He still hadn't answered me when we got to Big Sur a few days later.

After checking into our 1930s inn and cleaning up, we headed to our dinner reservations in the dining room. In Montpellier, Nico had worked long shifts, so I'd still been able to lie down and read books all day by myself; in this cozy, rustic restaurant, five hours of motorcycling and eight days of tour-guiding down, my exhaustion was setting in. I was unused to socializing that much those days, and I had marshaled all my energy to do it. Along with the stressful uncertainty of my pending proposal, I was starting to break down.

My agitation increased; by the time our entrées came, it was becoming unbearable to sit at the table. I was actively looking for distractions in the room when a woman appeared in the open top half of the restaurant's Dutch door.

She was easily in her eighties, and holding a little white dog. She seemed to be talking, or complaining, to no one. Our table was the closest to her. When I made eye contact, she said directly to me, "In France, you can take dogs in restaurants."

I smiled at her politely, but then stopped cutting up my duck. "Are you French?" I asked her.

She said she was.

"He's French," I said, nodding at Nico.

"*Vous êtes français?*" she exclaimed, bringing his attention suddenly to the conversation.

She had been a young woman during World War II, she told us, living in her town, trying her best to mind her own business, when the Americans arrived. One paratrooper fell in love with her immediately and started pursuing her. He asked her to tutor him in French, and she complied. As his lessons progressed, he asked her to marry him, and she refused. When the war ended, he went back home. But he returned, several times, to try to persuade her to come to America with him as his wife. Finally she consented. She'd been in California for sixty years, she said, given birth to some insane number of sons, gone on to live happily ever after.

"Oh, come *on*," I whispered to myself, my breakdown achieving completion with the appearance of the Ghost of Christmas Future here. I turned my head while Nico chatted her up in French, swallowing hard to keep the tears that were escaping my eyes minimal and quiet. The woman either didn't notice or didn't care, and one of her middle-aged sons appeared in the window alongside her; he was in the instrumental band that had been playing in the restaurant earlier that night, the two of them explained happily.

When we returned from Big Sur, I could barely drag myself out of bed anymore. I only did so fueled by the knowledge that I just had to keep it up for two, then one more day. Nico could feel it. It wasn't as if he didn't know about my illness. But he was still managing to escape the majority of the everyday, real-world worsts of it.

That would end on our next trip.

* * *

In the two weeks between the Montpellier and San Francisco rendezvous, I'd written and turned in the feature I'd reported in Ohio; after Nico left San Francisco, I wrote the piece I'd reported in Uganda, then went to report another piece in a state I couldn't publicly disclose because I was working undercover. At the same time, among that writing and editing and fact-checking schedule, I started doing some interior decorating.

When we got back from Big Sur, Nico had said yes. Yes, he said, he would move in with me, move to the United States for a while. He would take some time off work and get a six-month visitor's visa so we could see how it was to be together. But he had to go on a three-month deployment to Guadeloupe, in the Caribbean, first.

I wished I didn't have to wait so long, because I was a disaster, and dealing with our long-distance relationship in tandem with my emotional problems was more than I could manage. In the meantime, I tried to divert my longing into readying the apartment for a man with European-high standards for charm. Which is to say I got rid of all the furniture I had taken from other people's garbage. Which is to say I got rid of all my furniture.

The only problem was that I had total psychological paralysis around buying furniture. During the hurricane season after the hurricane season that had brought us Hurricane Katrina, my husband and I bought a couch. By this time, my relationship with my mistress was in full swing, and it was becoming ever clearer that my marriage wasn't sustainable. Given its vulnerability to natural disasters and homemade ones, I could not handle owning this couch. The day it was delivered, I locked myself in my bedroom with my dinner, refusing to look at the sofa I'd so painstakingly picked out, and called my father in hysterics. I remember him laughing at me. Was I being ridiculous? I suppose I was being ridiculous. I was having a hard time explaining to him why hysterics were warranted.

"It's just a couch," he kept saying.

"It's not," I kept saying. "It's really not."

I'd never wanted a ton of belongings, having worked at a moving company in high school and college and seen how much shit people had that they didn't need. Hurricane Katrina didn't help my aversion to possessing household goods. That was further validated later during the summer that I bought the couch, when I lived in Thailand with the refugees from Burma, whose explanation for not owning normal things like family photographs was invariably "I lost it when soldiers attacked and burned everything down." So here I was

in San Francisco with garbage furniture. But lots of other underpaid trans-
plants to San Francisco furnished their places with street and thrift-store junk.
At least I went to Bed Bath & Beyond when I needed new sheets and cook-
ware. Post-PTSD, though, my anti-furniture eccentricity crossed over into
the purview of psychosis.

"I saw you try to buy furniture before," Nico said over Skype, laughing at
me skeptically when I told him I'd paid a decorator to force me to prepare the
tiny studio apartment we'd share.

"That wasn't even furniture," I pointed out. After Nico had told me he was
going to move in, we went into a Sur La Table together before he went back to
France. He wanted to buy a celebratory teakettle. Our couple's first houseware.
As we stood in front of the selections, I refused to pick a color. All I could see
looking at the teakettles was the dollars we would need to fund our uncertain
future after all of our belongings were destroyed in a great earthquake or fire.
Why couldn't I just keep making water for my tea in a frying pan?

"I can stay here for two hours if you want," Nico said after twenty
minutes.

"Great. Let's go get some lunch and bring it here and eat on the floor in
front of this rack of teakettles," I said, hoping to wear him out of his interest
in the mission.

He said he was prepared to do that, and he wasn't bluffing. He pointed at
the black one for the fifth time with the patience of someone doing it for the
first, saying, "Zhis is classic, I think. Isn't it? Yes. It is." He got me to admit that
I liked the blue one. When he picked it up, I stopped breathing. He hugged it
to his chest and petted it. "Yes, zhis is lovely," he said. Then he grasped the
floor model more protectively, looked at me sternly, and said, "I take zhis. If
zhey say zhey don't have zhis one still because we take too long to decide, I
will die." And walked away from me toward the counter.

I gave chase and grabbed his arm. "No!"

He let me drag on his shirt like a toddler, but didn't slow his progress toward additional merchandise. He wanted bowls. Big silver bowls. "I love your
big bowl," he'd told me his first day in the States, the one I ate popcorn out of
or mixed cake batter in. "What is it?" he asked. "Silver? Everyone in American movies has bowl like zhis."

He picked out a whole set of them, nesting sizes, the "brothers and sisters"
of the one I already owned. I panicked at the counter as the gal rang the
stuff up and Nico handed her a debit card. The whole way home, I repeatedly

pointed at his shopping bags full of teakettle and "American bowls," saying, "I don't think you should have bought that stuff. Are you sure you want that stuff?"

He tried to blanket me with superhuman tolerance. "It's fine," he kept saying. "We will enjoy zhese bowls. If we lose zhe bowls zhat is fine too."

I shook my head to the contrary, choking on anxiety, choking back tears, as we got farther from the store and closer to my apartment.

"I'm so proud of you," Nico said over Skype, therefore, when he heard the decorator was on her way with swatches of couch fabrics.

There were two interceding months in our plans to see each other in person. I would go visit him over Thanksgiving in Guadeloupe. Before then, between each moment of mightily gathered and embarked-upon functioning, mostly what I did was, as Denise put it, "suffer."

My battle never to be able to feel anything at all won, I waged deeper into my new battle: dealing with my feelings. Keeping defense mechanisms such as dissociation from getting overwhelmed and kicking in—or, still, keeping from wishing I was dead. Like most other people, I never in my life had spent any time trying to ground myself, find my center, and feel the entirety of my emotions. To revisit Boulanger's *Wounded by Reality*, "As the psyche matures [after childhood] and self-regulation consolidates, the core self [of a normal person] becomes the unarticulated and unformulated ground against which the figure of experience is projected. Normally completely taken for granted and operating out of awareness . . . it is 'the primitive underbelly of experience,' like a heartbeat or regular breath." That was my life before. But: "catastrophe disrupts the core self, quite literally fixing it in place, changing biological and psychic experience. The 'bare autonomic faith in the body' . . . is lost. In its defensive retreat into dissociation, the psyche has broken faith with the consistency and resilience of its core. It is as if the core self's psychological support systems, agency, continuity, cohesiveness and affect—all of which were temporarily disconnected by dissociation during the actual trauma—cannot be reconnected seamlessly. The self has lost the familiar ground on which it stood."

I continued to try to practice groundedness and connectedness daily. When I got there, I continued letting my mind and body do whatever they needed. But none of those things felt good. The uncontrollable, intrusive images of things that did happen, in Oklahoma, or in my twenties, or in Haiti were now joining images of things I had never even seen. I woke up from a nightmare to have a picture of a girl on her back with dead eyes suddenly enter my mind. Her head was moving against the ground to the rhythm of whatever someone was raping her with. To stop thinking about that wasn't an option. It couldn't be made to go away. So then there came all the girls who were on their backs with dead eyes everywhere, maybe at that very moment, and I had no choice, however hard I closed my eyes, but to look at the hundreds of them all crowding into my vision in a collage.

Please start screaming, I asked them when I couldn't take it anymore. *Maybe you'll feel better if you resist at least that much.*

And they opened their mouths and scrunched up their eyebrows and started screaming, a thousand screaming faces. But then all I wanted them to do was stop.

I felt better briefly when I was reporting undercover. I was doing manual labor at an online-retail distribution center, hard hours and even harder productivity quotas, stress and adrenaline coursing through my limbs and propelling them along. Alex could hear it in my voice when we checked in over the phone. "You sound . . . shaky and amped up," she said.

When I got back, I explained my body's reaction to this combination of exhaustion and overstimulation to Denise as "Holy fuck this is terrible—and thank God," relieved for it, the familiarity of it, my comfort in its specific kind of productive, awful momentum.

"That's trauma," she shrugged, and I got onto the table.

Once on the table, I couldn't connect to my body, as I'd been training to do there for weeks and weeks before. I could either be functional or connected. One or the other. Either in touch and a disaster, or coiled and ready and deadened. It was the key aim of my ninja schooling to integrate these things, but at that point, I could not be both.

"How was therapy?" Nico would ask on Skype.

"A little bit hard," I said. "Sometimes I can't feel pieces of my body, you know."

"Yeah," he said. He knew. He was getting more regularly and more graphically briefed on the state of the crazy.

But he still knew only in theory. A few days after that conversation, and two months after he'd left California, I flew into Pointe-à-Pitre, the biggest city in Guadeloupe. Nico's unit was deployed to the Lesser Antilles island, an "overseas department" of France, for three months to help with routine police matters and do "interventions," they called them, SWAT raids of suspected drug dealers. He didn't know, he couldn't have known, what my episodes were truly like. I couldn't explain it even to people who did speak my language, so though I'd tried to let him know as much as possible, as I so wanted him to understand me, there was no way he was prepared for experiencing them firsthand.

Within hours of my landing, I had my first one. We got in bed, and all my limbs disappeared, and I became woozy, and panting, then tearful. The next morning, I woke up from a nightmare with the kind of shaky blackness that always started a day in which I could do nothing but count the minutes until the day was over and I could go back to sleep and try to start again.

My nightmares at that time were generally about murder—about someone getting murdered, a stranger or me, sometimes kidnapped and tortured first. Lately, though, I'd been going through a spate where I was the one torturing and murdering people. In one dream I'd had before leaving for Guadeloupe, I was in a big old house with a bunch of people, and we'd collectively decided to torture this middle-aged white guy to death. We were keeping him in a box full of dirt, like a coffin. I was the one who was most enthusiastic about adding more dirt to the box every day before we all went out for egg rolls so he'd keep suffocating. I could see his face, all dirt-covered, and hear him scratching around in there desperately while I knelt over the box, topping it off with more soil.

That first night in Guadeloupe brought another installment in the series. "I had a dream that I tortured two people to death," I told Nico when we woke up.

This time, I'd tied two people down to the floor, or someone else had. They were alive, and I was whipping a grappling hook into their faces. Its sharp metal points caught with a sure, soft thump in one face, and then I pulled it back and repeatedly cast it into the other until nothing was left but wet, hamburgery meat.

When I told Nico about this, he said simply, "Which two people?"

He was lying on his back in bed next to me, shoulders loose and wide. I pictured his perfect little organs in his torso, open to attack. He saw the envy in my face when I looked over and whispered, "I can't do that." In my terrible sleep, I'd bolted my arms across my chest. My hands remained locked onto my sides, reinforcing my skeleton.

When Nico rolled over on top of me, I didn't loosen my grip. He took my right wrist and pulled my arm back to my side, and panic rushed through my rib cage.

Danger, my body screamed, and my eyes welled up. *Dangerdangerdanger.*

Protect the midline. The skin that holds everything precious inside there is too delicate to do it alone.

My mind, knowing there was no danger here, repeated this knowledge as a mantra, chastising my body as usual. That internal disconnect, or the additional alarm when Nico took my other wrist and pressed that arm gently to my side, too, proved too much. I dissociated.

My mind refused to agree with my body on where I was.

I tried to force it to.

You are in a bed in Guadeloupe.

No. I'm not.

That looks like it's true, but I can't actually feel it.

My arms became numb below the elbows.

A therapist would probably not recommend Nico's forcibly if very lovingly undoing a trauma patient's contraction. When I contracted like this on the table, Denise often had me contract *more*, contract all the way, hold every muscle in my body tight with teeth gritted and braced until I felt like I was ready to let it go. That way, I was in control. I was empowered to pick the moment that I would release and she would start pushing on me from the side, shaking it out. But Nico wasn't a therapist. He was a guy who woke up next to a girl he loved whose nervous system didn't work normally and did the best he could.

What he did next actually was something my therapist did—he stroked my arms, toward my hands, toward the place that'd turned from weight-carrying blood and muscle to nothing but static. Eventually I relaxed. Then I sobbed profusely. When I started, Nico said matter-of-factly, "Yes," as though it was a thing that had been certain and necessary. Holding me, he encouraged me to stick with it, let it through. This was something therapists did, too. *Stay with the sensations,* Denise always said. *If you can.*

But the last thing I wanted was for my boyfriend to become my professional caretaker.

This trip was three weeks long. There was no sucking it up and hemming it in for that duration. It was too long to remain in a jet-lagged, sex-dizzy, touristic-drinking haze. Also, from now on, as far as Nico was concerned, the stakes were higher. Before, he'd been my fabulous if improbable hot young French boyfriend, who was to some extent a fantasy. Now he was moving into my house. It was likely this was lighting up a bunch of issues. Divorce. Fear. Potential for failure. Vulnerability, uncertainty, unreliability. The timing wasn't ideal, but I didn't want to lose him. If I did and ever managed to find another person I loved that much, I would have to confront the issues then, anyway.

We were just going to have to work together.

It quickly became clear that the only thing worse than dealing with myself during an episode was dealing with someone else trying to deal with me at the same time.

The next time, it started with a salad.

"How much onion do you want me to use?" Nico asked me a few days later, standing in the kitchen of the island cottage we'd rented. It was perched on a hill in a neighborhood of concrete homes, a carriage house at the end of someone's long driveway. I'd just stepped out of the little tiled shower and into the kitchen, which was open to the living room, which opened via a wall of glass doors to the outside. There, beyond the property's bushy greenery, bursting with flowers and palms, an ocean undulated in the distance, too far away to hear.

My body turned to static. I fucking hated dissociating, being lost in the clear light of a place I belonged, lost when I wasn't lost at all. Physically, this particular dissociation covered a lot of area: everything between my pelvic bones and my chin. Just, *gone*, dissipated instantly into a billion particles that I couldn't feel anymore as a part of me but could sense floating around, agitated, nearby. When the room started to move fast away from me, past me, I walked from the kitchen counter and into a dark corner of the bedroom.

"Baby?" Nico asked after me.

But I was very busy arguing with myself, one voice inside me saying that if I talked to Nico I'd be swept up in that disappearing, fast-moving room he was part of out there, and another voice saying that made no sense. I grasped for my tools, like trying to focus on something real. Like that I had fingers and they were holding on to a real mug I'd taken out of the kitchen.

"Baby," Nico said. He was standing in the doorway.

When I looked up at him, saying nothing, he started toward me as nonthreateningly as possible, crouching down to make himself small, reaching out to me on his knees. He touched my face, which softened with his warmth. He said he needed his *petite femme* to help him make dinner. He held me in his bare arms, and I was a real person in *there* this time, feeling my skin on his skin. And then I could suddenly feel what had set me off and sent most of my body away to escape it.

It was sadness. Regular old sadness. I started sobbing.

"*Mon bébé*," Nico whispered. "*Je t'aime tellement. Je suis là.*"

My baby. I love you so much. I'm here.

Later he would admit that this was terrifying for him, walking in and looking in my eyes to find them completely unmoored. But he held on and incanted his support like a lullaby anyway.

Je suis là, he repeated. *Je suis là, je suis là, je suis là.*

That was how it went.

Except for when it didn't.

When I started crying another time, he told me to try to smile, and I told him that really wasn't helpful, and he got mad that I called him unhelpful, and I got mad that I now had to manage someone else's drama along with my own, and he ended up yelling, "Why we are even together if this is how is our fucking time together?" Sometimes when I interrupted a make-out session to announce I was too crazy to have sex because my reaction to arousal that day was shame and disgust that made me fantasize about lopping his hands off with a machete so he'd stop touching me, he didn't pet my face and say "OK, my love." Sometimes it turned into an argument about not enough respect for each other's needs. Or his complaining that our relationship wasn't as passionate as it should be.

There's a steep learning curve for a couple dealing with trauma. It's hard enough for one person to withstand, and much of it is compounded with two.

Best-case scenario, when it didn't start a fight, I found his presence comforting—but then, at the same time, I was humiliated that a nice normal person was witnessing my being a maniac, then guilty about making such a nice normal person witness that. This time in Guadeloupe, too, we didn't just have our own relationship and my problems to contend with. This time, these long weeks, was real life. I had the undercover story I'd reported due; Nico had drug wars to perpetuate. So every day we woke up and went to work, and had to get the grocery shopping done, and figure out who would be in charge of making dinner.

"You have so many bad things inside you," Nico said to me at some point before the trip ended. He was acknowledging it as much to himself as to me. He meant collected fear and grief, not that I was some sort of hell spawn. At night, with his back smooth against my chest, I stayed awake to be ready for something terrible to happen. I didn't know what it was, but I knew it was coming.

Nico could feel my restlessness next to him, even when he was asleep. No matter how still I was, I made his slumber fidgety and choppy, too. "You know how you can feel other people's feelings?" he asked once, casually—because though hardly everyone can, it came perfectly naturally to him. He just let them land on him, other people's enthusiasm or nervousness. He could feel his lieutenant's anxiety prick up his skin, or his best friend's relationship trouble weigh down his muscles, unless he "cut the links," as he also casually put it, when this is a legitimate somatic practice that can take years to master. Meredith had prescribed visualizing the severing of the connection between others and myself sometimes; being oversensitive, I was prone to being subsumed in other people's intense emotions. Nico put it basically the same way Meredith did when he said, "Sometimes it's too much, or you don't want or need to feel that."

"He's an empath!" Tana said when I called her from Pointe-à-Pitre. "Like Deanna Troi." The *Star Trek: The Next Generation* analogy was not bad. Nico could sense the shifts in my shape and mood as easily as an expert like Denise. And spending so much time in his presence, I was starting to disturb him.

"You're so intense," he said.

Earlier in the trip, I'd found Nico going through my closet, and when I asked him what the hell he was doing, he said, "I was smelling all your clothes." This was a guy who sometimes said, "If you stop to love me, I will stop to live." Who, after he hurt my feelings once, after I retreated to the shower, stepped into the stream of water alongside me without bothering to take off his pants and belt first, lest one more moment pass without my understanding how sorry he was. It was not easy to out-intense the French. But here I was, being that unstable and extreme. Being that much work.

"Don't worry," he said with my face in his hands and his lips against my ear after I started crying about his comment. "*T'inquiete pas*. I will not stop to try to understand."

I didn't know how he could possibly understand me, when I not only lost the ability to locate my own self in space and time, I also no longer knew the person I was supposed to be looking for.

11.

Would you believe me if I said that those Guadeloupe episodes were relatively mild? That by the time I left Guadeloupe, after three weeks, we still hadn't hit the bottom of that PTSD-couple learning curve? If I said—again—that things only got worse from there?

Nico and I parted with plans to meet again in France in a couple of months, in the new year. France 2012, where I would hallucinate and rage and make Nico cry, and he would still see fit to propose to me.

In the meantime, I was back in San Francisco only briefly before it was Christmas, which I hated. Since The Fall, Christmas had involved my parents being some combination of homeless or despondent or drunk. But I always had to go back to Ohio for some reason. Two years earlier, my mother had developed an incurable degenerative cranial nerve disease that caused her so much pain she was put on a high, constant dosage of opiates, plus anticonvulsants and analgesics; I spent that Christmas at a Marriott behind a Cincinnati hospital where she was having brain surgery, then weaning her through painkiller withdrawal in our ugly room as she shivered and sweated, post-op, a dozen staples in her head, metal plate in her skull, a medication drawdown so elaborate I had to make a chart to remember which pills to give her when.

Now, I had to go back to Ohio because my father was getting remarried on Christmas Eve. He was still friends with his old mistress, who was invited and for some reason delivered a weepy toast about how many "obstacles" there had been in the beginning of her own relationship with my father—his still being married to my mother the main one. A friend from college I'd roped into being my date put her hands on my lap to keep me from getting out of my chair and making a scene. No fat middle-aged alcoholic man in the Midwest outdrank me that night. Back at my mom's little house, for which I'd lent her half the down payment, I spent the majority of the trip on her couch watching record-breaking amounts of HBO. Both of my parents had seen me openly weeping six months earlier, when I'd still been in Ohio for the PTSD-sex-essay publication. In the interim, my father regularly called to make me rate my morale on a scale of one to ten, encouraging me to hang in there and stay in therapy when I answered "three" or "four." But my mother and I hadn't talked about it since, and in front of her now I didn't bring it up.

I don't remember exactly when the stabbing fantasies started, but it was sometime around this time.

Or rather, I should say, that was when they evolved. In the initial broke-openness after the PTSD essay, I'd longed for a mortal wound, not unlike the injuries some cutters give themselves to distract them from their emotional pain. "I wish I would get stabbed," I'd told Isaac, my ex, when he'd been over for one of his babysitting shifts. I'd never seen him look so alarmed. It was breathtaking, dazzling, to me, how much pain a psychic ailment wrought. With my every nerve scraped, and a deep nausea that could neither be fed nor puked away, I thought of my worst previous physical hurt, the time I'd broken my arm when I was five. The surgery and the stitches and the post-anesthesia vomiting seemed calming compared with what I was now feeling, and I wished that I were in the hospital with a life-threatening stab wound instead.

Since then, stabbing had stuck with me. Now, I didn't wish for passive stabbing but regularly pictured myself plunging knives deep into my own flesh. The less I drank and the more I felt, the more often I wanted to cut myself open. And not for the distraction but for the bloodletting. In my head, it seemed I could feel better if I could just open up and pour some of this suffering out.

Denise and I stepped up our goals. When I'd first come to her, her primary concern had been damage control. Though she'd asked me what I ultimately wanted—*to be able to feel myself in the world and process those feelings*—achieving that from the state I was in would take a long time, and would require me to be open to feelings, first and foremost. As my body had locked itself up against feelings for good reason, Denise hadn't wanted to pry it apart then "just to throw you back to the wolves."

That is, she wouldn't facilitate my full undoing until she was sure I wasn't going to be put in danger at work—and that I could take the time and space I needed after being pried open to rest and take care of myself and fall apart and not function. Once, she'd been part of a therapists'-aid trip to a war zone. When she got there, she'd realized that the security situation—checkpoints, suicide bombers—didn't meet the requirement for healing from *post*-traumatic stress, because the trauma and threats to safety weren't over for anyone she treated. She and the other therapists had focused on alleviating the symptoms of PTSD rather than on treating their cause. Healing was luxurious. It was for those whose lives were not just about survival anymore. Denise and I had been venturing into plenty of uncomfortable emotional territory together already, but I had a lot more undoing to go before we could get all the way at those twin foundations of processing the trauma and rebuilding a life. And as long as I was doing my job full time and in unsympathetic and dangerous environments, Denise wouldn't do it.

I hadn't wanted to do it anyway, when I'd first started seeing her. I was in so much pain already. And when she'd told me that the second foundation was choosing not to stay a victim, I'd been appalled. I hadn't done anything wrong, so I shouldn't have been responsible for fixing it. Why should *I* have to put everything back together? And how could I possibly, when I felt too awful to carry on with even normal life? And if *I* couldn't, as that privileged white American person who went to college, who could?

"You say that like it's just a choice people make, easy as that," I said, scowling at her.

"It is a choice," she said. "You can't choose whether or not you're a victim. But what you choose to do with that is up to you."

"But I *am* a victim," I said, "and you spent all this time trying to make me feel OK about being a victim—it's not my fault, other people did bad things, it's OK for me to be traumatized—and then after I accept that, I have to renounce it and move on and refuse to be a victim."

"It is important to acknowledge what happened, and how awful it is that what happened, happened. In trauma, you need that validation and support," she said, because if you didn't get it from your community, you felt like you had to acknowledge and reinforce your own victimhood and got entrenched in it, holding that recognition yourself. "But you still have to make a choice to move on. If you stay there in that step of recognizing that you're a victim, you stay a victim."

"That choice only applies to people who are educated or lucky or rich enough to have someone like you tell them that they even *have* options for moving forward," I practically spit, "and then have the time and money to pay you to help them do it. This conceit that people have access even to awareness of that choice in this culture, and then to the help they'd need to make it, is insanely classist."

"I absolutely agree with you that the process you're going through, the way you're going through it, isn't available to everyone," Denise said, remaining calm.

But it was available to me, as long as I pumped every cent of not-so-disposable income into it until insurance accepted my claim. I hated Denise that day, more than the time she'd shown me how much my sideways, shrinking body language had made my "No" to Marc unbelievable our last night together in Haiti. What I heard her saying was that victims who weren't bettering themselves were self-pitying assholes, and that as long as I felt like a victim, it was because I wasn't choosing hard enough not to be one, and goddammit if I didn't feel like a victim of the world and fate and my own nervous system every day. But there were two types of people I could be: a stale victim, shut down and festering, at turns tough and crazy. Or I could be somebody who wasn't impossible to live with. With the means and the option and the safety to do it, I didn't have any excuse not to choose that.

I was so mad that I had to do this. Mad that I hadn't picked this disorder but now had to embark on a long and excruciating odyssey just to be able to love someone. But I did love him. I wanted him, and that life. I was a ways into my undoing now anyway, since I'd gone public with my symptoms, and with Nico coming and my growing sense that if I felt like this for much longer, I probably wouldn't survive, it was now or never to get to the bottom of it.

I couldn't heed Dr. Shere's advice to retire at the age of thirty-one, but after Christmas, I took my many accumulated weeks of vacation from work. When that was over, I took a pay cut and went part time. I cut a contract to do just two stories that year, and promised Denise that none of them would be in statistically dangerous territory. Whatever that meant, for a woman.

And however much of a difference working or not working made on that account. When I'd stopped in New York between Uganda and Paris, I'd gone to a magazine party. Numb enough not to have sad-girl feelings pulling my shoulders into a stoop, dressed up and peer-surrounded and feeling fantastic— wearing high heels, even, in which I stood proud and absurdly tall—I didn't make it through the night without an important editor following me when I went outside for a cigarette to tell me that I had an amazing body, that he could see from the shapes under my dress that it would stay amazing even as I got much older, and that he wasn't going to be able to help himself from touching me soon.

Still. Denise and I had a deal that I'd choose my assignments carefully, and arrange escorts and the utmost precautions no matter where I went.

So we delved deeper. Pressed on memory and trigger points that left me incapacitated for days. Doing table work where I "completed a movement" I hadn't at a crucial moment before—shoving and flailing at Denise from on my back, or kicking my legs maniacally, screaming "I *SAID* no" at her—whatever my body felt compelled to. Doing trauma release work, where I released contractions in my muscles by contracting them extra hard for long periods, fatiguing them until they gave out, forcing them into a prolonged shake. The theory behind trauma release work was that the natural response to trauma was to shake, to move the surge of stress and fear through so it didn't become trapped inside. Like some animals did—because they hadn't been socialized to stop it. Alex told me her dad had experienced this post-traumatic shaking-release, too, only recently, long after he'd incurred the mortal fear of his service in Vietnam. Though his therapist wasn't making him do it on purpose. At his children's urging, he'd finally been getting help for the psychic wounds they'd grown up watching him struggle with. Since the VA generally favors exposure therapy—being too vast and bureaucratic an institution to adapt to the changing and complex needs of trauma patients—it was no surprise that his therapist abruptly prompted him to talk about things he hadn't talked about or even let himself think about for decades. After each session, he walked back to his car, and couldn't go anywhere. He sat there in the parking lot and shook, crying. For hours.

Denise and I finally did EMDR. She handed me headphones that played beeping noises in one ear and then the other, and palm-size boxes hooked up to wires. They vibrated one at a time in alternating hands. She asked me a question, and I closed my eyes while my ears and hands were beeping and buzzing and she sat close across from me with the controller in her hand. After a few minutes, she turned everything off and asked me what I noticed now. We did this many times over, discussing the disjointed images that came up. There was a little girl, and she was under attack. Nico appeared and tried to help, but everyone else told him not to be nice to her. My father was there at some point, in the form of an immense and floating head. We didn't do EMDR much after that session, since Denise didn't think it was the best choice of treatment for me. I felt destroyed for more than a week afterward. If trauma exists on a severity spectrum, EMDR works best for those who are on the simple-trauma—versus the complex—end. And Denise was increasingly thinking I was "right in the middle there."

As we pressed ahead, my nightmares were constant. One night I had a nightmare in which my father was killed. I fainted in the dream when they told me, with these two unfamiliar people holding up my arms on each side. The next night, I dreamed I was infiltrating a pack of poor and extremely violent murderers, kind of like a gang, and I was terrified that they were going to figure out who I was and kill me. But I had to be there to help someone, maybe a friend, figure out who'd killed some relative. And so I had to fuck this guy, this slight, weaselly, disgusting greasy asshole guy, because whatever my cover was, it involved my being open to prostitution, and he had money and people were watching us. When it was over, my letting him touch my nipples and put a weaselly narrow tongue in my mouth and pretending that was OK, I caught wind that the gang knew something was amiss, and as I was leaving, walking through the parking lot, this heavy blond woman with a ponytail who murdered people was running up behind me.

The next day, I couldn't get out of bed. When I woke up, I'd bound myself, clutching my sides together, straitjacketing my hands across my chest. Protecting the midline. Exhausted and nauseated. For the rest of the day I remained fragile as a piece of paper with a tear already in it, needing just the slightest tug to rip open fast and wide.

Nico called as I lay there. "Why don't you try going outside?" he suggested.

You're weak is what I heard.

"You think I'm weak and this is my fault because I'm not trying hard enough," I said. I was furious. He didn't understand that I *couldn't* go outside, because he'd never felt like that—just as I wouldn't have been able to understand it before it started happening to me, either.

"No, my baby," he said. "No. I'm sorry. I didn't mean it like that. I thought maybe it would help you to go outside. OK if you can't go outside. I'm here. I love you so much. Anyone would feel like you feel if they lived what you lived. I love you even like this because you're perfect for me."

This would diffuse a normal person in a normal fight. This would diffuse a normal me, even a really pissed or hurt but non-episodic me. It addressed and quelled the insecurities feeding the outburst.

But I wasn't a normal me anymore.

"Fuck you," I said.

He tried a few more times, remarkably, before saying—and really earning—that he couldn't talk to me when I was like this. He got mad. Though I'd asked him not to a hundred times, it seemed to take more than a hundred times for a partner to stop taking episodes personally.

"My words are useless," he said angrily.

When we hung up, I did force myself to go outside, but hated it, and came back to count the minutes until darkness. When I closed my eyes to go to bed, my mind played images of a man in a military uniform very slowly knifing another young man to death until I fell asleep. Then I had a nightmare that I was lashing someone bloody with a whip. The next night, I dreamt about a young boy whose father woke him up every morning by punching him in the face until he vomited.

The following mornings, I woke up wrecked, continuing to be incapable of being open or loving or non-irritable even to anyone who was being nice to me—including Nico. By the time I arrived in France in February, the last time we were supposed to have to meet long distance, I had many times over-extended his patience.

After this trip to France, we wouldn't have to take long flights to see each other in various countries anymore. After this—hopefully just a month after this, if his temporary leave from the gendarmerie was granted—we would live together in San Francisco as I'd dreamed. For six months. But we didn't want to wait that long to see each other after Guadeloupe, which had already been two months ago. Plus, I had to meet Nico's mother.

I flew into Basel, the closest airport to Nico's hometown, near the borders of Switzerland and Germany. He picked me up, and together we drove into his region of Alsace. Wine country, with rolling vineyards everywhere between the mountains. Lovely country, full of hills and quaint villages.

But in that country, on his own soil, Nico behaved more as he'd been raised. Harder. Harsher. He'd already been growing tired of our melodramatic, episodic interactions before I'd arrived, and in France, he was less forgiving. If I'd felt my own culture to be lacking in compassion, the last place I should have gone was to one that widely regarded my countrymen to be coddled, oversensitive pussies.

I got the flu almost the moment we checked into our chalet. Years later, after hearing stories from Nico's French friends about how they lied when they got sick so their parents wouldn't yell at them for whining, it would all make sense. But at the time, it was like being slapped in the face when I asked Nico, who was otherwise a decent human, to bring me food and he narrowed his eyes and said, "You want to be treated like a queen? You're *sick*. It's not your fucking birthday."

I wasn't in France long before I feared our relationship, for all our new grand plans, might not be sustainable.

When I got better from being one kind of sick, I was still the other kind. And sometimes that was OK. One time when I woke up agitated in the middle of the night and started wandering the room, he called me over to him and wrapped his arms around me, breathing slow serenity into my face. I fell apart another time, after the first time we had sex that trip. The moment I came, I became so vulnerable that the post-sex panting turned into some deep breaths followed by ragged sighs. The breaths got deeper and the sighs sharper, the remaining pieces of my togetherness breaking up, until I was sobbing.

"I'm here," Nico said, holding me, waiting it out. He did the same thing several other times, once after we drove past a castle ruins—this part of France had endured heavy shelling during the First World War—and I asked Nico if he'd ever found any bombs. I'd recently been reading that more than 500 tons of unexploded ordnance were still collected and destroyed every year; more than 600 of the guys whose job it was to collect and destroy it had been killed. Nico said that he had discovered a big bomb in the woods when he was seven, yes, and though his friends had wanted to kick it, he had gone home to tell his parents so they could call the proper removal authorities, the way that they'd been taught in school. And then later when we were having sex I couldn't stop crying for a long time about war. And he'd again assured me that he was there.

But as in Guadeloupe, my episodes didn't always bring us together so cooperatively.

One morning when we woke up, he said something innocuous, but I instead heard that I wasn't good enough to be his girlfriend, and I started a fight. Jet-lagged again, I woke him up in the middle of the night; he told me I traveled too much; the reason I traveled half the time was because of stupid him, I said, seething. We got into a fight. I took a bath and hallucinated that I had a deficient and monstrous body. I screamed at Nico for lying that I was gorgeous. I found an end piece of a baguette that we'd forgotten about and let go stale and lit up with rage, stomping about the kitchen with the waste and senselessness of our irresponsibility. I started bitching at him for using a tone that sounded sexy with one of his friends on the phone. We went for a walk in the forest where he'd buried his father's ashes, and I was cold and mean. I went into a corner of the chalet bathroom to cry for hours. When Nico came in to drag me out, frustrated and worn down himself, I told him we needed to talk.

"This is what this is really like," I told him, sitting on our bed. I explained how sometimes I didn't have any feelings. And sometimes I had too many.

He became especially unhappy the night we had dinner plans with one of his friends and I couldn't go. I was not well. I was embarrassed, but had no choice but to admit it, the way I was aching and shaking and scared. Many times when this happened, he tried to reason me out of it, to bring me around by explaining why things were OK, however many times I told him that wouldn't work, still taking it personally when it didn't. One time he just walked away from me and went to do push-ups. Sometimes, like this time, he tried to bully me out of it.

"You need to control yourself," he said. "You need to work on yourself."

"Maybe I'll be fine at dinner," I said. We both knew it was a lie.

He called his friend to cancel. He stormed off into another room of the chalet and called another friend to holler in French about how awful I was. Something like "What am I supposed to do with a person who's acting like this?"

Alone, I closed myself in our bedroom and called Tana.

"We need to break up," I told her. "I'm ruining him. I'm not fit to be around other people. He's going to hate me because I'm insane."

"Don't make decisions on days when you're failing the coffee-cake test," she said. "Listen. No one does anything they don't want to do, and if Nico wants to stick it out because of all the good things you give him, that's his choice, and he'll evolve and adjust."

Nico and I had both called the right people.

"Don't be an asshole," Nico's friend was telling him at the same time. She had suffered a bout of major depression in recent years, so she was possibly the most sympathetic person in France. People didn't have control over their feelings, she admonished him, and especially not people who had medical conditions that were defined by a total lack of control over feelings, so if you're sticking this out, which you should because of all the good things she gives you, you need to get it into your head that she can't and you can't just make her problems go away.

When I came out of the bedroom, I found Nico sitting in a chair near the Christmas tree that the proprietors had left in our rented living room a month and a half past its date. The lights blinked white. I sat on the floor near his feet. Crying—bleh, again, like always, but more softly for the moment.

"You cry too much," he said, gently but sort of stunned.

I snorted, as I'd been telling him this all along. "True story!"

"I'm sorry I seemed mad. I didn't want that. It's not your fault."

I rested my head against his legs and breathed. "You won't get rid of me like that, just because you have a problem," he said. I'd taught him that phrase, *to get rid of.* He'd said the same sentence four other times already that day, and his resolve to not leave me remained unchanged. "If you want to get rid of me, try something else."

The next day, we were watching a Michael Jackson DVD on his aunt's couch when he half-proposed to me.

I was feeling better. I generally felt better after a day as bad as the previous day. My crazy seemed to work in a cycle: a bad day, then a worse day, then a couple of days so bad they were intolerable. After that, a little bit of a reprieve, maybe two or three days. Then it started all over again. That particular day, a week after I'd arrived in France, I was stable enough to leave the house. Easily.

And thank God, because Nico's favorite aunt and uncle had invited us over for lunch. They'd made a mountain of choucroute, a cabbage-based dish piled with sausages. It was sauerkraut by any measure, but in this region, which had been lost in the Franco-Prussian war and not given back to France until after World War I, people did not take to having their food called German.

At a table for seven crammed into a kitchen with just enough space for the chefs to squeeze their asses past en route to the stovetop, I sat against the wall. I was force-fed wine while the food finished, though it was ten-thirty in the morning. Nico's uncle's mother-in-law sat next to me and held my hand. In this part of France, rural and eastern, no one feigned pretentious non-fascination with America, so mostly Nico's family spent the morning asking me to explain every American custom they'd ever heard or didn't understand.

Was it true, Nico's uncle had him translate to me, that most Americans didn't drink wine around breakfast time?

"Not really," I said, and seeing me shake my head, the kitchen erupted in cries of *Why, why,* distressed for the state of American life. We stuffed ourselves with greasy meats, and then they invited me into the living room to watch Michael Jackson videos.

Nico and I took the futon, lying down close. With the proximity, and without the distraction of the five hollering French people, the peace I generally felt around Nico arrived. A gravity in my abdomen. A sense of being not lost. I could feel it even when we were fighting and in the midst of my most episodic and strongest convictions that we wouldn't make it. On the couch, chests together, limbs entwined, the inevitability and permanence of him spread a warm weight I could actually feel through my midsection.

Nico was petting my hair. His lips close, he kissed my head. I could feel his breath when he said quietly, "Do you want to make your life with me?"

My warmth was interrupted by fear. Was he nuts? Did he really want me to make his whole life as shitty as I'd made his past week?

"Maybe," I said.

When we got back to the chalet that night, Nico and I stayed close, positioning ourselves on another couch there. We pulled it over in front of the small wood-pellet stove, starting a puny fire.

"I didn't understand you before really when you said you cry all day sometime," he admitted.

"I know," I said. How could he have? What an adjustment! He'd started out with a girlfriend who, when he'd met her in Haiti, had seemed a capable professional and party gal, and now he had a mess who couldn't even pick herself up off his bathroom floor.

"I told you," I said, "that you didn't understand how bad it was. And I can see how it's impacting you." I started crying. (Obviously.) "I know what happens to couples like this. I know what happens when you expose another person to this all the time."

By then it had been months since I'd started talking to Brannan Vines and other military spouses. I told Nico about how they picked up depression and distress and hypervigilance—the heightened state of stimulation one develops from watching for danger all the time—from their veteran hus-bands. I told him about how one of them was recently having dinner at the Olive Garden when her husband's anxiety and her own new habit of waiting for the incoming, of waiting for something to happen, overwhelmed her right into a nervous breakdown. She was just trying to eat her Zuppa Toscana, and she could not stop the tears from coming.

"I could destroy you," I said.

By then, he'd pulled me on top of him and started kissing my cheeks, all his fingers tangled up in my hair.

"You can," he said heavily. "I don't care."

I turned my face away from him, crying harder. French people were so dramatic. There was nothing romantic about this. I shook my head.

"You're my life," he said. "I don't want to make it without you," even if it meant being dragged into my emotional world so deeply that he had to share it. But he didn't know what it felt like to feel like me, and knowing it myself, I knew this was a bad call. Tana was right; he was a grown-ass man who could make his own decisions, so I wasn't going to martyr myself by ending the relationship to save him, but maybe he would change his mind, I thought. I hoped he would change his mind, for his sake.

Instead, on the couch again another night, after more hours of more crying, after I exploded again because I couldn't uncoil any of that horrid winding-up in my torso—"My friend really likes you"; "I don't give a FUCK what your friend thinks!"—Nico slid to the floor and got on his knees in front of me.

He hesitated first, setting his face into resolve, anticipating resistance from the start. But he opened his mouth anyway and said clearly, unwaveringly, "Do you want to marry me?"

My midsection got hot and panicked, sending sparks up and all over. Perhaps I was going to throw up.

"I understand now this is as bad as it gets," he pressed on. "But I still want to make my life with you. You tell me this is what you're really like. And I tell you I'm still here. Nobody is better to do this with you than me."

"I should do it by myself," I said. "Where no one else has to go through it too or get hurt."

"No," Nico said. "I'm here. I'm ready."

That night, Nico's question unanswered, I woke up and watched him sleep. I convinced myself that I shouldn't touch him. That I should stay away from him. Though silently chanting to myself how poisonous I was achieved that goal, it did little to make me feel as if there were much reason to live.

At the end of every single session with Denise, she told me to call her if I needed her. I had never once invoked this right. I took it to mean "Call me if you are seriously about to kill yourself"; if I called her every time I needed psychiatric assistance, I would call her several times a day. Tonight, though, I *needed* her. It was three in the morning, but given the nine-hour time difference, it was only early evening where she was. I got out of bed and went to the chair next to the blinking Christmas tree. I called her up, and got no answer. Unsure what else to do, I wrote her an e-mail, then climbed back into bed, spending the rest of the night staring into darkness.

> To: Denise K. Benson
> From: Mac McClelland
> Date: Sat, Feb 4, 2012 at 6:04 PM
> Subject: hello!

I just rang your bell (I know, it's Saturday; I'm sorry about that, but I had to try), and here's what I wanted: for a person who spends so much time talking to women who talk about how awful it is to be married to a person with PTSD, I am surprisingly shocked to watch how awful it is for my partner to be in my vicinity when I have several rough days, as I generally do every week, in a row. As a healthy 26-year-old, Nico is not really prone to long bouts of sobbing, and you should have seen how surprised he was that he was doing it, but that's how he reacted when I was paranoid and panicked and totally overwhelmed with despair for a couple days in a row and just couldn't stop crying, which as you know happens to me all the time. I was better today, as I usually am after my weekly Grand Bad Day where everything becomes especially bad, and so he's better, too, he's great, but you can see that he's still recovering, honestly. And it's only a matter of days before I turn into that person again. I know, he'll probably adjust a little bit, but seeing what my sickness can do to him pretty much instantly doubled my grief, which was mostly self-pitying before, but now is also

alarmed and horrified about my potential to do real and lasting
harm to a person who's going to move into my apartment in
several weeks.

I'll give you a million dollars to tell me you think it's possible that
I'll get better. Alex's dad never got better, and Vietnam was a
really long time ago. Do you really think it's possible that I'm
going to get better?

No pressure or anything.

x!
Mac

I didn't have all the answers by the time I left France. I did have an answer
from Denise—"It does get better if you stay the course, do your practices and
take very good care of yourself. It's complex but healing can open up really
amazing places in one who is committed to turning and facing all that's
there"—but that didn't mean I knew if I could really pull it off and get
through it. And I didn't have answers for Nico about his proposal.

His mother, who we went to meet over a rabbit she had cooked, had
Nico translate to me that this was wise, my taking my time to consider. She
asked me to split a bottle of wine with her at eleven o'clock in the morning.
She smoked and approved that I was pretty enough. She said she hoped I
figured out the marriage thing relatively fast since I was getting old to have
a baby.

I left without committing to anything either way. But on my last day in
the country, Nico's lieutenant called to tell him his request for leave had finally, officially, been granted. He could use the six-month visitor's visa he'd
acquired and go to the United States in a month.

So we had that. Plus, we had a wee splash of hope. On one of the days in
the chalet that I spiraled the furthest away from sanity, free-falling away from
myself, lost in my own body, I flipped out and lashed out and bawled for
hours. And then: I got better. I recovered—without sleeping/drugging *and*
sleeping my way out of it, which I'd never once done before. I recovered enough
that we could go out for a late dinner. Having first searched the bistros of our

own village, the only people walking the brick streets out in the cold dark, we drove to an Italian-Alsatian restaurant.

"What do you think?" I asked Nico as we read our menus.

"I think I want to marry you," he said.

I laughed. "Still?"

We tried each other's entrées like regular people out to dinner. Back at the chalet, we made tea. We made fun of our uptight chalet owners for telling us when we checked in that only one person was allowed in the bathtub at a time. What kind of French people were they? We had sex in the bathtub, and on the bed, and went to sleep in a supportive tangle.

My first same-day episode recovery.

That victory was far from my last.

12.

Back in San Francisco, I had an episode in the canned-bean aisle of a grocery store. I became so hopeless and enraged that my limbs went numb and I could think only about how much calmer I would be if I cut open each forearm along the ridge of the ulna bone, from my wrist to my elbow, in one clean, long slice. Cleanse and purge. My hands wouldn't be able to disappear then! Not if they were on the other side of very real rivers of blood, seeping out and catching on my arm hair. Invoking the image pacified me, as usual. But it didn't seem like the most adjusted way I could be dealing with the situation.

This thought alone was a win. Though I spent huge amounts of my time with Denise talking about tools, developing and practicing tools, once I entered a crazy space, I failed to follow her advice most of the time. In an episode, nothing made sense, and I often couldn't remember that I even had tools, much less what they were, and when I did remember, I often couldn't persuade myself to use them anyway, or I tried to use them but quickly abandoned them. This time, holding a grocery basket in one hand, I decided to go for some grounding exercises—and not give up.

I rooted down through my feet, dropping my weight into my legs, toes spread, heavy contact with the ground. I took a deep breath, starting the first breath exercise. I pictured my skeleton, to give my contracted muscles a break by remembering it was there, how sturdy it was, concentrating on letting *it* hold me up while the muscles could just drape off, tall. . . .

Wait, I thought.

You look like a crazy person.

This was the canned-bean aisle. Nobody stood around contemplating beans. It didn't take that long to choose beans.

I relocated to the freezer aisle, and planted myself in front of the ice cream case.

There, concentrating on my breath, filling my rib cage with it and expanding across my shoulders, taking up space, my full space, the space I deserved, I visualized my energy stretching outward in all directions. Down past the floor, into the soil, into the earth's crust. To the left through my shoulders into the yogurt case, right, all the way into the bulk foods, reminding myself that this would pass, it would pass, it would eventually pass. And there, I achieved another victory.

I didn't feel better. But I convinced myself that I *would* feel better, later. Something moved just a little. Just enough. I convinced myself that a bad moment would end, and that I might someday be able to help bad moments end.

If only the post-trauma healing path always moved forward. My glimmers of progress were encouraging, but they were no safeguard against the constant threat of regression, or lack of progress in another sphere. Back in Denise's office, post-France, I'd put myself back into self-defensive lockdown. Nico had noticed it coming on and called me on it when I was leaving.

"I can feel you becoming *Mac McClelland*," he said—not the person but a byline, a flat persona of a tough and busy lady reporter—as we sat in the airport in Basel. I hadn't noticed it, but he was right; I had distanced myself from him on the bench where we were waiting and started making the transformation into A Girl On Guard Against The World Alone, my body becoming tenser, muscles turning rigid under my hardening candy shell. Until he said that, I hadn't realized that I was sitting at attention and gritting my teeth.

Now, in therapy, on the table, Denise was encouraging me to try to let my stiffness go some.

"OK," I said. "Let's do it."

She pressed on my chest, supporting the contraction there. Everything was about supporting, inviting, not forcing. To demonstrate how this worked, she would sometimes make me hold out my fist and clench it as hard as I could. Then she would have me use my other hand to try to pry the fist loose, which wouldn't work, but when she had me use my other hand to instead wrap it around the fist, squeezing gently and supporting it, it softened.

Now the tension in my chest softened as she put weight on it.

"I hate that," I said. I could feel my nervousness rise.

"OK," she said, stopping. "Should I move my hand away?"

"Depends what we're going for."

"*I want to feel myself in the world,*" she reminded me.

I started panicking as I thought about what that would feel like. People went through this process so they could have a fuller life, Denise always said. Reach their fullest emotional and professional potential. She said someday maybe I'd be glad this had happened to me; some addicts ended up grateful for their disease because trying to heal from it forced them to find a connection to themselves, a richness of experience they otherwise wouldn't have had. I thought these people sounded like idiots. They must have had shitty lives before. I'd easily have sacrificed whatever ninja properties I was going to get from this to have my non-crazy back. Used to be, when I'd go into the office, people I ran into in the kitchen would say—with varying degrees of enthusiasm—"I knew you were here; I could hear you laughing all the way over at my desk." What about *that*?

I tried to relax a bit, and started really panicking. *Oh my god Oh my god Oh my god.* "I changed my mind," I told Denise. Fuck this imperative I had to try to heal. "I changed my mind!"

"OK," Denise said. "What's going to happen?"

"Everything will fall apart," I said, starting to fall apart on cue, tears spilling out of the eyes I'd squeezed shut. "I won't be functional in the world. I won't be functional anywhere at all."

Denise asked me if I wanted to stop.

I did. I really did. But I took a deep breath. "No. It's fine," I said. "Let's fucking do it."

I had to learn to surrender. I had to master surrendering to myself—and to Nico, if I was going to be able to accept his love, not to mention accept him inside me. I'd been so good at this before. I'd loved so hard and so easily in my life, and I was either going to get good at surrendering again or I was going to stop trying, leave Nico, and screw a never-ending string of twenty-year-old poets like the other writers with intimacy issues I knew. Denise encouraged me to keep in mind the difference between surrender and submission. "They are not the same thing," she kept telling me. "You just have to surrender, You don't have to submit."

Denise pressed on me and prompted me some more, and I squirmed and resisted but then fell apart some more, and then it became too much and my hands disappeared.

"That's OK," Denise said. I lay on the table, crying. It was almost time to go. "It was uncomfortable but nobody died. It's really important to remember that nobody died. You didn't die."

I didn't die, but I still failed. Somewhere in this transition between brick person and open human person who was a complete mess was the key to getting better, and I was miserable at occupying that middle ground.

"Honor your defense mechanisms," Denise said. She told me this all the time. I was wasting my energy being angry with myself for not getting better fast enough, perpetuating my problems by trying to brace myself against them rather than embrace them. "It's a miracle that you're alive, and your defense mechanisms got you there. Don't be mad at them for coming up when it's not a good time. They're just trying to protect you."

This instruction was proving to be one of the least attainable of my therapy directives. As a ceaselessly high-performing perfectionist, I wasn't inclined to forgive such low achievement. When I was in first or second grade, I got a Ziggy calendar at the start of the school year (teddy bear calendars, Ziggy calendars; it says something about the kind of child I was that my favorite thing to play with was *calendars*), and set about writing in every foreseeable event. I had gym class once a week, so marked it four times a month, getting almost all the way through the school year before my mom walked over and said, "Who's Jim?" Homophones! I hadn't learned this one yet! I felt the hot flush of disgrace. For months, I had to look at the calendar as it hung on my wall full of crossed-out *jims*, cursing my stupidity.

Now I was supposed to turn into a crazy person and, instead of being pissed about my dysfunction, put my arm around my crazy and say, *Hey, man, welcome*? I recognized that doing otherwise was senseless and counterproductive. But I just wasn't built that way.

So, fine, I continued to try learning from zero the self-compassion I so urgently needed. As I had so much/too much empathy for others, I tried to sneak some of it over into my own camp. I imagined the compassion I would feel for Alex during a tough time, or a badly suffering animal, then tried to transfer that feeling to myself. The success of the practice was limited. My perfectionism was holding my head underwater in the shame and frustration pool, making my struggle harder and using up effort that could have been put to use healing. But as much as it was a hindrance, it became one of my greatest assets.

I was an accomplishment machine, goddammit. I was not going to give up, and I was not going to let this situation stand. Even Denise had to admit that she was impressed with my perseverance, a quality not always easy to come by in a majorly depressive and traumatized mind.

"You're so hungry to get better," she said.

"Aren't most people?" I asked.

"No. A lot of people who come here, even though they make the effort to go to therapy, they come in here, and they just kind of sit here, and won't or can't do the work. Sometimes I have to wonder, 'Do you even *want* this?'"

I did! *I* did! Denise consistently tried to convince me that that was courageous. So we pushed on. And sometimes, on the table, it would be bad, and I would be alarmed and upset and crying, but I would let go anyway—and when the crying stopped, there would be peace. I felt solid on the table, but not too heavy; my presence filled up my body, and my body felt like it was a part of everything else around me.

"Take a picture of this," Denise would say when I got to this place. "Take a snapshot in your head. Remember what it feels like." Usually, the feeling didn't last five minutes after I got off the table and into the world. Lately, I could take it outside with me and walk around with it for a while, but it still faded within a day, at the longest. "The more times you get here, the easier it will be to get here, and the longer you can stay here," Denise said.

"How many times do I have to do this before I can always feel like this?" I asked.

"Three thousand."

"*What?*"

There was a study Strozzi-Heckler cited in his writings and trainings that he said he'd seen while working with Special Operations Command and marines. An officer had shown him some research about combat readiness that concluded 3,000 repetitions were required for a person to nail down an action. The study was apparently impossible to cite specifically or verify. But I still preferred it over the better-documented theory that a person needs thousands of hours of very deliberate and goal-directed practice to gain mastery of an activity—an average of 10,000 hours for some domains. In any case, the point was that changing and mastering motor patterns were quite hard.

"That . . . is terrible news," I told Denise.

"The more you do it, the better you'll get at it," she said. "Think how easy it is for you to put on a shirt. Think about how much more complicated that was when you were little."

I did all the homework she gave me. When I went for walks with Alex, I walked from my center, leading with the spot an inch or two below my navel. When I found myself leading with my head forward, the way I'd always walked and that almost everyone else in the city walked, I corrected myself. Alex slowed her pace and practiced the posture with me in solidarity. To make myself remember to do grounding exercises, I tied them to daily habits, practicing every time I made tea or took a shower. At a minimum, that equaled two times a day, but they had to be *good* times, successful times—it wasn't about just quantity but quality—and I nailed it and actually achieved grounding only about a third of the times I tried, so I tried not to think about how it could be twelve years before it became second nature. The only thing Denise suggested to me that I didn't do was go on full-time medication.

When I got back from France, at that point, in that condition, she had to agree with Dr. Shere that it might be time for me to think about serious pharmaceutical intervention. I hadn't been surprised to hear a doctor like Dr. Shere recommend that, but avoiding doctors like that was why I'd gone to someone like Denise, who would approach healing holistically and thoroughly and wouldn't automatically try to put chemical Band-Aids over things. She broke my heart when she told me. "You're a somatic therapist," I whimpered, crying at the implications immediately. My situation must have seemed pretty dire for her to say that. "I thought you'd recommend we use healing crystals before you'd say I needed Prozac."

"I know," Denise said. "But we can't ignore at least the consideration when you're suffering this much. It could help you feel better while you work on getting better." Pills were not her go-to move. But they might help alleviate my symptoms while I was addressing the cause in therapy. "You don't have to take them forever; you could just take them for three months and see how it goes. Sometimes it resets something for people. It could lessen your suffering in the meantime."

I didn't want to do that. Whether it was the right move or not, I just wasn't ready to do that. Nobody was positive what the long-term or permanent ramifications of antidepressants were, if any, and I was already terrified about the future of my brain without adding in more variables. I kept prescription drugs on hand for emergencies, but wanted to keep that the extent of it; as it was, I almost never resorted to them. I wanted to try all the alternatives, try harder, before going the fully medicated route.

We upped my therapy sessions from once to twice a week. And so that I would be doing something proactive all five weekdays, any day I didn't go to therapy, I went to yoga.

I'd gone to yoga semi-regularly, maybe a couple times a month, on and off for years. I'd noticed after I got back from Haiti Part I that though I didn't necessarily feel better afterward, I always felt different. It was good to exercise in any circumstances, obviously, but the stretching and opening and breathing that make up a yoga class were more transformative than your average aerobics. The effects were tandem to some of my therapy goals of uncontracting, processing, moving things through. I'd noticed how much moving-through yoga facilitated when I'd started going more regularly after I got back from Ohio—one of the issues it let surface being, as mentioned, that I'd lost my will to live.

Now, pulling myself to a yoga studio every other day, emotions continued to arise. In the middle of some sun salutations, something inside me would break down, and there I'd be, crying in yoga again. Denise pointed me in the direction of some studies conducted by Bessel Van der Kolk, the somatics-loving pioneering neuroscientist, who also teaches psychiatry at Boston University School of Medicine. He got funding from the National Institutes of Health to study trauma and yoga. The trouble with trauma, according to Van der Kolk, was that it damaged sensory-processing and self-care parts of your brain. There was increasing evidence for the brain damage that trauma caused: The EEGs of Australian soldiers who'd been scanned after each deployment to Iraq and Afghanistan showed increasing hyperarousal, that coked-up inability for calm, as well as memory and attention-processing problems. Post-trauma, my limbic system, the part of the brain that regulated motivation, memory, and conditioned fear, overreacted in situations where it didn't need to—watching TV, having sex—a chemical and hormonal hangover. Learning to accept my nervous system's hyper-reactivity and help it calm down was one of my main goals. It would calm not only the fear I was unnecessarily producing, but the additional fear that accompanied not being able to control my own body. In the stillness of yoga poses, one could learn to connect to whatever sensations in the body came up and to invite them (never try to force them; they couldn't be forced) to relax. Breathing, for example, to regulate heart-rate variability. Even the Army eventually started giving out millions in grants for this kind of "alternative" research.

The very short of it was that Van der Kolk had designed studies where traumatized people did yoga that focused on these skills, and then he looked at their PTSD symptoms. After yoga, test subjects experienced more controlled heart rates, fewer intrusive memories, and less hyperarousal. Patients regained enhanced control over their arousal systems. One small neuroimaging study with his patients suggested that yoga might be able to affect the parts of the brain that trauma damaged.

Van der Kolk launched a neuroscience-based clinical practice and methodology, working with a yoga instructor to direct a yoga program that offers several classes for trauma patients every week. Ultimately he did another, groundbreaking study that showed how much yoga could help a group of people with some of the most difficult symptoms to treat: chronically abused women. More than half of the women who did trauma-sensitive yoga for ten weeks improved so much that they no longer qualified as PTSD-positive. It was the first study of its kind to show that yoga could be used as a clinical intervention. Van der Kolk's clinic's yoga staff currently runs programs at rape centers, domestic violence centers, and traumatized youth centers, and trains other yoga instructors around the nation to treat trauma.

I wanted Van der Kolk's results. So I kept going. As I kept running through poses, I didn't always get to a better place after whatever episode happened to kick in. Sometimes I did. Often I left raw or depleted or anxious or more of whatever unpleasant sensation had been lurking all day. But if I had to go through that to get through this, at least I was contributing to the process. And occasionally, at the end of class, I found that peace. Occasionally I lay on the ground during savasana—corpse pose—and felt solid. A thing on the ground, but also part of the ground, and the sky. Integrated within myself, integrated with the world.

My nightmares continued. A pack of coyotes ate my head while I was still alive. A huge man chased me around a college campus. A schoolboy slashed several of his classmates to death, then pushed their blood-splashing bodies into a pile in a bathroom stall I was hiding in.

"You're doing really good," Alex encouraged me.

I managed to leave the house every day. I told myself I had to if I was going to hang on to my one remaining, sappy source of joy. I had the opportunity to experience the greatest love I believed could exist. Nico loved fearlessly, the way he spoke English and did backflips into hotel pools in Haiti; he had so much love to give and no qualms about giving it, even though, frankly, he knew better. That was what I wanted, a life like that. Around that kind of person. I wanted to feel myself in the world so I could feel the best thing the world had to offer, and that was Nico's love.

"You *wanted* him," Denise would say years later, remarking on how hard I fought. "You really *wanted* him."

But that was later.

Now it was just a month after I left France, and I was working my therapeutic practices to their limit. Then after a month, any gains I made on healing, if there were any, were annihilated when that one thing I wanted arrived in my apartment.

"Two steps forward," Denise was always reminding me about trauma recovery. "And one step back."

I was elated to have Nico in the United States. I cleaned the house spotless, washing the walls even, and bought so many bourgeois food products to stock the fridge that the checkout gal at my grocery store asked me if I was having "a special party." We would have six months together. We weren't sure what would happen after that, but it was three times more time than we'd spent in person put together yet. After eighteen months of e-mails, and Skype chats, and ultra-long-distance multi-country dates, and all the pining, and aching, and misery that went with it, his face appearing in the arrivals hall outside of customs at San Francisco International was not just exciting—it was a complete relief.

However. We had overestimated two things.

The first was my ability to deal with the change of dealing with another human twenty-four hours a day.

It was always an adjustment, getting used to him and his touch and feel and smell after so long apart; most rendezvous, the first time we had sex involved a lot of stopping and starting as my body kept yelling, *Who the fuck is this guy?* I was often, as I was then, still wearing my emotional armor. So it wasn't totally shocking when we started making out that first day and my core turned to ice, and my hands disappeared.

Nico wrapped his hands around my fingers, pressing his warm fingers into my palms to try to connect them to reality. I tried to verbally coax the rest of my body into reality, too. "OK," I said out loud. "I'm in a bed. I'm in a bed," and it worked that time, actually, but the thing about reality was that it was a harrowing place to be for me. Reality was not sexy. The reality was that I was very sad inside, so when I rejoined reality I started crying. Nico was lovely, and strong, and his chest felt like home. I relaxed into him, into the space he was holding in the room, and some of the tightness strangling my throat thawed. It poured out of my mouth forming the syllables "Nobody's gonna die."

That was sort of a weird thing to say once during sex. But I wasn't finished.

"Nobody's gonna die. Nobody's gonna die. Nobody's gonna die."

Nico was taken aback a bit. Literally, he backed his head and chest away from me. "What?" he asked, because as often as this sort of thing happened, it was still a surprise every time, apparently, when your girlfriend went from sexy talk to talking about dying in an instant.

"To get personal, I don't even like sex anymore," my marine pen pal Chris had written to me after my PTSD-and-sex essay, when he'd been trying to support me by telling me how terrible he felt, too. "I can't get that personal with anyone. I guess I'm scared to lose anyone else that I get close to." You never knew what kind of excitement you might encounter when you got naked with me, and it dawned on me now that we were going to be having sex not just on vacation stints, but full time.

Wheeeeee!

A few days later, we were at home again and I was sitting on the couch. But then I jumped up, and stomped around, my nerves on fire, blood running venomous and agitated, storming into the bathroom and throwing my clothes on the ground, getting in the shower and trying my tools. The stall in my bathroom was two feet by two feet, and I rocked my weight from one foot to the next in it, my little containment tank. Breathing? No. Too shallow. I couldn't even get the breaths into a chest this tight. Grounding, envisioning, mantra-chanting, whatever, whatever, I couldn't calm down and couldn't stop pacing and rocking my weight back and forth so I pictured what I really wanted: a gigantic knife.

"The knife is huge and sort of curved," I explained to Denise, "like you would put in the hand of an Arab if you were making a racist movie."

"You know I'm Lebanese, right?" she said.

"Yeah. I said a *racist* movie. But you knew exactly what I was talking about."

Anyway I used both hands, in my mind, to place the tip square in the middle of my sternum, just between my breasts, before plunging it through my skin and bones and muscles to the hilt. That did provide some relief, let some pressure out, and I felt weak from it so held myself up against the wall. Ultimately I got down on the shower floor, and sobbed there for about half an hour with the water running.

"That's standard trauma, never knowing what the little thing is that's going to get you and set you off," Denise said when we talked about this. "Do you remember what it was?"

I thought about it for a second, what I'd been doing on the couch. And I did remember. We both laughed a little, that sad, snorting laugh, when I told her what it was.

"My Internet went out."

Before Nico had moved in, I had conducted all of my craziness alone, where no one else could see me, but for its very, very, very unfortunate emergence on our trips together. Living with him, I was mortified that my behavior was always on display for another person. I told the most about it to Tana and Alex, who listened and supported as best they could, but I still told them very little, trying to spare them from the monotony of chronic illness. For them to be able to get the whole picture of what was going on, I'd have had to be calling them every day to disclose truthfully, "Hi it's me. I *still* hate being alive. Yeah, I am still not coping with any of this." If I spoke about my disorder in direct proportion to its significance to my life, we would speak of nothing else. So I tried to have mostly normal conversations or just talk about it for a couple minutes before moving on, while I let it run always privately in the background and, to keep from bringing it up again—again, again, AGAIN—when I got desperate to go on about it for hours I sometimes called someone from grad school or even high school who I hadn't talked to in years and when they asked me how I was doing, just dropped it on them.

But there was no managing Nico's exposure as my housemate. I obsessively worried about its impact on him. He couldn't help feeling bad when he'd sidle up next to me without my hearing him, the surprise detonating a terror bomb in my guts that left my heart racing and me shaking and sometimes crying for ten minutes, saying, "You *scared* me." And he couldn't have been thrilled that he'd had to devise a time limit for how long he'd let me pace and pant and sob in the shower before coming in after me, startling me through my weepy, hallucinatory fog, and sometimes having to carry me out.

"I can't do this," I told Denise after probably the third time I'd sent Nico leaping up out of his sleep when I started screaming during a nightmare. "I can't take care of myself and someone else at the same time. I want to live in a cave by myself."

"Can you change that story to being that you just haven't *figured out* how to take care of yourself and your relationship at the same time *yet*?"

I did try telling myself that. But my self wasn't convinced. Because to further complicate matters, I was not the only troublemaker at my address anymore.

The second thing that Nico and I had overestimated was how well he was going to handle being an immigrant.

Sure, I'd seen him become frustrated before. But considering what he'd been through generally, and what I put him through specifically, Nico struck me as a walking reincarnated Buddha. He was a man with a stable foundation. Not to say he was unshakable. I'd seen that he had cracks, like everyone else. He had unresolved grief about his father. And he, too, had some issues about Haiti. I'd first noticed it in Montpellier, when he'd been flipping through pictures on a digital camera and come to an innocuous shot of a displacement camp. His reaction lasted just a second, but long enough for me to catch it: He winced and turned his face away.

When his unit had embarked to Port-au-Prince, Nico had been excited. Unlike many of the other guys, he wasn't upset when the brass told them, as they were leaving for the airport, that instead of staying one month as planned they'd be staying three. To Nico, his mission in Haiti was the same as the personal mission that had made him join the gendarmerie: to save lives. He arrived in a country where a lot of people did need help, but where many of those people saw MINUSTAH, the United Nations Stabilization Mission in Haiti, as pampered occupiers—some from former invader and slave master *France*—come to enforce the interests of the wealthiest, whitest class by tamping down legitimate unrest and keeping the masses in check. Haitians, including those in the camps MINUSTAH was dispatched to protect, protested their presence. Especially after a deadly cholera outbreak was linked to infected foreign peacekeepers. Nico was part of a force that created unrest as much as it calmed it, a literal plague on the country.

It wasn't true that grunts such as Nico lived luxuriously—their tents leaked on their faces at night when it rained and blew down in storms, and they showered six at a time under a horizontally strung hose with spouts stuck into it—and Nico knew his unit was made up of good working-class dudes trying to do a good job while doing what they were ordered. But he couldn't disagree with at least one of the protesters' accusations against them: that they were worthless. The moments when he intervened in machete fights or ran madly through camp under the weight of his guns and gear in the heat to detain a guy trying to kill his wife were, for Nico, outweighed by the ones where he and the rest of the troops ate their UN lunches in the back of a truck, in front of a bunch of hungry camp kids to whom they were forbidden to give any leftovers. When they returned their leftovers back at the compound, they were thrown away.

And then, after ninety days, they left, everything exactly the way it'd been when they arrived.

Maybe it wasn't surprising that for Nico—who'd seen his dad crying one afternoon, hadn't said anything about it, and had found him hanging dead the next night—there was no sin greater than uselessness. The most upset I'd seen him was one of the many times he couldn't pull me out of an episode. "I just want to feel like I'm helping you," he'd yelled. "I just want to feel like I can help you, I make it better for you. That's all!" He'd started weeping so hard, he shook. He started screaming at me. "*That's all!*"

I had learned that not being helpful or useful, which to him seemed to equal not being a good person, was Nico's primary issue. Its coincidence with my unhelpable disorder was the cause of nearly all of our real fights. "Ridiculous," I'd told Tana when we talked about this. "He sounds like a superhero. 'He gets really mad sometimes, but only when he can't help enough.' If I ever write about him, I'm going to mention how he thinks women are bad at parking so I'm not like 'Mleh, my boyfriend's perfect!' I'll have to include unflattering things about him so I don't sound like a total lunatic."

So let me take this opportunity, here, to say that when Nico got to San Francisco, he was a real dick.

Nico had adjusted to life just fine on his deployments. He'd shat in holes in the ground in French Guiana for months, breathed the gasoline-and-poop fumes as they burned the waste during breakfast, worked twenty-four-hour shifts, drank water full of iodine tablets and been away from his family, his girlfriend, his cocker spaniel.

But he did not adjust to this glittering American city. When Nico arrived in San Francisco that March, he was unit-less. He was comparatively language-less. He didn't belong. He was alone with his girlfriend, who did belong, nervous about using English with Americans aside from me, finding that other Americans weren't as good as deciphering his accent when he tried. In these circumstances, Nico could not help me, no. He could not call the phone company, or order in restaurants, or make conversation at parties. He could not even help himself.

Now he was a blind and staggering baby, too.

At this point, for me, with all the therapy and self-awareness-tuning and opening and purging, my response to being triggered was mostly to start crying. It was inconvenient, annoying, and maybe distressing—but not cruel. As a man, and a Frenchman, and a soldier, and a child whose father told him not to cry, who didn't cry after his father's death because he was busy holding his mother together, Nico's response to being very upset was not to cry.

It was to be a fucking asshole.

Cold, shut down, mean. Uncooperative and rude. Knocked way off center, lost from his own foundations, he was quick to argue or just stop speaking to me, even in public. I told Denise that he was ruining my life. I'd spent eighteen months wishing for nothing more, aside from my sanity, than to be close to him. Now that I was, I just wanted to get away.

He wasn't like that all the time. He was often delightful, everything I'd fallen in love with. He invited me to lunch; that was how he would say it, even though we lived together and were always sitting in the same studio apartment, "I would like to inveet you to lunch." He was adapting to my episodes—he'd stopped telling me to calm down or suck it up, and started waiting it out with me, supporting me through it.

Overall, though, his moods were unpredictable and extreme. I'd been in a relationship like that before and hated it, so I was extrasensitive to the dynamic, along with being extrasensitive to everything in general. In a way, his episodes were worse than mine. He hadn't been practicing acute self-awareness for a year. So another difference between us when we were being monsters was that he had defensive denial that wouldn't allow him to know he was being a monster. That knowledge cannot be pointed out to someone from the outside. And he did not have a coffee-cake test.

"You're being a monster," I would say to him when he'd turned hard and angry, snapping at me at breakfast, using that seething, scathing tone maladjusted spouses sometimes use.

"No," he said. "It's you." He could keep it up for hours, or days, or a week, that frightening hostility, before recognizing what had upset him (he hadn't been able to call the doctor to schedule a checkup for himself) and coming clean about his real issue (he felt like an impotent loser) and turning into his old self. Sometimes, his issue turned out to be the same as my issue: fear that we would lose each other. After one rough, mean weekend, he broke down, saying just, "So many bad things have happened in my life."

Your feelings are not for show, his father used to tell him when he was growing up. *Lock them into your belly, and you keep them there until you die.*

We took turns ruining things.

One day, we went for a sushi lunch, and Nico was happy and affectionate and sitting close to me and kissing my cheek. Since we were sitting at the sushi bar, the sushi chef—some hipster with a mustache and tattoos—couldn't avoid seeing that; I could sense him watching us out of the corner of his eye.

"Please get away from me," I said quietly to Nico, burning with agitation. He didn't move fast enough. "Get away from me!" I whisper-yelled. Outside, and back home, my anxiety at stabbing-fantasy levels, I barked at Nico. That kind of PDA, I hollered, didn't swing in America.

Nico wasn't buying that outburst. He'd been told that public Frenching wasn't normal but had seen plenty of other couples cheek-nuzzling. We fought about it, and I stayed tight and irritated, for days. A few nights later, lying next to him, I woke him up after he'd fallen asleep to fume, "You're always TOUCHING ME," with my jaw locked and my body tense and my fists in angry balls.

Had Denise been there, she would have pointed out that in that state of rigidity—against the world, against my own truths—whatever I was thinking was likely to be a defensive self-lie.

But Denise wasn't there. So.

"You're fucking SUFFOCATING ME," I said. "You can't just touch me in public whenever you want because you're fucking EUROPEAN. That's not how it fucking works here! I've *TOLD YOU*."

Eventually, another day—after days of this!—worn out and in his arms, with his warmth surrounding my rib cage in our bed, I softened up enough and there the truth was, sitting in my mouth.

"I didn't want the sushi guy to know that I'm in love," I said suddenly, out of nowhere for both of us.

"What?" Nico asked. "Why?"

"Because. Then he would know that I needed you."

Nico made a face. "And?"

"He would think I couldn't take care of myself," I said, and as the realization came together, I started crying. "And then he would think I would be easy to kill."

Wheeeeee!

Then I took Nico out for a rousing bout of karaoke one night, and he struggled to make English conversation and fit in, but decided that his problem instead was that he hated me. He spat rude answers at my friends when they tried to engage him. He stood apart from me in the bar, however I tried to draw him in and soothe him, continually moving away as I interacted with others so he could glare at me from a distance.

"I think we're the right people for each other, but it's just not the right time," he said. It was after another time he'd been pissy and mean, over an entire weekend trip with Tana. "I can't help you, and you can't help me." He was in a tailspin. The guy who'd waved away our language difference and all other obstacles was now suggesting that we call it quits and write it off as bad timing.

He was right. About the timing. There was a reason they told you not to date or make any major changes for the first year in AA. The stress of new recovery is too hard on a relationship, and the stress of a new relationship is too hard on recovery. The path of my healing was complicated, inching onward but then doubling way back on itself, constantly surprising me with how much worse *all the way worse* could keep getting, or staying at previously reached depths of worse but then moving in a new direction, toward ground that hadn't yet been covered. But there could only be one trajectory for our relationship. It was forward or nothing. We were already in love. We couldn't live without one another as long as we were in touch, and maybe even if we weren't, and we couldn't take it slow or casual even if we wanted to, which we didn't, because we lived in different countries. We were going to make it through this together, or we weren't going to make it together.

I didn't think Monster Nico was the real him, at his boiled-down essence. I considered it a layer of temporary maladjustment and unresolved pain. Underneath, I was certain there was his shining, perfect core. And I was hardly one to be accused of schoolgirl optimism. Somehow, generously, Nico believed the same thing about me. Even when I couldn't anymore.

Submerged as we were in it already, we were getting ready to dive deeper still into the PTSD pool. Since before my own PTSD essay had come out, I'd been laying the groundwork for a story about the impact veterans' PTSD had on their relationships. Though I'd intended to focus on sex, the spouses I talked to were eager to get the word out about something else: that living with someone with PTSD was giving them PTSD, too. "Secondary trauma." After regular phone and e-mail check-ins over nearly a year, I was finally going to meet Brannan Vines, founder of Family of a Vet. And I was taking Nico, who'd been in the United States just a month, to her Alabama hometown with me.

T'inquiete pas, he had always said to me. *Don't worry. I won't stop to try to understand.*

Trying out our relationship full time, and trying to do it in tandem with our issues, we tested the limits of Nico's promise. Lately, we couldn't ignore that it was more easily whispered than kept.

13.

Navy SEALs are screened carefully for vulnerability to PTSD.
They're resistant to it.

—FBI Special Agent David Rossi, *Criminal Minds,*
Season Seven, Episode Three

My first morning at work on the secondary-trauma story, I was already
taking to dramatic journaling while I sat on the sidewalk outside my hotel.

4.2.12

> *Good morning, Alabama.*
> *"Remember, if you do this story, it's not so you'll get worse," Nico says
> in the car. "You don't have to absorb it to understand," he says last night,
> stroking my hair. "Because you have the same."*
> *This morning I ask where my hugs are. "Where's my hug?"*
> *"What?"*
> *Repeat.*
> *"What? I'm sorry, I was speaking French in my dream, I need one mo-
> ment to switch."*
> This relationship is a certain failure, *I think.* You will never be dili-
> gent enough or free-time-having enough to learn French, and a rela-
> tionship cannot survive this language barrier.
> *Oh, no. I woke up crazy.*
> *I shuffle frantically through my toolbox—breathing? No. Some kind
> of mantra? Yes. "This will pass"? No. "Do not be seduced by your thoughts."
> Propels me to the bathroom. "You need to relax," he says at breakfast. "You
> can't be like this. And if I can feel it, other people can too."*

False. Sources find me universally charming, *I counter internally, though out loud, I say the marginally less friendly,* "Don't tell me how to do my fucking job." *Bleh. But it's too late, he's put his hand on my leg and extended his calming presence and now I'm more grounded and can feel what I really feel like.*

I feel sad.

Cures at this point still kind of limited to crying it out through my face or drinking it down. Visualize dropping tears into the hotel cheddar cheese scrambled eggs. That seems right. But I don't have time for that shit, so I'm gonna wear it.

Brannan would understand. But I'm not here to tax her.

Before we left for Alabama, I had been taking it way easier than I had during my previous schedule now that I was part time. Haiti I was eighteen months in the past. The last story I'd reported was the undercover work in the distribution warehouse, before I left for Guadeloupe—five months ago. But I had to work again sometime.

As I'd been pursuing it over the months before Nico moved in, the content of the secondary-trauma story had started worrying the people around me. One morning, I'd talked to a veteran's wife. She had a handful of young kids in the house and a husband who, after Iraq, looked out the window more than a hundred times a day. For the past couple of weeks he had been sleeping in the garage he boarded up, which was sort of fine with her since during the nights he started screaming or hitting "things." And more than once had sexually assaulted her. A lot more than once.

"You need to quit!" my father yelled at me when he called later that day and I happened to be crying about this. The next day, he admitted he'd been drunk and apologized for being rash. "You cannot get enough distance from these subjects, and it's tearing you apart!"

He was extra-mad that day because of how upset I'd been earlier that month, when I e-mailed Chris, my marine buddy, my validation hero, who'd shared his symptoms and told me to fuck all what anyone said about me. I hadn't heard from him since we'd been scheduled to talk on the phone. Though that wasn't a big deal—he was busy, and I figured he'd changed his mind or wasn't up to talking about his psychiatric secrets—I wanted to let him know I'd been thinking about him and was still ready to talk whenever, if ever, he was. It was his wife who wrote me back. She said she knew that we'd been talking, and she thought it was helpful to him, so thanks for that. But she thought I should know that he was dead.

"No, no," I said to no one, sitting alone on my bed reading her message. It was shortly after Nico had left his first visit to San Francisco, the previous fall. "No no no no no no no."

Breakdown. Normal-person breakdown: totally appropriate breakdown. I dropped into a quick deep hole of grief, shaking my head, gasping and sobbing, wondering what had happened. But I knew what had happened. Every day, the VA said, eighteen veterans committed suicide. One every eighty minutes. It was the pinnacle of bullshit: The very things that made the ones with PTSD want to die were the symptoms their body produced because it had so badly wanted to survive. Chris had PTSD, and PTSD was regularly fatal. They never said it like that, and I didn't understand why. When you had cancer, they told you that you had x percent chance of dying, especially if you didn't get y and z treatments. No one says that unresolved trauma can kill you. If anyone did, maybe people would take it more seriously. Serious as cancer.

I Googled a news clip, and indeed, Chris had committed suicide, after barricading himself inside his house and engaging the Tucson SWAT team in a standoff. In the story, his ex-wife was quoted as saying he'd called her from inside and sounded like he'd lost his mind. "All they give you is pills," he hollered at the officers outside, railing against the Department of Veterans Affairs. I looked at the dates on the clips. The day before, he'd asked me for my phone number. The day of, he'd e-mailed me, saying, "Just give me a day or two. Please"—no ending punctuation. He'd written it hours before he shot himself in the face.

I called off work. I stayed in bed even more than usual that September.

"I can't tell you not to do this," Nico said when we talked about my continuing to work on the story. "But I'm glad your father said it."

I knew I needed to watch my limits. But I didn't know what my limits were anymore. There seemed to be nothing within my limits. It wasn't just the horrors my war sources were dealing with—or, say, one of my sources from Congo updating me that a colonel had cornered him in a grocery store when he went to pick up bread and mentioned how *eeaaaasy* it was for people to disappear around there. The story I'd done undercover was not about war, or genocide, or murder. But though it was about working in a warehouse, I had still started crying—just for a few minutes, but still—one night after a ten and a half hour shift. The job involved laboring in ergonomic conditions that should've been illegal, and I cried because it hurt, because everyone I worked with said it hurt, and because they all had to do it for real and for almost no money. I cried because the company had fired this one guy because he'd missed work the day his baby was born. That was perfectly regular life, that people treated people like that for maximum profitability, and still, it was enough to break me down.

This was why Dr. Shere had said that for her money she wouldn't think I'd get better as long as I had a job, unless I could find a job that paid enough to live but produced zero stress or grief and let me take hours and hours off every week for therapy and for yoga and for the days when I lapsed into psychosis or depression. This was why Dr. Shere had suggested that I not work at all.

"Ohhh, *fuck* that," Denise had said when I'd passed this advice along.

Alright. So, not *everybody* around me didn't want me doing the secondary-trauma story.

Denise didn't take kindly to anyone, least of all me, acting as if I were an invalid. She wasn't against my working. In physical therapy, you had to find a balance between doing too much and doing too little; you couldn't heal your post-surgery knee just sitting around. You had to exercise your muscle to make it work right again. You had to take it easy, but still try it out. Denise supported my doing the emotional equivalent. But she wasn't without her concerns. "We need to take really good care of you," she said every time I saw her in the run-up to leaving for Alabama. I'd been with her for nine months by then. "We need to watch how you're doing, and make sure you have all the tools and support you need."

She thought there were some encouraging signs that I could handle it. One being the vast amounts of time and money I was pouring into recovery, but also more internal signs. That I'd known I wasn't up for Haiti, for example. That I'd done it anyway was another matter, and a matter of employment, but having recognized that I was too burned out for the assignment at the time and resisted it, and that I'd given myself at least one day to take it easy when I got there rather than running around from the moment I landed like I was supposed to, and forced myself to go swimming when I didn't want to, indicated a good baseline of instincts for my needs. When I'd got home,

I'd recognized I had a drinking problem, and at least tried to stop. I'd tried to take care of myself back in San Francisco, by immediately going to therapy. And by cooking. If I couldn't bring myself to do many things then, I did walk back and forth to my neighborhood grocery store to make pot after pot of wholesome, elaborate soup. "Well chosen for a post-Haiti PTSD pot," I wrote in my cookbook above the recipe for Black Bean With Rice and Guacamole, just days after coming home. "Still a little watery with modification but a delicious and warming lunch," I wrote a month later next to Cauliflower Vichyssoise.

My history of self-care plus lessons learned equaled the potential to work with my PTSD, a necessary if not ideal partnership. It'd been a year and a half since my diagnosis. Since PTSD can alter your physiology indefinitely, I was going to learn to work with some extent of it or another eventually, or maybe never work again. And I had to work to eat, of course. But that wasn't the only way I needed it. It was also kind of the only thing I had left.

A partial list of things I was terrible at for the moment: Sleeping. Sexing. Breathing. Not turning into a maniac without warning. I was a constant disappointment to myself, the cause of endless gut-wrenching derision, that I'd become this way and would always be this way. But work! There was something I could do. Something I loved to do. Assign me a story, and maybe there would be some nervous breakdowns in between then and the deadline these days, but I would get it done, and it would be good. When Denise had had me put the things that were important to me, that made me who I was, two fingers' widths below my navel in my somatic core, to be pressed on and remembered and invoked in times of groundless insanity, there'd only been a few things in there. One of them was Nico. One of the others was work.

My job was important to me. I didn't have any illusions that I was saving lives, but part of me still believed, especially after being inundated with letters from people who said my admission of post-trauma sex dysfunction made them less inclined to feel like killing themselves, that good stories contributed something. Information, awareness, solidarity, the seeds of acceptance or movement toward change. My refugee roommates in Thailand hadn't got peace from war out of my writing a book about them, but it brought them some personal relief. They just wanted a witness. They just, at least, wanted someone to *know*.

I wasn't trying to sacrifice myself for a cause. But neither was I interested, in the case of this story in particular, in getting better at the expense of turning my back on other traumatized people. One of the members of my impromptu e-mail support group, who himself had felt like no one understood him, was dead. He had done what he could for a stranger despite his own suffering. I had to do what I could. Plus I didn't care to be ruled by fear, which I'd never let govern me before. I wasn't being reckless. When a magazine editor got in touch to offer me an assignment in Iraq ("I don't think the story would involve an active war zone, but it would probably involve witnessing some gruesome stuff"), I didn't fool myself for one second into thinking I was ready for that. Though I wanted the job—and hated myself for not being capable of taking it—I turned it down.

"This is your conviction," Nico would always concede when we argued over Skype about whether I should still be professionally chronicling other people's problems. ("You don't have enough problems of your own?" was one of his lines.) "This is who you are. I have a lot of respect for it. And," he'd add, "it won't be as hard as when you were alone."

So with Denise having trained me and committed me to monitoring myself in the run-up, and Nico in tow with me on the ground, I was back in the field for a couple of weeks. Back to work on the Gulf Coast.

Brannan Vines picked me up outside our southwest-Alabama Homewood Suites while I was scribbling the previous diary entry onto a piece of paper. If she noticed that I was in emotional free fall, she didn't say anything. Instead, she drawled, "Aren't you cute!" like a grandma, though we were the same age, and I was five inches taller than she was.

Over the past year, Brannan and I had conversed about intimate topics even old friends might not—failings at sex, sanity, optimism, personal maintenance—but we were seeing each other for the first time. She was pale, with well-styled, chin-length, dirty-blond hair. She wore loose clothes, baggy top and pants, but lipstick. Her nails were done. I was amazed that she managed to make that happen, since Brannan had several jobs. One of them was taking care of her husband, Caleb, who was three years older than she was, but since he'd come back from his second tour in Iraq had frequent falls and walked with a cane. That was not a job figuratively: Recently, the Department of Veterans Affairs had started a program to pay spouses of veterans who ended up as default but essential caretakers. After a lot of paperwork, home visits, and assessments, given Caleb's level of disability, the VA paid

Brannan to take care of him full time. In the VA's estimation, that was worth $400 a week.

The first thing Brannan and I did together was drive to Florida. Every week, she and Caleb drove to the Pensacola VA hospital, because though there was one in Alabama, it had once prescribed Caleb a drug to which he was allergic and he'd nearly died. He didn't trust the place now, and Brannan hadn't been able to get him to set foot in there since. So every week, at least once, they drove an hour to Florida for doctor's appointments. Speech therapy for Caleb's traumatic brain injury, or TBI, from the twenty-plus explosions he experienced between IEDs, vehicle-born IEDs, and rocket-propelled grenades. Physical therapy for the degenerative joint disease he came back with, that lots of guys were coming back with for reasons they said they hadn't figured out yet—missing cartilage in one of his knees, several disintegrating spinal discs. Appointments related to the twelve medications he was on—antidepressants, sleep aids, anxiety meds, pain meds, nerve meds, stomach meds. Tests for mysterious cysts, tests for his lungs, which were mysteriously only 48 percent functional. Usually Brannan and Caleb drove together, but today he had group therapy after his appointment and then lunch with the small handful of old 'Nam guys from therapy after that.

"I'm so sorry my car is so filthy," she kept saying on the ride over. "I wanted to clean it before you came but things just got . . ."

"Please," I said.

In a waiting room at the Pensacola VA, which looks like any other large doctor's waiting room except for the gun magazines lying around, we met her husband. Round and long-haired and bearded, he looked much older than her and extremely tough, but he shook my hand and said hello politely. I also met Shilo, the German shepherd at Caleb's side. Shilo was a PTSD service dog—a product of one of those many treatment studies the government was funding. She was trained to bark at Caleb's triggers and jump up on his chest when she could sense it coiling with the anxiety of an episode, providing instant warm pressure and sympathy. When all three Vineses were whisked in to see the doctor, I stayed behind and read about firearms.

After the appointment, Brannan and I drove home so she could work her other job. A sweet and spacious three-bedroom in a leafy subdivision, the Vines' residence did double duty as Brannan's office. She'd set up a desk and computer in what was supposed to be the dining room; it'd never been finished as a dining room, since they'd bought the house with the intention of fixing it up as they had with another house before the war but obviously weren't up for that now. She sat down and got to work immediately. The stated mission of Family of a Vet, or FOV, was "to help you find your way, find the information you need, and find a way not only to *cope* with life after combat . . . but to survive and *thrive!*" It had a hundred volunteers and thousands of Facebook users, who met up in groups to compare and commiserate. If she wasn't answering e-mails, Brannan was on the phone, which started ringing soon after we walked in.

"Deep breath, Helen," she said to the caller. "Deep breath."

Brannan worked, then filled me in on what was going on, and I took notes.

Helen's veteran son was committed to a non-VA psychiatric facility, but he did not want to be there, because he, a severe-PTSD sufferer, was already paranoid, and one of the other resident loons had threatened to kill him. Also, he had fought for his country, he was screaming at Helen, and they promised they wouldn't abandon him, and he swore to God and to his mother that if the VA didn't put him in with the other soldiers, he was going to kill himself. Helen had already made as many phone calls to hospital administrators as she knew how but wasn't getting anywhere; did Brannan know what to do?

"Breathe," Brannan said to the next caller, too, a veteran's wife who was calling from the parking lot of a Dairy Queen to which she'd fled because it looked as if her husband's episode was about to become violent. Brannan said the same thing to the woman whose husband's service dog had died in the night; waking up to the death smell had triggered him, and the wife thought he was on the verge of hurting himself or someone else if she couldn't get him into a VA hospital. But the closest major clinic was four hours away, and she was eight and a half months pregnant and got three hours of sleep, and the clinic's Web site said its case manager position for veterans of Iraq or Afghanistan was currently unstaffed.

"Breathe," Brannan told everybody. Even as she said it, her voice was shaky and thin. I could practically taste the constriction in her throat from my place on the couch in the adjacent living room. When she had a break between phone calls and joined me there, I asked her if she ever took the deep breaths she herself was advising.

She readily admitted that she didn't. "If I stopped, and started breathing," she said, "I would be too sad."

The house was quiet. We could hear the cat padding around. The air-conditioning whooshed, and a clock ticked. Usually, the place was ensconced in darkness even during the day; they kept all the blinds closed for Caleb's light sensitivity and for privacy. But alone in the house, Brannan and I had opened them to the sunshine. Even when the phone rang, and she started talking and pacing, it somehow didn't penetrate the stillness.

Discourse about trauma may have been ghettoized to support groups and private therapy in the outside world—and even then, sometimes couched in euphemisms and veiled terms—but in Brannan's world, it was all trauma, all the time. Together, FOV volunteers and users normalized their experiences by collecting and sharing them. Everyone who had something "crazy" to say about what was happening in their house found that the same thing was happening in someone else's. No punches were pulled. This was the place where you could admit addiction and rehab, relapses and spousal abuse, fear of getting assaulted in your own bed, and not getting divorced anyway. No judgments.

"My Husband entered the Marines shy and quiet," someone had written in the comments of my PTSD-sex essay, "looking for educational assistance; but he came back angry, scared, and expressing violence that he, I, our 4 kids, nor the VA seems to understand. When everything is quiet in the forefront of our home . . . trust me, our bedroom can be frightening."

This woman and I had been in touch in the meantime, and Brannan knew about it. "I heard you talked to Christine!" she said; turned out she was a member of FOV.

Sometimes people complained to Brannan that her organization was making veterans with PTSD look bad by discussing these issues ("tired and depressed and very sore, PTSD episodes with violence suck . . ." a typical Facebook posting read), but she of all people wasn't trying to stigmatize. She knew how stigma contributed to Caleb's condition, to the way he felt about himself and the way other people interacted with him, but she also knew that honesty and awareness were the keys to spouses' survival and to overcoming stigma. It was a fine line she was walking.

She'd been lost without PTSD awareness once herself, she told me on the couch. It wasn't like she was born with the information, with taking it all in stride. When Caleb had come home from his second tour, in 2006, she didn't know what to do with him. He was wound up and on a hair trigger. He had outbursts that scared her, when she'd never been close to being scared of him before. He hadn't yet been diagnosed with TBI, so there was no explanation for why he was forgetting whole conversations minutes after they'd happened. When they had sex, sometimes it was great. But sometimes, he suddenly froze. Brannan didn't know what he was experiencing when that happened, because when it did he got up and walked wordlessly out the door.

She could have been warned. Countless, documented multitudes had experienced what they were going through before them. They would have been less unsettled if the decades of research about it were systematically shared or spread. Instead, some panicked Googling led Brannan to the Web site of Vietnam Veteran Wives, where she ended up talking to its founder much the way that today's phone callers ended up talking to Brannan. VVW's founder, Danna Hughes, had been through the same turmoil decades ago and had opened a center to help get Vietnam vets benefits and educate their spouses and communities about their condition. Danna guessed what Brannan's symptoms were before Brannan even admitted them. It wasn't just Caleb who was different now. Danna knew that it was Brannan, too.

Secondary Traumatic Stress Disorder (STSD) is, as one medical journal puts it, "almost identical to PTSD except that indirect exposure to the traumatic event through close contact with the primary victim of trauma" is the cause. It's been well documented in the spouses of veterans with PTSD from Vietnam. And the spouses of Israeli veterans with PTSD and Dutch veterans with PTSD. In one study, the incidence of secondary trauma in wives of Croatian war vets with PTSD was 30 percent. In another there, it was 39 percent. Kids have been studied, too, with researchers finding in offspring of veterans from World War II, Korea, and Vietnam such symptoms as a "higher rate of psychiatric treatment," "more dysfunctional social and emotional behavior," and "difficulties in establishing and maintaining friendships." Forty-five percent of kids in one study "reported significant PTSD signs"; "83 percent reported elevated hostility scores." The symptoms were similar to those researchers had seen before, in perhaps the most analyzed and important population in the field of secondary traumatization: the children of Holocaust survivors.

In 2003, though, a team of Dutch and Israeli researchers meta-analyzed thirty-one of the papers on Holocaust survivors' families and concluded—to the fury of Holocaust families and clinicians alike—that when more rigorous controls were applied, there was no evidence for the intergenerational transmission of trauma. When I called the lead scientist and asked him about his results, he told me that he also wondered if the studies about veterans would hold up. But he speculated that if they did, the many differences between veterans and Holocaust survivors might account for it. Namely, that the survivors' community rallied around them with support and resources and did not make them feel as though they were expected to sack up and get over it. To this day, Jewish groups offer home care and counseling to Holocaust survivors, as well as support groups to second- and third-generation members of their family.

Another, recent study of PTSD combat veterans' spouses concluded that more than 15 percent showed signs of STSD, while most of them were generically psychologically distressed. As I sat in Brannan's living room, a 20-year, 10,000-family study of Iraq and Afghanistan veterans' kin, the largest of its kind ever conducted, was under way to settle the question more definitively. Meanwhile, the social-work programs manager for U.S. Army Medical Command conceded to me that "in a family system, every member of that system is going to be impacted, most often in a negative way, by mental health issues." But though that was the sort of thing they told reporters who called asking specific questions about secondary trauma, they didn't provide that information to soldiers and their families as a matter of course.

Back in those dark confusing days, psychiatrists and social workers could've told Brannan how contagious trauma was. People who worked with traumatized people needed support groups of their own, and families' exposure was a hundredfold. Studies that did or didn't validate this wouldn't impact Brannan either way. She knew what her life was like. And Danna had known what her life was like. Danna had guessed, correctly, that she'd stopped being a whole person. That she'd lost herself in constantly orienting herself around her unpredictable husband, and that she'd developed new, unrecognizable emotional tendencies. In her living room, Brannan told me what it was like when hypervigilance overtook her. She remembered a time she was at a drugstore and was standing behind a sweet old lady counting out change when Brannan suddenly became so furious her ears started ringing. Being too cognizant of every sound—every coin dropping becoming an echo—she exploded inwardly, her fury incinerating any normal tolerance for a fellow patron with a couple of dollars in quarters and dimes.

Brannan had never been to war, but she had a warrior's sense of hyperawareness and stimuli-sensitivity. They were skills on a battlefield, but crazy-person behavior in a drugstore.

We laughed about this sitting in her living room. We laughed about it together because she knew I had the same kind of problems sweeping my floor, or writing e-mails, or missing a train.

After talking to Danna and finding out she wasn't the only freak show in the universe, Brannan took it upon herself to found her own organization and pass the information on to as many people as she could. She wanted to give people hope by surrounding them with other people like themselves; she wanted to show people how other people were making it. She'd made herself familiar with all the research and history. It was the stuff about the kids that worried her most, because she and Caleb had a six-year-old, Katie, who was at school now. It was a lot for Brannan to juggle, FOV and the caretaking and their daughter. Especially when her symptoms overwhelmed her normal cognitive functioning.

"Sometimes I can't do the laundry," she said. "And it's not like, 'Oh, I'm too tired to do the laundry'; it's like 'Um, I don't understand how to turn the washing machine on.' I am looking at a washing machine and a pile of laundry and my brain is literally overwhelmed by trying to figure out how to reconcile them."

She used to be different. She used to travel, just up and flying to France one time. Now new places and new people stressed her out rather than excited her. Caleb had been through intensive in-patient government therapy twice, and Brannan was bummed good treatment wasn't available to her. Now she didn't even like going to Walmart, because she remembered the time Caleb went into scary meltdown there; because she was always hypervigilant watching for triggers for him there; because maybe these days Walmart was too overwhelming for her, too.

Soon Caleb came home. When we heard him pulling into the driveway, we jumped up and drew the blinds, plunging the house back into its usual darkness.

I arrived back at our hotel later in the evening. I'd left Nico with a rental car and to his own devices. He had southern Alabama to explore if he was so inclined. He had access to a hotel pool and a gym. He had his mom to talk to—they'd been having hours-long Skype conversations since he left France. He had unlimited amounts of Netflix to binge-watch, using it to practice

English-listening and -reading comprehension with the closed captions on. When I got there, he was in our room.

I didn't realize until I saw him that I was hoping he would be gone. Being my affectionate boyfriend, he wanted to wrap me up in hugs and kisses and hellos as soon as I walked in the door, and I needed a minute. I needed ten minutes. I needed maybe forty-five to ninety minutes to myself. Or maybe like a week.

I excused myself to take a shower. I sat on the floor of the tub waiting for the water to heat up, huddling around the hot faucet for a while before I pulled the metal tab to send it up to the showerhead. I'd hemmed up a melt-down earlier in the morning when I'd felt it coming on but hadn't had time to deal with it. Now it escaped fast as I took deep, gulping breaths and cried. I thought about Caleb. I thought about how we'd talked when he came home, how mad he was when he told me that someone at the VA had once said to him, "Kids in Congo and Uganda don't have PTSD," as if those kids were tougher than he was and proof that he was making it up. I thought about Katie Vines, who had been in trouble when I met her that afternoon. Brannan and I had gone to her school to pick her up, and she'd bounded into the car, her blondish bob flying, her face nice and round like her daddy's. We didn't realize she was in trouble until she handed Brannan a folder from the back-seat that had notes about the day from her teacher.

"It says here," Brannan had said, the folder open on the steering wheel, her eyes narrowing incredulously, "that you *spit* on somebody today."

"Yes, ma'am," Katie admitted, lowering her voice and her eyes.

Brannan had conferenced with Katie's teacher many times about her behavior. Brannan said she mirrored her dad's overreacting and yelling. She said she was "not a normal, carefree six-year-old." In the car, she'd asked Katie to name the alternatives to lashing out that they'd talked about. Sometimes, Brannan had told me, Katie asked her to pray with her that her teacher would like her. Once, she'd asked Brannan to take her to a hypnotist so he could use his powers to turn her into a good girl. Looking in the rearview mirror as she drove, Brannan occasionally turned around and swatted lightly at Katie, trying to get her to stop picking at the open sores she dug into her own legs with tiny anxious fingers.

Back at the house, Shilo had barked at Katie a lot. Shilo barked at triggers, and Katie was a trigger, with her loudness and impulsive kid-ness. There was something else about kids, too, for Caleb. One of the memories that caused him the most trouble was the time he picked up the pieces of Baghdad bombing victims and found that lady who appeared to have thrown herself on top of her child to save him, only to find the child dead underneath.

Katie remained cheerful despite Shilo's barking. She ate her afterschool pancake snack and went and got dressed for tap-dance class. She came downstairs looking sweet as pie in a black leotard, pink tights, and shiny black tap shoes. On the way to class, where we dropped her before Brannan dropped me off, she said, apropos of nothing, "One time, a bad guy in Iraq had a knife and my dad killed him."

Brannan scolded her, but kindly. She didn't know why Katie adapted this story about Caleb's confiscating a weapon from an insurgent into a story about bloodshed, but she wasn't happy that she kept repeating it. She'd recently ruined one of her classmate's birthday parties by bringing it up, there at the Chick-fil-A.

Back in my hotel room, I stayed in the shower a long time. When I came out, I tried to engage with Nico. But I was still full of searing agitation. I told him I wanted to watch TV.

"I get that," my father had said on the phone when I told him about my TV needs once. "When I was doing all the bad things I was doing, and I knew I was eventually going to get caught, I remember sometimes when we were all watching TV together I could forget about it for a little while."

I just wanted to watch TV for an hour, I told Nico—I wasn't allowed to shut down for the whole time I was working anymore, making it harder to process everything and open up later. This time I had Nico for optimum safety and emotional support. I wasn't going to wander the hotels and restaurants of a strange city by myself. I was going to process as I went. But I was invoking my Denise-approved right to one hour of reprieve. I took it, staring at some show on my laptop in bed while Nico continued his English studies on his. Then I felt better. More decompressed.

We talked. We lay next to each other. We kissed. As soon as he put his hands on me, I panicked.

No no no! my body cried.

At the very least, if there were no dissociation or breakdown to be had, active excitement ruined me. When Nico and I kissed, my heart started beating faster. When my heart started beating faster, I wanted to stop and run from the apartment, or hurt or dismember him in a rage.

"Slow it down," Denise always said, as we were deconstructing these moments on the table. The point was so that I could start to recognize them better as they were happening, learn to listen to what my body was saying about them, and eventually, see them coming. "Go back to that moment. What happened in that moment?"

What happened in the moment, when my heart started beating faster, was that my body didn't associate being excited with sexiness anymore. It was a sign of mortal fear or encroaching episodes.

It made my body think, *Get out of there.*

This, it occurred to me in a sad moment there in the Homewood Suites, would not be happening if I were drunk.

I lay back, sighing angrily, sadly, accepting defeat. Sometimes it passed; this time it didn't. We would try again later or the next day. Nico remained undeterred and always ready to try again. His resilience was stunning. I didn't know how many times I could put my hands on someone and watch her flip out before deciding I never wanted to try touching her again, but I doubted it was very many.

Though Nico constantly struggled for balance in his new uprootedness, he managed to find a foothold some days. Luckily, this seemed to be one of those days. You could feel it in him, even around him, the ground stronger underneath your own feet in his proximity. I accredited some of it to his natural-born qualities, and some of it to his nationality. He had been raised to experience the present. I had been raised to live in the future: I ate breakfast so I could get ready for school, I sat through school so I could go home, I did my homework so I could get ready for dinner, I ate dinner so I could watch *Full House.* Nico ate dinner so he could *wring every available bit of pleasure and taste and human company* out of an evening. When he could locate himself in the present, it was as if he carried the weight of centuries, the bricks of a whole village, inside him. Those times, when he lay down next to me, he sunk like a thousand pounds of soft, rare stone.

Today, he said, "It's OK, no problem." He held onto me while I cried.

And so we spent our time. I went to work, and came home. As in California, how I felt in Alabama depended on the day. One day, we drove to a BBQ shack on Mobile Bay for dinner and I ordered rum and pineapple juice, like someone who drank for fun, not someone who drank because she wished she were dead. Another day, I came home and changed and we ran laughing to the pool. Another night, when we tried to have sex, it went so poorly that it ignited a huge fight.

"You should get a *non*-crazy slut," I was spitting at him toward the end of it, because I had used to be one of those, and I wanted to be one again so badly. What beautiful, virile Nico needed was the old me. I had been able to go from zero to sixty and back in twenty hot, fast minutes. I had desire, and then I had orgasms. Ta-da! Now I kept thinking I had desire, but when I went after it, I ended up feeling terrified and gross. At first, I wished that would stop, but since it was increasingly appearing like that wasn't going to happen soon, I started wishing I'd never liked sex in the first place.

"There's no permission or accepted precedent," Denise said sympathetically about this once, "socially, for a woman to just approach sex like 'I wanna FUCK.'"

Oh, but I had. Whether because of my overtly lusty parents or the unapologetically smutty dykes I'd come up with, I had used to do that, and what a miracle I had been. I hadn't realized the miracle at the time. How I missed that girl now. Nico had been the last person to kiss her, and I was glad he'd only barely met her. If he'd known her well, he would've missed her, too, and I couldn't have dealt with that.

There was the time in Alabama where we drove past a haunted house together and I tried to explain to him what a haunted house was, and he said, "They grab you like *this*?" and caught me off-guard with a hand to my right breast, and I curled up into a strict ball, knees into my chest, sliding my back down to the seat of the passenger seat, arms wrapped around my legs, a weird low, involuntary moan escaping my mouth.

But hey, man: Don't take it personally.

Nico retracted and turned rigid, and like that we drove for blocks, a cold silence settled between us. When we got back to the hotel, he said he felt sick and took a nap. After he woke up, he was tense and cold until bedtime.

Possibly I should mention here that in addition to being worried about me, and the immigration thing, the ninth anniversary of Nico's father's suicide fell in the middle of our trip to Alabama.

Every morning, I woke up and drove to Brannan's house. There I sat in her living room, observing or doing my own work as she worked, and going with her wherever she went. Whenever Caleb emerged from his room, I'd chat with him, and he would tell me he felt like shit, or how he was glad Brannan did the work she did, because it was good for her big heart and for other people who were going through what they were. When Katie came home from school, I'd play games with her. When Shilo came through the room, sure as a dope hound would've gone for pockets stuffed with junk, the trained PTSD service dog jumped onto the couch and put her paws on my chest.

When Brannan took breaks, she came and sat by me, and we talked about her work or who'd had what kind of recent episode. Whenever that person was me, she saw my guilt about the impact on Nico.

"It's his choice," she said, whether to stay with me or not.

Brannan was an avid defender of that choice, and not a fan of people telling other people they shouldn't be in their relationships. People asked her all the time why she didn't get divorced. Even when they didn't have the balls to say it, she knew that's what they were thinking. She admitted that she'd thought about it. Vietnam veterans with severe PTSD are 69 percent more likely than other vets to have their marriages fail. Brannan knew plenty of spouses from more recent wars who'd done it. She also knew that 65 percent of active-duty suicides, which were so high as to outpace combat deaths, were precipitated by broken relationships. But it wasn't the concern that Caleb would kill himself that kept Brannan with him—it'd happened before that he'd downed so much medication and booze that she told him he was going to die and he said, "Well, what if I don't care?" Her fear that he'd commit suicide and leave her guilty and their child fatherless wasn't her reason.

"I love him," she said. "I have enormous respect for Caleb. He has never stopped fighting for this family. Now, we've had little *breaks* from therapy, but he never stopped going to therapy." On FOV's Web site, she once published a love letter to Caleb that explained all the reasons she wanted to stay with him. Because the person who most often asked Brannan why she stayed with her husband was her husband.

She said he was her friend, and her first love, and her rock, and her lifeline. Her young daughter's blossoming father, her ally, her hero.

She told me she'd learned not to take his symptoms personally, most of the time. She told everyone they had to learn how to do that.

Still, one morning when I walked in, she was exhausted and haggard-looking already. "It's been one of those mornings," she said. And that morning was the fourth morning in a row she had said that. She walked upstairs to rouse her husband, which she always did at arm's length in case he woke up swinging, and I heard his voice bellow through the house as he screamed at her to leave him alone NOW. They had a doctor's appointment this morning, but Brannan was going to have to cancel it. She told me he'd had a particularly rough and screamy batch of nightmares last night.

When Katie came home from school, as we were playing a game, I asked her if her dad had woken her up last night, being that she was in the next room over.

She said nothing.

Her lack of response made me think that she hadn't heard me. I tried one more time. "Katie, did you hear your dad last night, did he wake you up?"

Katie, rambunctious and wild, impossible to quiet or calm down, acted as if I hadn't said anything.

But things would get better that night. Tonight was Lasagna Night. I'd gone and picked up the ingredients that Brannan needed after work last night. This morning, Brannan had browned the meat for Caleb's favorite dish, talking to Shilo about it. "Daddy will be really happy," she told the dog sitting on her kitchen floor. "Of course, he's too cranky to be happy about anything, and he'll be mad because Katie won't eat it because I spent all day makin' it and the only thing she wants to eat right now is pancakes." The Vineses had invited Nico and me to join them for dinner; I would go back to the hotel later and pick him up. They didn't make plans to hang out with other couples often, or even relatives, because people didn't understand that things could come apart in an instant if Caleb had a "bad PTSD moment." Brannan knew we already knew how that worked.

And dinner was a smashing success! Nico walked into the house in his nice button-down and right out to Caleb on the back porch, the men shaking hands. Brannan put a big bowl of salad and an array of dressings on the kitchen counter with the lasagna, and a frosted Bundt cake with chocolate chips in it. We made ourselves plates, then huddled around the coffee table in the living room. Katie bounced around us, unable to keep her seat in the excitement of the visitors, running to and from her room to bring and show me games and drawings. The men talked about weapons. We made fun of Caleb for being so old. Caleb told Brannan that she should learn a little something about gift expectations from watching us when I asked Nico what he was getting me for my birthday and he said, "Love."

We talked about our engagement.

We had got engaged.

One day, I had said to Nico, "Yes, I want to marry you." He was silent for a while as a slow smile permeated his face. He cried a little bit.

"I will make you happy," he said. Some days later, we woke up smiling at each other and he said, "I was dreaming we were shopping for engagement rings."

"Oh, yeah?" I said. "I was dreaming I stepped in a decomposing face."

Brannan and Caleb were happy for us. Though Caleb warned Nico that if he thought I stole a lot of food off his plate now, it was only going to get worse after I was his wife. The evening was long, and loud with laughter. There was one mildly uncomfortable thing where Caleb told us that the Iraqis were the worst people in the world to deal with, specifically because one time someone fired a missile at his unit and it didn't explode but lodged in the side of a building and little Iraqi kids were running up and kicking it. He was in charge of making sure everyone stayed back, but the kids kept coming, unsupervised. No one in their community or family was watching or stopping these kids. He became very worked up while telling us about this.

There was his thing about kids again.

But tonight, everyone was in good form. After the plates were cleared, Brannan curled herself against Caleb's side with his arm around her on the couch. They reclined there together, close, playing the old experienced couple. They'd been married for more than ten years already—"for-EVER," I explained to Nico.

"Feels like it!" Caleb said, and everyone laughed, and Brannan batted at him.

Leaving that night, we all beamed at one another at the front door in the warm way people do when they're separating after a nice meal. Nico and I drove home, the pleasantness carrying over in the car.

Back at the hotel, I crouched in the bathtub near the stream of warming water, washing off the day, as was becoming my ritual in addition to my bathing-time grounding practice. I was filled with sympathy for Caleb. I couldn't get myself out of the bathroom for it. I thought how epic my struggle for wellness was, and I had never even killed anyone. And I didn't have a traumatic brain injury to treat at the same time that would exacerbate my problems. And I had the disposable income to get treatment outside what my insurance allowed (the group therapy sessions, like Caleb went to—where, from what everyone told me, no soldier wanted to tell other soldiers about the emotional hell he was going through). And my struggle for maintaining my relationship benefitted from childlessness and loads of free time to work on connecting—"We have to find each other every day," was Nico's rule—and we had a hard enough time doing it all the same. And my main outlet was crying, an outlet veterans were less likely to take up. Imagine if for every time I started crying, I started yelling or throwing things instead. If instead of my energy behind a breakdown, it was a man's, and a trained soldier's.

"It's not a contest," Brannan reminded me when we talked about these things. But she admitted that she, like all traumatized people, always questioning the validity of their pain, thought my struggle was worse than hers. I stared at her in disbelief every time she started or ended her sentences with "Not that I have any right to complain to *you*."

Caleb had told me how he wanted to go back to Iraq. He said he would if they'd take him, which they wouldn't because of his disability. Chris had told me the same thing. He said Iraq was horrible, but in a simpler way. "I wish I could go back to war," he had written me at the end of an e-mail about how much he hated being at war. His system was built around it now. "I enjoyed it, the Camaraderie, the adrenalin and knowing that I was great at being a United States Marine."

While I was in the bathtub after Lasagna Night, back at the Vines residence, Caleb was in such a good mood after dinner that Brannan asked him if he was up for putting Katie to bed so she could go lie down. He said he was. Forty-five minutes later, he woke her up screaming. Not two days after that, he told her he was leaving her. "I'm going to get it over with and do it so you don't have to," he said, because that's just the way the scale went that day, when he weighed the pain of being alone versus the pain of being a burden.

14.

The letters, they kept coming. I read each one several times when I opened it, and re-opened random ones frequently. When I needed solidarity or support. When I was low on energy to work. Or to live.

> To: Mac McClelland
> Date: Thu, Jul 7, 2011 at 10:17 PM
> Subject: Your article
>
> Hi Mac,
>
> A friend recently sent me this article and I can't tell you how much I needed it and how much it moved me. I hope you don't mind me writing, it's just that I feel like you wrote the story of my life and recent struggles in that article.
>
> I have worked on issues of gender for the past 10 years, with the early part of my career spent as a domestic violence and rape counselor for both adult and children victims. I currently work in the field of human rights on a national level, with a good majority of my recent work focused on sex trafficking. While I am still young (27) and aspire to be the best in my field, I have in the past year struggled with the ghosts of my work. I am haunted by the women I've met and the case studies I must sort

through each day. My emotions, my mind, my feelings towards sex, the panicking, the vomiting, it all sounds so familiar.

As women in this field, we don't discuss enough the toll this work takes on us—how I'm afraid sometimes it molds us, into something we may or may not want to be.

Thank you again.

All the best,

Maria

> To: Mac McClelland
> Date: Mon, Sep 5, 2011 at 5:09 PM
> Subject: Thank you - your article about PTSD

Hi,

I've never been raped but I've had a difficult life, growing up in a war zone and other stuff later. Nothing even remotely as bad as what women are going through in Africa, though. You've made me realize one of the aspects of PTSD, the way you stop functioning in normal situations and just expect shit to keep happening. I realized how much was buried underneath the 'brave face' that I'm keeping up. Thank you for describing and publicizing this aspect of PTSD, and your unorthodox way to cope with it.

Anyway, thank you again, this was very helpful.

Ivana

> To: Mac McClelland
> Date: Mon, Mar 12, 2012 at 7:45 PM
> Subject: I'm Gonna Need You to Fight Me On This:
> How Violent Sex Helped Ease My PTSD.

Hi Ms. McClelland,

My name is Emily and I am eighteen years old and I go to a
small university. I want to thank you for your article. I was raped
last fall, during Frosh Week. For a long time, I was okay and I
put it to the back of my mind and I didn't think about it. I'm not
really okay right now. I have nightmares and daymares and
anxiety and insomnia and random bouts of crying hysteria. I'm
in treatment now, but it's not easy. It's never easy. I want to
thank you because of the approach you took to your PTSD. Very
rough (not necessarily violent) sex with my boyfriend has proven
to be a settling ease for my disorder. I thought that was really
fucked up, to be honest, but after reading your article, I realize
that coping with what has happened to me, and what has
happened to you, and what happens to a lot of people isn't
really simple and easy to deal with. There's no right way to help
yourself feel better. Anyway, thank you so much, and best of
luck with your future endeavors.

Emily

I had a nervous breakdown in New Orleans. That's where we drove to get
our flight back to San Francisco after Alabama. There, eating takeout, I
started crying and couldn't stop. We were in a tiny pied-à-terre borrowed
from one of my friends, and Nico had to take a step back from me, leaning
away in his chair at the table, cringing and shaking his head. It went on for
quite a while.

But I'm tired of writing scenes like that.

And when we returned from Alabama, we were increasingly having a different kind of scene.

The day after we got home, I stood by the bed of our studio apartment
watching Nico make tea. I walked over to him in the kitchen and wrapped
my arms around his waist from behind. Before he could finish squeezing his
tea bag, I'd pulled his pants down.

Ha-HA!

Yes. THERE was that slut that I knew and loved! Whose desire wasn't constantly superseded by the terror of becoming psychotic in bed! As we pressed against each other against the counter, my crazy failed to show up. It wasn't every time that it did, but lately, it'd been often enough that I forgot what it was like when it didn't.

I led him to the bed with abject glee. Radiating joy that reached to the walls and ceilings of my apartment. *Make way for this girl; she's got FUNC-TIONAL SEXUALITY.*

That night, as we went to sleep, I started seeing scenes of people being disemboweled. But rather than finding it calming, as I usually did, I winced and thought, *Gross. I don't want to think about* that.

"Victory!" I hollered at Denise the next day, throwing my arms up in the air.

She started laughing. "We'll take it," she said. Denise had advised me to have a plan ready (get up and walk around, take a break, switch positions) for when sex triggered me, per the suggestions of Staci Haines, a revolutionary somatic therapist who'd greatly influenced Denise's work and had written a sort of *Joy of Sex* for survivors called *Healing Sex*. (Just glancing at its table of contents subheads—"Self-Trust and Compassion" "Do I Deserve Pleasure?" "It's Not Your Fault"—was enough to make me weep.) Denise and I had devised a load of different plans—my God, in our time together we would come up with and try so many different plans—and though this wasn't an example of my having successfully employed one, anytime I had sex without being triggered was a celebration-worthy event. "We'll fuckin' take it," Denise said.

It was our first session after I got back. I confessed to the New Orleans meltdown.

"What did you need when you felt like that?" she asked. Nico had asked me that, too, when it was happening. The answer was that I needed to lie in a dark room and read a cookbook. So I lay in a dark room in New Orleans and read a cookbook off my friend's shelf, a beautiful glossy one called *Cooking My Way Back Home*, and as long as that was the only thing I was doing, I was fine.

Denise smiled because that was random. But whatever worked. Still, it didn't satisfy her curiosities about the million-dollar question, which she proceeded to ask.

"Should you be doing this work? Should you continue doing it?"

I wasn't done with the story yet. I had to report another piece of it yet, plus write everything up. And I felt fine about that.

New Orleans wasn't worse than anything I had undergone in San Francisco when I was not working. I felt weighed down by the Vineses' struggle, and what their struggle said about how many people were having that struggle, but it struck me as appropriate levels of weight.

"How do you feel in your body when you talk about it?" Denise asked.

Well, yeah. I kind of felt like dying. I'd spent a lot of time on the trip in the bathtub, processing, stealing glances at the closed door while I cried, like an alcoholic closeted away with a bottle, hoping Nico wouldn't come in. But I dared anyone to spend that much time in a house full of traumatized strangers and come out feeling much differently. In my totally unbiased opinion, I was doing a pretty good job.

Two days after that session with Denise, I woke up and said, "I feel like a regular person today."

Nico looked over at me.

"I just feel like—" I thought about it, trying to describe how I felt. "A person."

A). I had feelings. B). My feelings were along the lines of "Ooh, it's sunny out," and not anything like "I can't understand why everyone doesn't commit suicide en masse." I didn't feel like a piece of cardboard, which was what I called a "weird" day because I didn't feel real and couldn't connect to anything, and while I generally considered a weird day to be better than a bad day, despite its own unpleasantness, a weird day tended to end in a bad day sooner or later.

Not today. That day, I woke up person-like.

Nico smiled and rolled over onto me. "You will have to get used to it, my love," he said. He planted congratulatory kisses all over my face. "You will start to feel that more and more." Not two hours later, my rib cage was in a vise and I announced that everybody had to stop all movements please because I couldn't breathe, all stimuli throwing me into a panic so nasty that my body wanted to escape from it with a fast dissociation. Which I knew would itself be so nasty that I'd spiral into the false certainty that I would always be this way; I would never connect to the earth again in a meaningful much less joyful way; I would never be functional.

But Nico blanketed me then. He dropped me to the bed and covered me with his weight, and it worked. I could feel him. I could connect to him. I gave into him, and the panic, and moved right through it. Victory!

That night, as I stood in the kitchen, my blood suddenly felt like it was on fire, lit by a tiny insignificant trigger.

Breathe, I told myself. *You're not that deep into the episode yet. It feels like there could be a way out still so breeaaaathe in. And oouuuut, two, three, four. Let's name it. Let's finger it so we're just looking at it out in the open. You are just mad because something didn't go your way. Breathe. OK. Now honor it. Your body feels terrible but for a reason. It's misguided at the moment but it's how you've survived.*

Nope. I stopped there. By trying to honor my systems, I was reminding myself how broken they were, how much they hurt, which was starting to tug me into a space where I didn't believe the blood-fire would end. *Try something else. Remind yourself: This will pass. This* will *pass.* I tried to remember a time when I didn't feel like this and struggled, though it was like, five minutes ago. *OK, forget trying to remember. This will pass. And then you can join the real present. Focus on the present. Try to acknowledge what's really happening around you, in reality.*

Fortunately for me, what was happening in my reality was that Nico was dancing at the kitchen sink while he rinsed lettuce. When I looked over at him, he wiggled his butt harder, in the happy, arrhythmic, uninhibited and unashamed way that European men can, beaming. I sat down at the kitchen table near him. He started talking to me, but I wasn't having it; his first few sentences hit a force field and dropped to the ground. I wanted to swat at them, to bat them away as if they were an insect, but he kept talking, and he said something funny, and his laugh touched me and I laughed.

And I was back.

"The more you do that, the more trust you'll build that you can do it," Denise said.

One morning, when Nico woke up with tears spilling slowly onto his cheeks, elegant little tears falling quietly and one at a time, I was there for *him*. Just a few weeks before, he'd woken up in the middle of the night unhappy, unable to sleep and ultimately getting out of bed because we'd been looking up San Francisco real estate for fun, and no matter that we couldn't afford any of it, he realized that if he took out a thirty-year mortgage at the age of twenty-six, he would if he were like his father be dead before it was paid off. And that night, I couldn't help him. I'd been at capacity with trying to hang on to myself, and had growled at him angrily, "I can't *help* you."

But this morning, I was able. That day was my thirteenth lucid and regular-person day in a row. So I wrapped Nico up in 125 pounds of sheer compassion while he caught his breath, exhaling his sorrow that when he saw his father in a dream last night, he didn't have time to tell him he missed him.

"If I were a gambling woman," Denise said, trying to lessen the shock of it even as we were celebrating my victories, "I'd bet you were going to have another bad day this month."

Just a few days later, I did. Nico said, "It's been a long time I didn't feel you like this." I was dreadfully disappointed and angry to feel it again. I wasn't the only one who was impatient with my progress—now that my employer's insurance company had accepted my workers' comp claim, they were making Denise submit all her notes about our confidential and private sessions if she wanted to get paid, and started to call her regularly to ask if I was better yet, how much better I had to get yet, and when she thought I would be better. Sometimes they contacted me with a similar line of questioning.

But the continuing struggle was just the inevitability of the process, the ebb and flow of it. That was how far I still had to go. In the meantime, mindful of how far I'd come, I set off to finish the story about secondary trauma. Having met Brannan, it was time to go profile Brannan's salvation and inspiration, the founder of Vietnam Veteran Wives, who was such a pioneer on the issue that thirty years after Vietnam and several years into two whole new wars, when Brannan went looking for understanding with all the tools of modern Internet technology at her fingers, what she found was Danna Hughes.

Way up North, and nearly as far west as you can go, in Ferry County, Washington, there's a little town with no stoplights by the name of Republic. Nico and I arrived via the Spokane airport and three hours in a rental car to find an abundance of parks and lakes and campgrounds. No sooner had we got there than people warned us against hiking any unknown path because of all the trip wire and booby traps.

"They do *not* like to be bothered," Danna Hughes told us of the high proportion of Vietnam veterans who lived around there, many of whom holed up in the woods. She used to go out there, after the war, to find them and make sure they filed for their VA benefits. Drove her husband nuts, the way she wandered into the forest to track down guys living on the dirt under cardboard boxes, trying to get them to fill out paperwork.

We met Danna at the grounds of VVW, where she was preparing for a Memorial Day fundraiser the next day. Back in the nineties, Danna served three counties and some 5,000 former soldiers via the center she founded, established nonprofit status for, and got the VA to recognize and reimburse. She'd started it because, like Brannan, she had a PTSD-disabled veteran in her life—only her husband had a violent incident that had landed him in prison. When he got out, he was still a ball of anxiety, and despite the prevalence of other suffering veterans' spouses in this county, which had the fifth-highest percentage of vets of any county in this vet-heavy state, there was no organization for the families. Danna didn't actually know what she was dealing with, because there wasn't a lot of talk about PTSD then. "I didn't know what it was," she told me. "I just lived it."

That experience was enough for her to feel that she knew what people needed. "*She*," Danna said, meaning any wife—nearly all the vets around here were men—"NEEDS therapy." She talked about how spouses of PTSD veterans lost themselves, were wrapped up and overwhelmed by the space the trauma took up, swallowed up by it. Dressed in blue jeans and moccasins and with short, well-styled silver hair, Danna smiled easy but moved pretty slow because she'd thrown her back out again. She used to be in beauty pageants, and it showed, in the subtly flirty but no-nonsense way she addressed everyone. She knew how it felt to have your nervous system turn against you, and that it was harder for veterans to get better if their spouses didn't get treated. Danna's husband was checking into in-patient psych treatments for almost three weeks at a time, she said, only to come back to his untreated wife and "within three seconds" be re-exposed to the same bad emotional environment he'd left. In 2001, he killed himself.

After a 2000 VA budget crunch, the contract for Danna's clinic was terminated. Now VVW had more modest but no less determined facilities: a camouflage-painted mobile home planted among tree-dotted hills. Tomorrow at the fundraiser the community would dedicate a new, second building, a log safe house open twenty-four hours a day so vets who felt themselves becoming episodic had someplace to go—it was better than driving to VVW's parking lot and sleeping in their trucks, as they often did. The closest VA hospital was 130 miles away. VVW offered help with filing for medical care and benefits—"Money has to be first. You can't breathe without it," Danna said—but also offered counseling. To *everyone* in the family.

"They will hang in there until the last dog is dead," she said of military spouses. She wanted to do everything she could to make that easier. She'd once been shot at, when a veteran with severe PTSD came in with his wife and in a strung-out rage, but that wasn't a deal-breaker for Danna, and she didn't think it should necessarily be a deal-breaker for the wife. Like Brannan, Danna was frank and unapologetic about her decision to stay with her husband despite the difficulties. "If you love somebody, you stick with them," she said, and there it was, naive, and beautiful, and impractically pure.

As if to prove that good results could come of it, Danna introduced me to Steve and Charlene Holt, an unbearably sweet couple helping out with the setup around the grounds. She was a local artist with long, feathered gray hair and serious eyes; he was a handsome guy in his sixties with a white beard and cargo pants. He'd got divorced from his first wife after Vietnam, drinking wildly and warring with her, but he had met Charlene in 2001 and with that inspiration checked into in-patient in Seattle several times. He had quit getting drunk, and found Jesus, and every time they passed each other as they worked that day, they touched and kissed. A decade into their marriage, Steve called Charlene "my bride."

"I've never known love like this," she told me, looking like she was going to cry. "He is awesome."

Everybody was chipping in with donated services and labor to get the fundraiser off the ground. Danna's late husband's best friend and war buddy Mike had come in from Montana. There were posters for it in the windows of the few shops along the main street. The nearby Indian reservation, which had 450 veterans of its own, sent military flag-bearers. And on the day of the event, between 200 and 300 people showed up, a big turnout in a county of 7,500 spread among 2,000 square miles. Nico walked around wearing an American-flag armband Danna gave him.

Throughout the afternoon, veterans and local politicians and musicians took the stage. Mike's daughter, who was a few years older than I, drove all the way from somewhere with her drummer boyfriend, who filled out one of the acts at the last minute. One after another, the people who stood up to the microphone thanked Danna. They thanked her for saving their lives, for keeping them from suicide, for keeping them off the streets—or out of the woods.

Their paperwork had been complicated or backlogged or lost or ignored, but Danna had kept advocating for them until they had what they needed to survive. She stood in the back against the trailer in a patriotic-red dress shirt, waving off their sentiments.

In the audience, Nico and I sat behind an elderly guy who, according to the badges on his cap, had served in World War II. When the color guard paraded onto the grounds, he barely had the strength and range of motion to salute. He started to put up his arm; he stalled, wavered and shook, then gave up. He tried again a few moments later, swinging his arm wider and harder, and his hand made it to his forehead. He managed to keep it there by cupping his palm around his big old-man glasses.

Vietnam vets still made up the bulk of Danna's clients, though increasingly she was serving Iraq and Afghanistan returnees. She also told me she assisted more than one veteran of World War II—in which a third of the medical disability discharges were psychiatric. Some of those men still showed up to Danna's office, having never been treated for anything, and cried, and cried, and cried. "So," Nico asked me during the fund-raiser, making sure he was following everything correctly through his ESL filter. "These people fight war but when they come back if they're sick they have to fight to get money, and sometimes they get nothing?"

Back at the hotel that night, I hit my wall. I started crying, lying on the bed, and I knew that I couldn't take in any more for this story. I was full. "I can't do this anymore," I told Nico. It was my birthday weekend again, two years after the birthday I'd cried in a petroleum-soaked Louisiana. Nico stroked my face and said that was fine. And it was. I'd mostly finished my reporting. Other than briefly stopping by Steve and Charlene's house, the only thing we had to do that Sunday was go out for breakfast.

Nico and Mike had exchanged phone numbers. They'd bonded over the senselessness of the work they'd been ordered to do, though they'd obviously been issued very different kinds of orders. Mike had become upset when Nico told him that other units in the gendarmerie had been sent to Afghanistan, and that he'd been ready to go himself. "There was no point," Mike said. No point to his being in Vietnam, no point to Nico's being in Afghanistan, or even Haiti, or anywhere. I saw Mike tell Nico that he was glad he hadn't gone to war, and Mike looked genuinely relieved.

They wanted to spend more time together. Mike's obligations to helping Danna tied him up, so they hadn't been able to go for coffee in the short time they were in town. Even that Sunday morning, he had breakfast commitments, but he invited us along. Nico and I stepped out of the car in the parking lot of a shabby diner—the only kind of diner in Republic. The sun was out, but the late-May air was cool; that far north, the sun never seemed to penetrate the skin. It shined down to just a couple of inches out of reach.

Inside, our long table was packed with weirdos. There was me, and my French military-police boyfriend, and Danna the frisky savior, and her niece, who'd also come in from out of state, where she taught kids at a school for the extremely behaviorally challenged—often resulting from trauma. There was Mike the surly but kind-faced Vietnam vet, and his considerable brown mustache. There was his daughter, who looked much older than I with her chin-length dyed hair and a faded tattoo on her face but had the clearest, brightest crystal eyes. There was her boyfriend, lanky and older-looking than she was and apparently a serious musician.

"Is that your coping mechanism?" Danna asked him in regard to playing drums, as though coping mechanisms were regular, polite breakfast conversation. I didn't know what he'd gone through that made Danna ask him that, but he nodded. Mike's daughter, I quickly understood on the other hand, had been arrested a lot.

"I always tried to be nice about it when the cops came to get her as a kid," Mike said, "since it was my fault that she was screwed up from living with me." When I asked him what had happened to "wife number one," he said, "War stuff." Wife number two as well. He gave cohabitating one more go with gal number three—"How could I help it? She's blond and six foot one"—before giving up. He couldn't keep a woman, not with the killing he'd done, he said, and since "the war *really* starts when you get home," he was committed to staying noncommitted for life. He hadn't been on so much as a date since 2005. Now he ran a one-man security company, escorting American businesspeople to scary corners of Russia and Sudan. "Where it's dangerous, I feel a peace come over me," he said.

As I said: what a bunch of weirdos.

Only that we weren't. It was getting so that everywhere I looked, I saw trauma. From Brannan's coffee table to this breakfast table, I was surrounded by family members who would never be counted or offered treatment. They were the collateral damage that didn't end with veterans, that everyone pretended didn't exist in a case of that clinical and cultural amnesia Judith Lewis Herman talked about. Their soldiers were the one group that did get recognition for their PTSD, and even they, after serving in a war, often got neglected, or judged, or outright fucked over. Their treatment didn't bode well for other traumatized people's. They were owed, and they still didn't get what was coming to them. All rape victims did was get raped.

And what *about* rape victims? Sexual assault and child molestation victims? They were a bigger proportion of the PTSD population, and without as many government resources behind them. Among men, the rate of PTSD for rape survivors was 65 percent, versus 31 percent for in-theater Vietnam veterans. (For women, the rate was 45.9 and 27 percent, respectively.) Looking at rape victims or veterans alone was enough to overwhelm someone, and they weren't the end of the epidemic. There were the children that Danna's niece taught. There were the reports about the severe impairments of children from violent backgrounds; scientific conclusions that unresolved early life trauma could equal emotional-awareness problems, substance abuse, problems regulating emotions, self-harm, inabilities to feel safe, trusting, secure, or worth anything. Brain damage. There was the book about multigenerational post-slavery trauma among African-Americans (exacerbated, according to its thesis, by the fact that no one was ever held accountable). An entire field of academia called postcolonial trauma studies. An estimated thirty percent of children who've suffered sexual abuse develop PTSD. Thirty-five percent who are exposed to violent neighborhoods. As many as 2.9 million American kids are abused and neglected a year, and PTSD drops an abused kid's verbal IQ by 30 percent, with the fear centers of their brains overdeveloped and self-care, self-understanding, and self-reflection centers underdeveloped—their symptoms severe and specific enough that there's a movement to get developmental trauma its own designation in the *DSM*. Ninety percent of "juvenile delinquents" have been exposed to trauma. Thirty percent have PTSD. A large proportion of the national prison population does, too.

I once read a study that found a PTSD rate of 21.6 percent in venomous-snakebite survivors.

"I was born with Hemophilia and those in my generation who have not been wiped out by AIDS or Hepatitis C also have PTSD. Many of the symptoms you describe I and my friends have experienced . . ." read one e-mail I received. I got another from a man whose wife abused him, which so shamed him that he'd stopped leaving his house, subsequently losing his job and becoming homeless. Another from a man who treated his PTSD with an Oxycontin addiction after his neighbor's house caught fire and he stood outside of it listening to him call for help while he burned to death. Another from a college student who was raped several times as a ten-year-old boy and wanted to stop spending his freshman year curled in a ball sobbing on Saturday nights while his friends were out having fun.

I meant it when I wondered: Why didn't the whole world commit suicide en masse?

To put some numbers on the rippling costs of veteran PTSD for the story, I interviewed Charles Marmar, the New York University professor who was on the team of the National Vietnam Veterans Readjustment Study, the most comprehensive study of combat stress ever completed. He was also conducting the new, 10,000-family Iraq and Afghanistan study. The simplest quantifiable story was that the VA was footing $600 million that year for mental health treatment for PTSD vets of Iraq and Afghanistan. Plus $25 million on funding studies. Plus disability checks; if Caleb lived until he was eighty, he alone would cost the VA $1.7 million, not including any of his treatment or prescriptions.

But while those costs of treatment sounded like a lot, Marmar said, it was impossible to spend too much treating PTSD, since the costs of not treating it were so much higher. "Personal tragedy, suicide, depression, alcohol and drug use, terror," he rattled off. "Stress-related health problems—cardiovascular, immunologic. Heart attacks, stroke, and even dementia. Residential rehab programs and motor vehicle accidents because people with PTSD self-medicate and crash cars; the cost of domestic violence; the cost of children and grandchildren of combat vets witnessing domestic violence. The treatment and compensation disability programs have cost billions. And the costs of the untreated are probably in the tens of billions. Or trillions! They're enormous." Police time, court costs, prison time for sick vets who came home to commit soldier-style shoot-'em-ups or plain desperate crimes. Lost wages. Nonprofit assistance, outreach, social services. There were an estimated 100,000 homeless vets on the street on any given night. Veterans made up 1 percent of the United States population, but 20 percent of its suicides.

Regardless, many people acted as if going to therapy were for the wishy-washy and weak. They'd say "He goes to *therapy*" with comically widened or rolling eyes. Despite the money the VA was spending on it, even the VA seemed as if it didn't take trauma seriously sometimes. "I guess we're just used to dealing with people with more severe injuries," a VA nurse had once told

Brannan upon seeing Caleb. I had downloaded the VA-developed PTSD Coach app to my phone, hoping that it would offer useful advice. When I tapped it and selected that I was feeling "Sad/Hopeless" off the menu of symptoms, a picture of a blue butterfly popped up. "Distract yourself," it said. "Word scramble your full name and see how many words you can make out of it!"

My ex-girlfriend who'd been assaulted in that hotel had also been molested as a child. That made her twice as likely to be assaulted as someone who hadn't, and had left her with textbook unresolved-trauma compulsions and self-sabotaging behaviors that she still struggled with. I couldn't help wondering if trauma's multi-generation ripple effects had shaped my own past. One of my father's earliest memories was of standing in a crib while his father drunkenly roughed up my grandmother. And listening to him pound and pound on the door, screaming, when she locked him out. But he said that he'd had no feelings about it. Might it have been harder for my father to dissociate from those bad things he did, if he hadn't been doing it since he was a baby because my grandfather was a wife-beater?

The only thing that separated the people at my breakfast table in Republic from a lot of people was their openness about their trauma, after years of discussing and managing it. To this crowd, it was the most natural and obvious conversation in the world.

Danna presented me with a brooch she'd made. It was a hand-beaded turtle—she had Native American blood, and it was significant to her heritage—that she gave to the veterans' wives she helped.

"I'm not a combat spouse," I said.

"You fight your battles," she said.

When the food came, the discussion effortlessly switched to Mike's daughter's habit of putting peanut butter on her pancakes.

One day, when I'd been sitting on the couch with Brannan, she'd fretted that the picture she was giving me was too bleak. "The whole point of Family of a Vet is trying to give people hope," she said. "Give people the tools to not give up." Concerned about how I was going to frame the story, she said, "I don't want to put out 8,000 words about how hopeless it is."

"OK," I'd said. "So what's your hope?"

"In a perfect world, everyone would know and understand what my family is going through," she said. "That would make people help, and I'd be less stressed, and the veteran would be less stressed." In a perfect world, spouses would be prepared, so they could manage both their expectations and their responses to their recovering partners. They would know that the sound of fireworks on the Fourth of July might make for a bad day. They would know that a plane flying too close to their house during Fleet Week might lead to their loved one's cowering under a table or pinning them to a table by their neck. If people were prepared, they wouldn't spend the run-up to their veteran's return counting on Hollywood-style reunions with ecstatic hugging and kissing and days of passionate making-up-for-lost-time sex, then call Brannan saying they were going to leave their veteran husband because he'd come home and locked himself in a closet for a week. Brannan's coaching sometimes kept families together, and that was rewarding for her to watch.

That night after our dinner, Brannan persuaded Caleb not to leave her. She persuaded him that she still wanted to be married to him. It wasn't the first time she'd talked him into staying, and she doubted it would be the last. But for the time being, they were still together. That was one example of a hopeful story. She posted as many as she could on her blog, so other people could take heart.

"Two nights ago," she wrote in one post, "I was doing my normal nightly running around like crazy to get laundry and school bags and lunches ready for the next day, when the hubby found me in the laundry room. To the sound of the running washing machine, the 'thump, thump, thump' of tennis shoes in the dryer, and the not so romantic smell of the kitty litter box, he held me for a moment and rocked me back and forth . . . and we danced. It lasted maybe 30 seconds . . . a brief moment in the middle of a chaotic day and a difficult week . . . but a brief moment that I've stored in my heart. A light in the darkness."

"We can reach a deeper love," Brannan had insisted to me when I was at her house. She didn't mean just her and Caleb; that "we" included Nico and me. "When you share this sort of thing with a person, and you make it through it, it's a deeper love, really." But I remained unconvinced, by her or Danna, that PTSD spouses could always identify and honor the line between being supportive and being subsumed and sacrificing too much.

After breakfast, Nico and I drove back through the Washington wilderness. We were shocked to find that the rooms in our airport hotel, which was attached to a casino, were beautifully appointed and brand-new. The default channel on the TV showed a repeating video about how the Kalispel tribe that owned it had nearly been genocided out of existence by whites but was now a thriving community with prosperous business ventures. The room had a gourmet single-cup coffee machine and a shower with multiple spray jets. It was the end of another assignment leg, completed without going crazy. There'd been less dissociating and weeping, while still staying connected to Nico, my bring-along bodyguard and emotional barometer. It hadn't been perfect, but I'd done better in Republic than in Alabama. And you know who had hot but loving sex on the Northern Quest Resort and Casino's 350-thread-count sheets?

Me.

"I don't just get to see the bad stuff," Danna had said. "I get to see the good stuff, too." I mulled various frameworks for including both in the story while Nico and I hung out in the departures lounge the next morning. Some-one had left a local newspaper on our seat. It had pictures of all the area sol-diers who'd been killed in Iraq and Afghanistan on the front because it was Memorial Day. There was a restaurant-ad sticker to buy any two sandwiches or salads and get the third one free at the top of the page, and it covered some of the guys' faces. Nico shook his head at America. Were all holidays honor-ing veterans and presidents here, he asked, celebrated with sales?

We were bored and tired. Nico took to his smartphone as I stared into space. I felt exhausted, given our wake-up time, but normalish. That is: gloomy about reality, but not like I didn't exist or didn't want to be alive. I don't know why I noticed that Nico had been sitting too still for too long, but at some point it seemed like something was off. When I looked over, he was reading an e-mail. It was a long, dense wall of text on his screen. His eyebrows were furrowed, and he started scrolling faster, not reading anymore, toward the end.

"*Non*," he said.

"*Non. Non. Non. Non. Non*," and as I asked him what was going on, he was standing up and taking a big gasping breath and looked like he'd been kicked in the stomach. It was a suicide note, from his mother.

15.

When Nico's family members gathered around their kitchen tables to Skype with him at our apartment, they came grave-faced.

In the Spokane airport, I'd thrust Nico my phone, and he'd called his aunt and uncle. They lived near his mother; he told them they had to rush to her house. "I think she would do this with something like medicine," he said to me, shaky and far-away-sounding, angry, but hoping she'd taken pills so there was some chance she could be taken to a hospital before she died.

She had. And she didn't, thank God: Eventually she came out of the coma. After her health stabilized, her doctor committed her to a psych hospital. When we got back to San Francisco, Nico was on the phone all day, for days, to France. Talking to the hospital, to his family. Talking, at last, to his mother. I could hear the way his throat closed up when she came on the line. She said he didn't have to come. She said it in the same way that she'd said in her suicide note that he shouldn't blame himself and his absence at all. He paced and made more phone calls. He was freaking out and worried and furious and terrified.

I cried to Denise in her office. I made this, somehow, about myself. "I feel like Nico and I must be trauma magnets," I wailed.

Denise tried to be gentle with me despite my cross of self-pity. But she let it be known that she was not wild about this analysis. "The way you interpret events is very important," she said. When researchers went back to survey 9/11 survivors about how they felt six weeks later, the results said that "having made sense [of the tragedy] was related to less distress." Some of the leaders of the field of post-traumatic growth (PTG), a phenomenon that the rosy-cheeked liked to bring up in every conversation about PTSD to remind people not just that it could get better, but that it could end up even better than before the trauma, thought that post-traumatic stress disorder was over-diagnosed and sort of overdramatized. The diagnosis was stigmatizing and victimizing. It did not need to be called an illness or a disease. Some studies suggested that a majority of trauma survivors could experience PTG, and, it was said, many maintained an enhanced spirituality and life appreciation and sense of possibility long after the trauma. The whole ordeal was natural and temporary, and should be viewed as an opportunity for big, optimistic life changes.

Denise didn't take her philosophy quite this far. Which was good, because while I intellectually agreed with the PTG movement's message of hope and fighting against stigma, as a crazy person I found it irritating and reductive. I was truly happy that most 9/11 survivors had found increased gratitude just two months later. Elevated levels of hope, and of kindness, leadership, love, spirituality, and teamwork. Excellent for them. But comparatively, I felt like a loser. Denise reminded me sometimes that I'd likely feel better and possibly enhanced later, but there was only so much cheerleading that people in the throes of the worst emotional pain they'd ever experienced could take.

Denise wasn't letting my negative interpretation of this slide, though. "Can we come up with a new interpretation?" she asked. "One you can really adopt in your body, that will work on a cellular level for you, about your future?"

"We got married," I told her.

"You *what*?"

We got married.

Because we had already decided to get married, Nico couldn't leave the country and walk back in with that intent without a fiancé visa, which could take a year to get. If he did leave and come back on his tourist visa, and we got married in the fall as we'd been intending, Citizenship and Immigration Services of the Department of Homeland Security could count entering the country on a tourist visa with that intent as fraud. If we got married immediately, immigration lawyers said, we could apply for an emergency travel permit that would allow him to leave and come back.

While Nico talked on the phone deciding whether to go to France, I was talking on the phone to lawyers.

He decided to go.

And. I. *Hated*. Him.

After the dramatic, drastic, tearing-lives-apart sadness of my divorce, I'd assumed I wouldn't get married again. But here I'd met a partner who was a miracle, and only a fool doubled down on remaining a hard-ass spinster when given a partner who was a miracle, even if the timing sucked. I'd re-given myself over to the radical idea of a life of partnership. Of surrender. To love and to another imperfect human.

But here I was getting married in Alex's kitchen. No words and no ceremony. I'd biked over there in mom jeans—literally, a pair of ill-fitting jeans my mother had given me during the Hurricane Katrina evacuation—and Alex signed the marriage license I'd biked to City Hall to pick up. She'd got ordained on the Internet. Nico met me at her house, and Alex, who'd put on high heels with her yoga pants for the occasion, set her pen down and shook our hands. We went to her neighborhood café and split a celebratory doughnut. The girl who sold it to us seemed to feel bad that that was our wedding party; she gave it to us on a plate with chocolate syrup and a scoop of ice cream to make it fancier, though it was already organic, local, and made with sustainably farmed palm oil that didn't threaten orangutan habitats.

I hated Nico for making me get emergency married on a day that was tinged with the gloom of damaged family and dangerous instability. But really, I hated Nico for leaving me. For deciding to go to France even though his aunt and uncle had told him they would take care of everything and that he shouldn't disrupt his life and his future to help his mother, who clearly, desperately needed some help. In all the stress and distress, we got married and then spent our newlywed days fighting like dogs.

"Who's going to take care of *me*?" I screamed.

I was sick! *I* was fighting and barely overcoming the urge to be dead all the time! I was trying, I swear I was trying, so hard, to support him through this impossible thing to be going through, calling the lawyers, getting the paperwork in order, writing the checks for the government applications, attempting to stay calm. Every time I looked at him, his head hung low with defeat and confusion, I wanted to scoop him up and hold him in a ball against me and rock him and say I was sorry for him and it would be OK. And I did that sometimes. But however hard I tried, I could not stop my true feelings from bursting through my containment systems at other times and screaming at him, "What about *ME*?"

And I had thought I was disgusting before.

The fights we started having the moment we got married were deep and scary. They were foul and foundation-shaking. "I don't *care* about your fucking mother!" I yelled at him during one of them.

Even my friends couldn't take my side. My behavior was inexcusable. Unforgivable. And totally uncontrollable. I knew I owed it to Nico's mother that he was as open and loving and secure as he was—his father, by all accounts, had been a little frightening and a lot cold. But I hated Nico's mother even more than I hated him.

"Who does she remind you of?" Denise asked me, and I wanted to blow up her office.

The day we got married, after we'd eaten our dressed-up doughnut, we'd gone home and got into bed for a nap. Somehow, amid everything else, we both had the emotional wherewithal to have sex. When it was over, though, I started crying.

"I don't want to be that kind of woman," I said.

"What?" my brand-new husband asked.

I didn't want to be the kind of woman who lost it so much that she took a medicine cabinet full of pills and ruined a young man's life. I didn't want to be the kind of woman who lost it to the extent that she couldn't keep an eye on the impact it had on another person, as Denise and I constantly monitored that Nico wasn't becoming a casualty of my illness, wasn't lost as himself, was remaining my partner, not my nurse. I didn't want my illness to cause pain to Nico at all. But of course it did.

I didn't want to be a woman who fell apart. Who couldn't take care of her children instead of making them take care of her. I didn't want to be a woman who was so undone when her husband left her and she went broke that she had to be seriously medicated, like my mother was after The Fall. My father had taken one of her heavy antidepressants from her stash once, "Just to see," and he said that it left him so numb that he wouldn't have cared if someone shot his mother in the face right in front of him. Still, under that dosage, my mother had taken our plates and bowls outside by the armload, walked them to the end of the driveway, and smashed them on the concrete one by one.

I didn't want to be that kind of woman. But I knew that I wasn't then in a position to manage the additional trauma of something happening to Nico. I knew that if he died or was taken away from me, I would be that kind of woman. I would go from passively, feebly wishing I were dead to slitting my own throat.

"Can you have compassion for her instead?" Denise asked about Nico's mother. "You know what it's like to not be able to control your emotions. You know she can't help it. You can be mad at the situation, but could you extend compassion to her, which would be good practice for the compassion you need to extend to yourself?"

The answer was no. I couldn't. I tried. Actually, maybe I didn't try; I don't remember. I feel confident that even if I had tried, I would have failed. On top of her having triggered my worst fears, I had always been a grudge-holder. I'd learned it from birth, and taken to it famously at a young age. I'd reveled in being wrapped up in my own sense of justice—angry and uncomfortable, but pleased by my own superior disappointment. It was a bad habit that was hard to kick, one that grew stronger when I was triggered, as in France, or now. Now, when I became furious at someone else's trespass (as opposed to over a stale baguette), I was often also soothed and excited. Atrocity was the one thing in which I still had complete faith. When a bad thing happened, I received the transgression with my eyes and ears, and then the realization of it sunk down to my core like something I'd swallowed, landing with a satisfying thud in my stomach. *Yes*, it said there. *You were right. Everything is exactly as horrible as you think it is.*

Every conversation Nico and I had, stressed and sad and burning money on immigration lawyers and Department of Homeland Security fees and last-minute airfare, turned into a fight. Screaming, severe, relationship-threatening fights. One day after leaving our new lawyer's office, we started yelling at each other downtown, incapable of heeding our surroundings like the incurably crazed or heavily addicted, hurling loud insults at each other on the street below the bricks of respectable office buildings. My workplace was among them, just a few blocks away, and as we headed in that direction to pick up more paperwork, I panted, intolerably hyperaroused. I fantasized about bloodletting. This time, I was going to do it. This time, I had to really do it.

What was in my office that I could use? There were scissors on my desk. I could take them to the bathroom and wash them—a nerd to the end!—and gouge open my thigh. I could just drive the scissors right into the fatty side there, gash in a good hole, then pull my black pants back on and let the blood and badness seep out as I continued on with my day. It wouldn't be that no-ticeable.

Denise and I had an agreement about this. She'd made me acknowledge multiple times that this was a line I was not to cross, from fantasizing to do-ing. But I thought my heart might explode with fury, and anyway, it was none of her business. The only problem, I realized as I stood at my desk eye-ing my scissors, was that there was no place on my body where Nico's affec-tionate hand or mouth or gaze wouldn't land for long enough for it to heal.

Because the fights always ended. *The* fight wasn't over, but the fights always tired themselves out, giving way to an understanding—if not a reconciliation—of each other's positions, and every day, no matter what else happened that day, we found each other at least once. That day, back outside my office, scissors not having been buried in any part of my anatomy, I felt backed into a corner as I leaned back against the building. Married for only a few days, Nico said, "Do you want we get divorced? I will go to France and stay in fucking France." It sounded pretty good to me. But the relief would be false and unlasting, and I knew it.

"I'm having a bad day," I admitted.

Nico softened immediately. In our world, this was shorthand for "I am not trying to be combative but am moments away from self-harm." He put his arms around me, and though we were both still angry, we held on to the hope that it, like everything else, would pass.

"I just want to live in a cave," I told Denise.

It was becoming my standby solution. Feel better by dealing with no one but myself. Make getting better and staying better easier by closing myself off to anyone else. Take fewer chances and suffer less. Love no one. Control the variables, or at least whittle the source of them down to one.

But I couldn't do that. Technically, I mean.

"The core experiences of psychological trauma are disempowerment and disconnection from others," Judith Lewis Herman says. "Recovery, therefore, is based upon the empowerment of the survivor and the creation of new con-nections. Recovery can take place only within the context of relationships; it cannot occur in isolation."

I couldn't get better by avoiding humans—in a cave, on a gorgeous and eventless beach, in my apartment—because recovery was defined and measured by my ability to interact meaningfully with them.

It was facilitated by them, too. Isolation was anathema to healing. The Lakota Indians knew that. When one of their warriors had a wounded spirit or ailing heart, as they variably called it, the tribe might attend to him for weeks, then throw him a ceremony when he felt better. At the turn of the twentieth century, the Russians, the modern pioneers of military PTSD treatment, figured out this personal-support modality and sent friendly psychiatrists to accompany soldiers throughout their war with Japan. Brannan had lately been watching a miniature, short-term experiment of this methodology unfold in her house, when another veteran and his family came to stay for a while. Katie had seemed calmer and more adjusted since their arrival, and Brannan realized why when she saw that one day, when Katie had a breakdown and cowered under the bed, the visiting veteran's kids didn't ostracize her as her classmates would. They gathered around her, climbing under the bed and hugging her. What Brannan knew, research increasingly confirmed. Perhaps unsurprisingly for a tribal species, support networks were vital components of healing from mental illnesses. In India, schizophrenics, some of the supposed sickest of the brain sick, were not sequestered in group homes but remained with family and often never even informed of their diagnosis. They performed better than schizophrenic Westerners on recovery metrics. And functioning metrics. They were less continuously medicated, less severely symptomatic, and more often had jobs. And spouses.

It wasn't what I wanted anyway, to be alone. When I'd met Nico I'd had that trite but nonetheless true sense that I'd been looking for him for centuries. But that wasn't going to stop me from whining about how hard it was to keep him.

"This is why you don't surrender to people," I told Denise the day she urged me to adopt new interpretations. Nico was at home, pacing our apartment with worry about his mother. "They fuck you over. Or they die." At the end of every relationship, and oftentimes throughout the middle, somebody ended up doubled over in agony. Somehow, I'd used to be fine with this. Now it struck me as definite grounds for cave dwelling.

Denise responded with a shrug. "Yeah," she said. "Everybody dies." And living in a cave was an option, but as much as I brought it up, it wasn't the one I had chosen. I had got *married*. So could we construct a more adaptable interpretation than that I was full of magnets that drew all the trauma of the universe toward me?

"I'm not going to argue with you that Nico's going to die, eventually," Denise said. "But as you know, worrying is not preparation. And he's not dead. So could you think of this as your chance? An imperative to love him big while you're both still alive?"

"That's what I'm doing!" I yelled. Could I love him any bigger? Had anyone ever loved anyone as much as I loved him? No. My love for him was limitless. Unfortunately, so was my capacity for fear of vulnerability and obsession with disaster.

Denise always said I had earned that. She wasn't going to argue with me, either, that Nico and I had a lot of bad shit around us and behind us. She reminded me of my goal, to feel myself in the world. We reaffirmed that I was committed to a fulfilling life. We agreed that I would interpret all that shit as compost for growing it beautifully.

I took a deep breath and smiled while I wiped tears off my face. "That sounds good," I said. "But I still think it would be easier to be alone."

As soon as I said it, though, I changed my mind. "Actually, not really." I knew people who lived like that, not alone exactly, but without intimacy. I neither envied nor admired them. Theirs was certainly not a life I'd ever strove for, or wanted to start striving for now. "I wouldn't say that what they're doing is easy, either."

"Yeah," Denise said. She laughed as she continued, starting to pantomime struggling with something off to the side of her chair. "It's kind of like trying to hold a beach ball underwater."

16.

Alright.

Let's try that again.

On a sunny, San Francisco–crisp afternoon in August, 2012, I stepped out of a taxi on Van Ness Avenue. From the opposite door of the car, my father got out and circled around to join me. There, waiting on the sidewalk, was Nico. He was holding something behind his back. He revealed it to be a bouquet. He stood with Alex, a dozen other friends, and my mother. She and my father didn't break their ten-year nonspeaking streak, but after initial protest agreed to stand on either side of me for a photo. My lawyer had advised it was important for establishing marriage legitimacy in our immigration file.

Before getting emergency married in Alex's kitchen, Nico and I had planned on doing it at San Francisco City Hall, that hundred-year-old, gold-domed Beaux Arts block at the edge of downtown. On almost any afternoon, you could watch couples in wedding clothes and in love, from the city and all over, line up for their licenses. Suits and tuxedos and all manner of dresses—big traditional ones, little cocktail ones, white ones and blue ones and gold ones—wandered around the marble all day, lingering for pictures and for the stately but sweet ambience. As a reporter, I'd watched a lot of gay couples get married there, if that happened to be a year in which they weren't blocked by legislation. After each time the legislation was overturned, couples flocked to the building, love and justice prevailing. The judges performed short ceremonies at various scenic points in the architecture: in the rotunda, on the midway landing of the cascading grand staircase, under an arch. In their black robes, they looked kind and no less sincere for the facts that they didn't know the couples and performed dozens of the ceremonies a week. San Franciscans running errands in the building stopped to watch respectfully. Everyone involved in the weddings at City Hall felt like a constantly evolving and expanding community. It was secular, and full of strangers, but we were all united by our belief in this one thing.

Nico and I couldn't get married by a judge anymore because we were already married. But San Francisco's City Hall is for everyone—you could do pretty much whatever you wanted there, not excluding cartwheels or protesting in the nude. So we stuck with the planned venue, having Alex remarry us under the 300-foot dome. Nico and I hadn't been in touch much when he was in France, and when we had, we'd continued to fight. He'd been gone for three weeks, as planned, taking care of his mom, painting her apartment, doing whatever she needed. They'd talked. She said she'd made a mistake and promised she wouldn't again. They parted on good terms, if tense. When he got back, we stopped questioning our relationship. We concerned ourselves now with finding the best way forward.

I didn't write my vows. We had decided to write our vows, but I failed to prepare much. "I wrote vows for you in February when you asked me to marry you originally in France," I admitted, standing there on the pink marble in an ivory lace gown, "when I had jet lag and you were sleeping and I wasn't." The dress was heavy, unwieldy, with a train—exactly the kind of to-do we wanted. The weight of it tried to compensate for more important elements that were missing, the out-of-town friends and relatives and reception. The night before, Nico's best friend Jimmy, who I'd met with him in the pool in Haiti, had called and put together his best English to say he wished he would be there and asking me to take care of Nico please. He may have been crying. I wished he were there, too; Nico was surrounded entirely by my friends and my family, and it didn't seem right to have a party with only my loved ones. His mother said she didn't feel up to it.

"When you asked me to marry you I was having a lot of very, very bad days in a row and was in the middle of a serious nervous breakdown," I continued. "So most of those vows that I wrote were about having nervous breakdowns." Those nights I'd lain next to him in France, keeping myself from touching him by telling myself how toxic I was, I'd passed some of the hours by writing in my head what vows I *would* say if I were ever in a position to accept his proposal. In them I brought up the way I could feel the certainty and rightness of him even in the depths of my deepest spells. As I composed

and recited the sentences, I'd squeezed hot tears all over my pillow, silent, my face twisted with the pain that I'd never get better enough to say them.

I decided not to use them now. I was making our audience uncomfortable enough with my multiple mentions of nervous breakdowns, and the following sentence: "We don't have to do the sickness-and-health thing, because you were around for plenty of sickness already."

Instead, I said that he was a miracle, and that I would hold him, keep him, and respect him like the miracle that he was, forever.

When it was his turn, Nico said he wouldn't forget what a beautiful creature I was, every day, and that he would let me put my fingers into his glass of milk to dip Oreos even though he hated that. He said his conscience and all his body and spirit were engaged in keeping me satisfied and making me happy for the rest of his life. "I'm not a military yet," he said, then paused. One of the many absurdities of the French language was that *yet*, *still*, and *again* were expressed by the same word. "Anymore," he corrected himself. "But this is my mission now."

At the end of his speech, Nico said that destiny put me in his way in Haiti. I thought about that as we abandoned our guests after the ceremony, driving north out of the city in a rented car. Nico sometimes said that if his father hadn't died, he wouldn't be the man he was now. He wouldn't have been lost and listless and joined the gendarmes; he wouldn't have been sent to Haiti; he wouldn't have met me. I had the same connection between him and the worst event of my life. If I hadn't gone through the exact set of experiences in Haiti exactly when I went through them, I probably wouldn't have got PTSD, not then, and quite possibly not ever. But I also wouldn't have met Nico. Without all our stinky, sticking, death-black compost, we wouldn't have each other at all.

San Francisco seemed whitewashed under a bright sun, passing by our windows as we sat, overdressed and holding hands, on leather seats. We stopped on the Golden Gate Bridge, delighting the tourists with the opportunity to add pictures of strangers in wedding clothes to their catalog of snapshots. Suddenly starved, we drove to a taco shack in Sausalito before continuing north. Up into the hills, up past the pastures, into the eucalyptus and redwoods and sequoias. We celebrated in the stillness at a cabin there, my dress, spilling over a chair, a reminder of what we'd done, but the feeling around us the same as in my hotel room that night in Haiti: relief that we were near. Permanently relieved, now, that we would never be another way.

* * *

Over that honeymoon weekend, we may have had an episode, between us.

Maybe one and a half.

Maybe it had been sex-related, as sex was turning out to be one of the most lingering problem spaces for me, as it was for many like me, every surrender an effort. Maybe not all of it had been about sex. "Maybe this is just what I'm like now," I'd been starting to think. I ran that by Denise in her office a few weeks later.

We'd cut our sessions to once a week, with the agreement that we'd see how it went. Two years after my diagnosis, sometimes I had long strings of days where I felt fine. I also had days where I woke up not-fine. A day where I woke up with Chris in my bones, and let him in and sang to him softly out loud, feeling static start to crawl through my limbs, a light threat to disappear, but opening up across my shoulders and letting it ride, the tingling in my nerves, breathing deep, singing, then crying, then up and out the door and on with the day holding on to the thought that the sadness would pass. And then a day where I strode through our apartment and rolled up my sleeves, not to accomplish anything but because they were too long, regardless feeling nothing but tall, broad power and openness and possibility.

"Maybe that's how it is now, fine sometimes, and not-fine sometimes," I told Denise. Some wonderful honeymoon afternoons, one bumpy honeymoon night. "Maybe my Tootsie Roll center is half darkness, and it's going to surface, but then it will recede, and that will be my life. Maybe it will always be like this."

I realized I would have preferred for her to contradict me—to tell me that eventually, PTSD patients who worked hard enough always emerged like a perfectly buffed and eternally gleaming coin—when she asked, "And how would that be? Could you accept that?"

I would think about that a lot, in the coming years.

"Maybe," I said. "Maybe I can accept being destined for that degree of grief sometimes. I feel pretty good right now. I get more used to the bad days and get better at rolling with them, and, you know, my depth of experience will be better in the end. Like you always say, if you can feel the force of sadness and if you weren't freaking out about it, there could be an exquisiteness to it, like it's valid and amazing as its own emotion." This would not have been one of the riches I'd yet attained. "Obviously I still think it's better not

to get traumatized in the first place," I said, because I still wasted a lot of energy bemoaning both that the world was unfair and evil, and my reactions to that—which were, in my defense and thanks to my disorder, quite drastic. "Mac's problem," Denise showed me she had written in her notes once, "is not that she can't fix it but that it shouldn't be that way."

But I had acquired some personal enhancements over my pre-trauma self. I enumerated them regularly for Denise. My self-awareness was vastly improved. My patience and compassion with myself and others were more developed and advanced. I had an increased presence in the present, and an increased consciousness of whether I was present or not. I was starting to accept Denise's assertions that negative emotions were acceptable and appropriate and could come on regularly. She encouraged me to picture them like a wave. Picture letting myself be taken up in their swell, relaxing into them. After they crested, everything would wash out level again on the shore. I was still bitter, because I probably could have acquired those qualities less painfully, but in general everyone said people with trauma should be optimistic. The vice president of the International Society for Traumatic Stress Studies, whom I interviewed for Brannan's story, felt optimistic about the field, because there are treatments that work, and a lot of people get better, even *better* better. On good days I did feel relieved that I wasn't suffering as I did on bad days, which made good days even better in a way. The flip side to that was that I was always in mind of suffering, even when I wasn't.

But as Denise always said, "Your room gets messy, and you clean it up."

And just days after that calm, collected session, I was a disaster again. Suddenly, I struggled to stay on the right side of nihilism again. Hard. I took nihilistic showers, shifting my weight neurotically, psychotically, from one leg to the other, repeating to myself a combination of a mantra about nature being evil by nature and the International Society for Traumatic Stress Studies VP's quote that the normative response to trauma is healing and that even for the non-normative healing could be attained. I alternated these with Denise's oft-repeated aphorism: Your room gets messy, you clean it up. That was the cycle of physical and emotional life. Your room gets messy, you clean it up. The moments of enjoyment when you weren't cleaning made it worth it. When you weren't cleaning, you were free to relish in love and beauty.

If you got really good, you could relish the cleaning itself.

You couldn't avoid suffering. The trick was accepting it. Not fighting against it. Not trying to escape it. Not wishing it was something else. Integration of trauma was the goal, Herman wrote, not exorcism. Not flying to a faraway cave and establishing residency there; just being with reality as it was. The simplest-sounding trick. And how hard it was to perform it. You could never stop practicing. And just because you pulled it off once didn't mean you'd pull it off every other time.

Demoralized as I was, I was more on the path to accepting it than usual. I wasn't yelling at anybody, or drunk. I wasn't numb, though continuing to inhabit my body was still depressing me half to death. But the more I did it, the better I got at seeing my emotions and feeling and moving them through.

Even in the midst of my nihilism relapse, I brought Denise good news. The day before, I told her (in the second half of our session—obviously I spent at least the first half bawling), I'd been making out with Nico when I knew I had to stop. "Something's wrong," I told him.

I took a minute to breathe, and realized I couldn't feel the connection between my torso and my limbs. I was dissociated. Lost. I stayed with it, and could name the nature of the dissociation in minutes.

"I don't know who I am," I said to Nico.

I reached into my belly for the things I put there. Work was there, but I couldn't get hold of it in any meaningful way. Nico was there. I knew I loved him, but if I didn't know who I was, what was my sexual identity? Did I even like having sex? I knew I did, or had at some point, so tried to conjure a time I'd desired my husband, picturing a moment that resonated. I pressed my belly to his and kissed him, putting my hands on him, and the connection brought my limbs back, plus one little piece of my identity: I was a woman. I was a woman with a body and desire.

It worked.

It was the first time I'd used sex to get *out* of dissociation, rather than sex being an activity that threw me unwillingly and miserably into it.

"You *wanted* him," Denise would say about Nico after we'd been married for more than a year.

I had. He was the centerpiece of my second foundation of healing: choosing the life I wanted to live going forward. And going for it.

As the months passed after our (second) wedding, I shed the concern that I would never be healthy enough to share a life. After our second wedding, my only regret about getting married was that we'd already got married and couldn't get married anymore. I plotted a lot of remarriages for our future. I asked him to marry me again every couple of weeks.

But as my biggest reward, he was also the source of my biggest challenges. I woke up in the middle of the night often to make sure he was still breathing. Often when he left the house I was paralyzed with fear that he'd die and never return. I continued struggling to surrender as fiercely and easily as he did.

"That's my gal," Denise said a few months into my marriage, when, on the table, I for the first time achieved the magic mix I'd been striving for. At the end of that session, I was completely open and connected. But completely together and ready for anything.

Just 2,999 more times of nailing it until I embodied the state I'd set as my goal to exist in. Maybe. Probably at least. I was still a year away from attaining even once a sadness that felt not alarming or awful, but exquisite. From feeling as if suffering and sadness were natural and intriguing, thinking righteously, *Who* said *I shouldn't feel like this sometimes? That anyone shouldn't?*

In the meantime, Nico did everything he could to help.

Two years into my disorder, I extended acceptance and understanding to others, to sources and to the strangers who e-mailed me. But I still cursed my own symptoms when they showed up. It was Nico who tried to foster acceptance for my irritable heart.

"Who are you?" I asked him once as we lay in bed in the afternoon. He'd given me a kiss, and my body had disappeared, and when I looked at him, I didn't know who he was. I *knew* who he was. But I couldn't feel like I knew who he was.

"I'm your husband," he said.

That made me cry for not having recognized him. In addition to feeling lost, I became very sad and scared.

"What's wrong with me?" I asked.

"Nothing," he said, cradling my head into his shoulder.

I heard this, and considered the current evidence. "Doesn't seem like it."

Nico hated it when I condemned my crazy. He had long ago reached the space I needed to be in, the one where I wouldn't judge, the one where I wouldn't hate myself or my emotions, where I felt like they were OK. He didn't miss a beat, creating a soft cloud of compassion around us by revising his answer, which he delivered with a kiss.

"Nothing bad."

EPILOGUE

That night, a year or so into our marriage, Nico was working late at the bistro.

That night, I got home from the office building I rented with other writers downtown and got in the shower. And at the end, I did my exercises.

I tried to invite my body to take up space under the stream of water, starting with the hardest direction: breadth. Width. I breathed expansively across my chest. Or tried; I couldn't do it. My shoulders were tight. I shook out like a loopy child, one doing a chimpanzee impression, naked, arms swinging low but hard around me, back to front by swooping around the sides.

I tried again. *Breathe.* I envisioned myself wide. Out past the confines of the shower stall, and already something softened and gave, wetting my eyes.

Keep going.

Visualize expanding across the street, right down San Jose Avenue to the right, past Mission Street toward San Francisco Bay to the left.

Oh, there it is, the obstruction. After everything else started to soften and relax, the hardest part stood out, a tense pit in my abdomen that today, like perhaps most days, was made up of fear and shame.

Where did that come from? I wondered, scanning automatically for some disgusting behavior in my recent or distant past.

I abandoned that, remembering, for once, that it wasn't my fault that it was there. *Try to be nice to it*, I remembered, too, and tried it. Again.

I put my hands over it, below my belly button and to the right where it seemed to live. I started picking my weight up off of one foot, then the other. Left foot up, right foot up. My shoulders swayed side to side into the movement, so that eventually I was rocking it. Holding it and rocking it like a baby, not like an unwanted one, saying to it, "It's OK."

It's OK, I repeated internally, *you can be here. You deserve to be here.* Rocking, rocking. Left, right. Hands cupping my abdomen. *I don't know why you're here but I'll take care of you*, I said, then stopped, the realization of what I was about to say next, and mean it, knocking me back into the wall.

I understand you're just trying to take care of me, too.

SOURCE NOTES

This book contains a lot of private information that was taken from my personal notes or history and corroborated, whenever possible, with friends, family members, and other relevant sources. The rest of it was fact-checked to hell and back. All printed sources, expert interviews, previously published reporting, studies, consultants, and statistics are identified in these notes. My fact-checker—fellow reporter and fellow fiercely trained fact-checker Sydney Brownstone—and I have indicated instances in which we found the "facts" to be particularly contentious and have in some cases offered extra explanation. I put that word in scare quotes because estimating something even as concrete and measurable as a body count is complicated enough (indeed, see a disagreement about Haiti's earthquake casualties in the notes for Chapter One); estimates are necessarily more nebulous with rates of traumatization in a world or national population. Still, they are valuable in attempting to understand truths about our world, and so are humbly presented for further scrutiny here. I've also presented them and other citations as a resource for anyone, traumatized or otherwise, who might want to learn more. The most frequent source of these citations is the sensitive, revolutionary, invaluable volume that stands as my trauma Bible, Judith Lewis Herman's *Trauma and Recovery*.

One further note about sources: A few names in this book have been changed, and each for very good reasons. I didn't modify any other identifying details about people but omitted plenty in the service of their anonymity.

PART I

7. "If your heart turned away . . .": Moore, p. 120.

CHAPTER ONE

9. 7.0 earthquake: U.S. Geological Survey.
9. 290,000 buildings: Disasters Emergency Committee.
9. There's some controversy over the number of casualties from the Haiti quake. The Haitian government immediately estimated deaths at 230,000; a year later, it estimated 316,000. An outside study said the number was 158,000 (Kolbe et al. 2010). An unpublished U.S. Agency for International Development study (Schwartz et al) estimated 46,000 to 85,000 deaths. In the immediate aftermath of the quake, Edmond Mulet, head of the UN mission in Haiti, estimated 300,000 wounded, and the Disasters Emergency Committee stands by that figure. A June 2013 study estimated the true number of injuries to be far less: 124,577 (Doocy et al). My "at least" 290,000 strikes a middle ground between the estimates. See also Maura O'Connor; Archibold.
9. three and a half million affected: Disasters Emergency Committee.
9. fewer than 10 million lived there: Central Intelligence Agency.
10. more than a million Haitians displaced in camps: U.S. Agency for International Development.
10. 1,300 camps: U.S. Department of State.
10. one of the largest UN forces on the planet: Center for Economic Policy and Research.
10. Nineteen million cubic meters of rubble/from London to Beirut: United Nations Environment Programme.
10. people liked to say that: Desvarieux, for one example.
11. most national government buildings damaged: Disasters Emergency Committee.

CHAPTER TWO

17. Haiti reporting scenes/Haiti feature: McClelland 12.
19. "we have double problems": Amnesty International for additional sourcing on this issue.

19. 50 rapes and sexual assaults a day/more than half of minors: Kolbe and Hutson.

21. no comprehensive protection plan: Amnesty International, p. 3; Kaelin.

21. 55,000 homeless on a golf course: The Petionville Club; Galloway.

26. one of the deadliest earthquakes: International Federation of Red Cross and Red Crescent Societies.

26. more than 10,000 peacekeepers: United Nations 2.

29. power went out frequently: McClelland 8.

29. five camp dwellers died: Logistics Cluster.

30. write about it in an unrelated story: McClelland 22.

31. went on for more than half an hour: McClelland 9.

31. eighteen rape cases tried: Beliard.

32. "Mac, you're done": McClelland 9.

CHAPTER THREE

35. "you will tell everybody in America": McClelland 1, p. 150.

37. standing in oil: Mechanic.

38. "In St. Bernard Parish . . .": McClelland 5.

38. information about sessions with and methodology of Meredith Broome: Broome.

39. largest accidental oil spill in history: Farzaneh.

39. collusion of local police: McClelland 3.

39. moonlighting as BP private security: McClelland 4, 6.

39. Deepwater Horizon gushed for 87 days: Federal On-Scene Coordinators, p. xiv.

39. journalists not always trained in trauma-related self-care: Some organizations provide mental health advice and resources, notably the Dart Center for Journalism and Trauma and the Committee to Protect Journalists.

39. rates of PTSD among journalists: Range from 5.9 percent to 28.6 percent. Conditional risk in general population is 9 percent. Smith and Newman; Breslau et al.

40. side reporting trip to Oklahoma feature: McClelland 11.

40. 3,000 BIA officers patrolling 56 million acres of Indian territory in 35 states: Bulzomi.

40. nearly two-thirds of Indian crime victims described their offenders as white: Perry, p. v.
40. tribes don't have jurisdiction over non-Indians: Unless Congress grants that power. *Oliphant.*
40. American Indians experience twice the national rate of violent crime: Perry.
40. some tribes 20 times the rate: Fletcher.
40. more than one in three American Indian and Alaska Native women raped: Amnesty International USA, p. 2.
41. federal attorneys turned down 65 percent of reservation cases: Between 1997 and 2006: Garcia, p. 7.
42. defining goal of somatics: Strozzi-Heckler 1, p. 9.

CHAPTER FOUR

45. dissociation: Dell and O'Neill.
45. "partial or complete disruption of the normal integration of a person's psychological functioning": Dell and O'Neill, p. xxi.
45. cognitive, psychological, neurological, and affective systems triggered by an event: Boulanger, p. 79.
45. common response and coping mechanism: Brunet 2; Acierno.
45. an escape from feelings: Strozzi-Heckler 1, p. 131.
45. "Terror leading to catastrophic dissociation . . .": Boulanger, p. 74.
46. PTSD symptoms must persist a month in order to qualify: Weathers et al; American Psychiatric Association.
47. definition of trauma criteria: Weathers et al; American Psychiatric Association.
47. helplessness, fear, and horror don't necessarily predict PTSD: Friedman et al.
47. sudden, unexpected death of a loved one/emotional disasters can cause PTSD: National Institute of Mental Health; Lilienfeld and Arkowitz.
47. hearing about or being continuously exposed to other people's trauma: Weathers et al; American Psychiatric Association.
47. PTSD complicated even within psychology: For a few recent disputes, see Lynn O'Connor; Lilienfeld and Arkowitz; and Wylie 2.
47. lack of openness and regular conversation about trauma: The Ochberg Society for Trauma Journalism devoted an issue to this matter in Summer

2014. Again, some organizations provide mental health advice and resources, notably the Dart Center for Journalism and Trauma and the Committee to Protect Journalists.

47. failure to include sexual harassment and sexual violence: CPJ's comments on that, McClelland 21.

47. Herman on Freud: Herman 1, p. 10-20.

48. Freud's breakthrough 1896 paper: Freud.

48. Freud's attribution of hysteria: ". . . the symptoms of hysteria are determined by certain experiences of the patient's which have operated in a traumatic fashion and which are being reproduced in his psychical life in the form of mnemic symbols." Freud.

48. strongest, smartest minds susceptible to hysteria: Freud; Masson 2.

48. strongest, smartest minds *especially* susceptible to hysteria: Breuer and Freud, p. 240.

48. Freud on the frequency of childhood sexual abuse: "It seems to me certain that our children are far more often exposed to sexual assault than the few precautions taken by parents in this connection would lead us to expect." Freud.

48. statistics bear out high rates of rape and molestation a hundred years later: Rates of child sexual abuse are estimated to be between 7 percent and 36 percent for women, between 3 percent and 29 percent for men. Finkelhor. For rape statistics, see below in this chapter's notes.

48. Freud ostracized: Freud scholar Jeffrey Moussaieff Masson cites Freud's personal letters, which he had exclusive access to as former head of the Sigmund Freud Archives, to describe why Freud might abandon his early seduction theory. "I felt as though I were despised and universally shunned," Freud wrote to Wilhelm Fliess after his 1896 presentation. Eventually, Freud reversed his earlier ideas, and concluded that the psychological distress arose from suppressed perversions—impressions in the patient's mind rather than real experience. Seduction theory, and Masson's scholarship of it, remains controversial in the psychoanalytic community. Masson 1, Chapter 4.

48. shell shock: Sharp.

48. shell shock didn't pan out per evidence: Herman 1, p. 20-21; Crocq and Crocq.

48. "moral invalids": Courtesy of French neurologist Andre Leri. Leri, p. 118; Herman 1, p. 20.

48. General George S. Patton gets slappy: Report from Lt. Col. Perrin H. Long cited in letter from General Eisenhower to Patton. Blumenson, p. 330.

48. British Ministry of Defence pardons soldiers: Fenton.

48. Greeks "out of heart" and "unwilling to encounter danger": Herodotus; Bentley.

49. Civil War doctors diagnosed Union troops as suffering from nostalgia: 5,547 between 1861 and 1866. Anderson, p. 258.

49. Da Costa and irritable heart: Hyams, Wignall, and Roswell; Wooley.

49. Herman on how women's liberation and human rights movements have facilitated the discussion of trauma: Herman 1, pp. 2-4.

49. rape trauma syndrome and accident neurosis: Rosen and Frueh, p. 6.

49. similar symptoms for rape and combat veterans: Burgess and Holmstrom; Herman 1, p. 31.

49. number of assignments, intensity, and social and organizational stress risk factors for journalists: Smith and Newman; Newman, Simpson, and Handschuh; Pyevich, Newman, and Daleiden.

49. entering a dissociative state strong predictor of long-term PTSD: Brunet 2; Schore; Brewin, Andrews, and Valentine; DePrince, Chu, and Visvanathan.

50. at least 4 billion trauma survivors in the world: Estimates in the U.S. range from 60 percent to 89.7 percent. The world population is 7.1 billion. Extrapolating from the lowest U.S. estimate, at least 4.26 billion people have experienced trauma—and some experts argue that many other countries present more traumatizing conditions. Norris 1992; Kilpatrick et al. 2013; Acierno.

50. 89.7 percent of Americans exposed to trauma by *DSM-5*'s standard: Kilpatrick et al. 2013.

50. 9 percent develop PTSD: The best estimate of conditional risk for PTSD in Americans. Breslau et al; Brunet 2.

50. violence against women more common cause of PTSD than war: Kessler et al. 1995; Herman 2. A study looking at the epidemiology of PTSD from the National Comorbidity Survey in 1995 found that of a nationally representative sample with PTSD, 49 percent of women reported rape and molestation as their most upsetting traumas, as did 7.2 percent of men. Combat ranked high for 28.8 percent of men. Additional sources: Acierno; Black et al; *NIH Medline Plus*. Additional math: There are nearly 125 million women over the age of 18 in the United States. In 2011, the National In-

timate Partner and Sexual Violence Survey estimated that nearly one in five, or 18.3 percent, of women over 18 in the U.S. had been raped—42.2 percent of which had first occurred before the age of 18. Of those, 45.9 percent are likely to develop PTSD—10.3 million. There are 21.2 million veterans in the United States. Going by the highest estimate of PTSD using the highest rate from any of the recent wars (Vietnam's), 31 percent of those veterans may have had PTSD—6.6 million. See Black et al; Kulka et al. The NISVS also estimated that 4.3 million women had suffered physical violence perpetrated by an intimate partner in the year prior to taking the survey alone. Between 45 and 84 percent of women who have been battered are estimated to develop PTSD, and nearly 33 percent of women in the United States will suffer physical violence at the hands of a partner in their lifetime. Black et al; DeJonghe et al. Note that the alarming numbers discussed here do not even include such crimes against men and boys, who are also far too often victims of sexual and domestic violence. For statistics see Black et al.

50. car accidents a leading cause of PTSD: Coffey et al; Norris 1992.
50. National Urban Search and Rescue left codes on Katrina houses: FEMA; Moye.
51. hazards in the spray paint quadrant: Moye.
51. "two dead cats": West End Animal Hospital; Animal Legal Defense Fund; Perlstein.
51. PTSD one of the most common and debilitating psychological disorders following natural disasters: Galea, Nandi, and Vlahov; Norris et al. 2002.
51. tens of thousands of New Orleans homes destroyed: Plyer.
51. Katrina death toll: Graumman et al.
51. Haiti earthquake causes upswing in mental health calls in New Orleans: McClelland 5.
51. quarter of the post-Katrina population had PTSD: Kessler et al. 2008.
51. if PTSD were measles, public health crisis: Hassig.
52. post-Katrina PTSD hardly better in New Orleans after nearly two years, worse in Gulf Coast overall: Kessler et al. 2008.
52. 6.4 percent of population thinking about suicide, 2.5 percent had a plan: Kessler et al. 2008.
52. suicide rates 56 percent higher, 85 percent higher in 2008 and 2009, respectively: Barrow; Louisiana Department of Health and Hospitals; Moving Forward Gulf Coast Inc.

52. need to establish safety before treatment/recovery: Herman 1, p. 3.

52. one- and two-year PTSD window where majority of population recovers/ doubling of prevalence of PTSD in most affected Katrina area: Spiegel.

52. Twenty percent PTSD in New Yorkers near Ground Zero: Galea et al. 2002.

52. Thirty percent (28.9) of New Yorkers in general recovered six months later: From two or more PTSD symptoms. Out of a representative NYC sample: Bonanno et al.

53. 65.1 percent of New Yorkers showed resilience; 30 percent to 50 percent recovery and 20 percent to 40 percent resilience in most exposed PTSD population: Bonanno et al, table 3.

53. New Yorkers still susceptible to symptoms later (as of 2011): Brackbill et al; Hartocollis; Galea interview.

53. resilience as triumph of human spirit: Bloomberg; Bush 1, 2.

53. more than 40,000 crisis counseling sessions after 9/11: Felton; Lewin.

53. fire department sextupled number of full-time counselors: New York City Fire Department 1, 2; Lachmann.

53. employers and community centers offered therapy: Felton; Lewin.

53. no food and water for some Katrina survivors for up to five days: *Frontline*; Clarice B.; American Civil Liberties Union; U.S. Department of Homeland Security, p. 36.

53. New Orleans eliminated nearly a quarter of in-patient psych beds: Rudowitz, Rowland, and Shartzer.

53. Van der Kolk comparing aftermath of 9/11 and Katrina: Harryman; Babbel.

53. New Yorkers represented as heroes: Anker; Bush 1; Office of the White House Press Secretary.

53. New Orleans crime-rate spike: In 2007. Evans et al, p. 34.

54. levees remain compromised for years: Even after $22 million in repairs, a repaired levee was leaking in 2008. Burdeau; Goodman.

CHAPTER FIVE

62. people sometimes driven to reenactments: Survivors of incest, rape, and combat trauma, specifically, in Herman 1, p. 40.

62. Janet and controversy: Interlandi, for one.

62. reenactments restore agency/"efficacy and power": Janet, p. 603.

62. "flooding": Herman 1, p. 181.

CHAPTER SIX

68. progress in Haiti in early 2011 was a joke: McClelland 13.
68. rebuilding happening only for the rich: McClelland 14.
68. reported rapes increased: McClelland 18.
68. female reporters and sexual harassment/assault: Matloff; Ann Friedman.
68. female oil wrestling night: McClelland 7.
68. The Doctor's demonstrative rape tips: McClelland 13.
69. Bill Clinton, tent-city movie house: McClelland 15.
69. chasing Baby Doc: McClelland 16.
69. orphanages: McClelland 17.
69. spending a Saturday with The Robber Baron: McClelland 19.
71. "whiskey": KERA, at 38:30.
72. freezing: The lateral nucleus of the amygdala takes in sensory input, and sends it to the central nucleus, which then activates instinctual response. The process lights up the autonomic nervous system (brain stem), while connections from the amygdala to other parts of the brain control freezing, immobility, and adrenaline. Van der Kolk 1; Wilensky et al.
72. people not taught to set their own boundaries: Herman 1, p. 69. "Traditional socialization virtually ensures that women will be poorly prepared for danger, surprised by attack, and ill equipped to protect themselves."
73. women who respond with physical aggression to violent physical attack more likely to avoid rape: Ullman. Kleck and Tark say that according to data from the National Crime Victimization Survey, self-protection actions (including forceful and non-forceful actions) "significantly reduce the risk of rape completions" and do not significantly increase risk of serious injury. Self-defense interventions for teenage girls in Nigeria and college women in the United States also showed decreased sexual assaults: Sarnquist et al; Hollander.
73. worse off if your rapist is a sadist: Kilpatrick interview.
73. female victims of intimate-partner assaults twice as likely to sustain injury if they used physical or verbal self-protective behavior: Bachman and Carmody.
73. victims are revictimized: Two of three sexual assault victims; women sexually assaulted in childhood are twice as likely to be sexually assaulted in adulthood. Sarkar and Sarkar; Campbell, Dworkin, and Cabral.
73. mountain lions prey on wasted mule deer: Krumm et al.

73. pleading makes it worse: Kleck and Tark, pp. 6, 18, and 19.

73. victims should look at own behavior only after it's clear that perpetrator is responsible for the crime: Herman 1, p. 199.

73. "thus did I take it upon myself . . .": Full self-defense stories in McClelland 20, 22.

73. full-force self-defense backstory and philosophy: Wagner.

75. women can be triggered into paralysis with words: Marx et al; Marx interview; Bovin; Gallup; Forsyth.

79. angry town hall meetings in New Orleans: McClelland 23.

CHAPTER SEVEN

82. International Criminal Court trial of Congolese politician: McClelland 24.

84. unveiling of Qaddafi's arrest warrant: McClelland 25, 26.

85. "rapid and dramatic return to the appearance of normal functioning . . .": Herman 1, p. 165. See also 173, 183.

85. scenes and details from the reported Congo feature: McClelland 29.

85. Bosco Ntaganda's fighters integrated into Congolese army in 2009: Human Rights Watch 1.

85. Ntaganda's outstanding warrant for arrest: International Criminal Court.

85. 800 civilians killed in Mongbwalu and neighboring villages in 2002; 150 in North Kivu in 2008; recruiting children: Human Rights Watch 2.

85. UN peacekeeper allegedly killed by M23 troops led by Ntaganda: United Nations 1.

87. "Private Eyes": McClelland 30.

87. Scenes and details from the Uganda feature: McClelland 33.

89. 213 survivors of antigay violence in San Francisco in 2010: National Coalition of Anti-Violence Programs.

90. Alec Baldwin movie: *Heaven's Prisoners*!

92. emotional anesthesia: Constriction of affect/numbing of general responsiveness. European Society for Traumatic Stress.

CHAPTER EIGHT

93. "Equally as powerful . . .": Herman 1, p 1.

94. Lara Logan garners jokes: McClelland 21.

94. —dismissals: Schechner; Hallett.

94. —blame: Mary Elizabeth Williams.

95. "abatement of many of my symptoms": See Herman 1, p. 183, about flooding and intensive treatments helping with intrusive symptoms but not constrictive ones, such as numbing and withdrawal. Reconstruction "is a necessary part of the recovery process," she says, "but it is not sufficient."

95. Ohio union rights recently demolished: links to this and other Ohio dispatches in McClelland 28. Scenes and details from the reported feature in McClelland 32.

98. oscillation between extreme and opposite symptoms: Herman 1, p. 162.

98. rape survivors with PTSD 26 times more likely to have serious drug abuse problems: National Crime Victim Center. For a great volume on the relationship between trauma and addiction, check out Gabor Maté's *In the Realm of Hungry Ghosts*.

98. 75 percent to 85 percent of veterans with PTSD turn to booze: Herman 1, p. 44; Kulka et al.

98. probably wasn't the first person in history to experience PTSD-related sex dysfunction: Herman 1 discusses it on p. 48. See also Haines.

99. essay I wrote about my PTSD: McClelland 27.

99. "What's Happening in Haiti Is Not About You": Valbrun.

100. "She makes use of stereotypes about Haiti . . .": Open Letter.

100. UN prostitute: Cave.

100. other side of article war (examples): Filipovic; Friedersdorf; Gay.

101. about 30 percent of Vietnam vets have had PTSD: *NIH Medline Plus*; Kulka et al.

101. Herman on PTSD deniability, sharing burden with victims, discrediting victims and their therapists: Herman 1, pp. 2, 7, 8, 115, 246.

101. people love stories about murderers: For an excellent article on this see Schlosser. Also discussion in Howard, specifically p. 136.

102. 1964 study of battered women, 1998 study of ER doctors, "masochistic personality disorder": Herman 1, p. 117.

102. people think they would have done a better job in traumatizing situations than victims did: Herman 1, p. 115.

102. "denial, repression . . .": Herman 1, p. 2.

102. trauma specialists harassed for taking victims' sides: Herman 1, p. 246. There's a famous case where daughter accused father of rape, then father sued daughter's therapist. Butler.

102. "In spite of a vast literature . . .": Herman 1, p. 8. See also footnote 7 on Herman 1, p. 279.

103. Haitian rape victim's published note: Danticat.

104. "I am bad," etc.: American Psychiatric Association.

104. persistent negative beliefs about the self being characteristic of PTSD: Dyer et al; American Psychiatric Association.

104. "geisha to the NGO republic": Cave.

107. concern between me and other traumatized people mutual: E-mails used with permission.

114. "healing does not always mean that we will feel better": Donald Epstein, p. 99.

PART TWO

115. "You do not have to be good . . .": Oliver, p. 110.

CHAPTER NINE

117. all information about sessions with and methodology of Denise Benson: Benson.

117. "person is a composite functioning . . .": Strozzi-Heckler 1, p. ix.

117. Special Forces to professional athletes: Strozzi-Heckler 1, back-page bio.

118. Levine's Somatic Experiencing: Levine.

118. Van der Kolk's treatment of a car accident victim with EMDR: Van der Kolk 2.

118. visual, tactile, and auditory stimuli while thinking about trauma: Roger Solomon.

118. Van der Kolk used neuroimaging to discover that frontal lobes went off-line during the re-creation of traumatic experiences: Korn; Van der Kolk 5.

118. importance of getting the body to feel safe: Korn. Says Van der Kolk, "I think medications are necessary if therapists have exhausted other techniques of calming people's bodies down."

118. can't treat trauma just by talking about it: Wylie 1. Also: ". . . fundamentally, words can't integrate the disorganized sensations and action patterns that form the core imprint of the trauma," according to Van der Kolk.

118. Van der Kolk training legions of practitioners to treat PTSD through body: His organization, the Trauma Center at Justice Resource Insti-

tute, has trained 20,000 according to the 2011 brochure. Trauma Center at Justice Resource Institute.

121. mind tells an anorexic he's fat: Park.

122. "just because our feet and legs are on the ground . . .": Strozzi-Heckler 1, p. 119.

123. "like I wasn't a victim of my own system": Van der Kolk 3, p. 8. "The core idea [with calming practices] is that I am not a victim of what happens. I can do things to change my own thoughts . . ."

123. "hatred never ceases by hatred": Chodron, p. 7.

124. dissociating is the opposite of processing: Van der Kolk 3, p. 6. "[T]he work with traumatized people consists of helping them to field the present as it is and to tolerate whatever goes on."

124. parts of the brain go off-line during trauma: Decreased activity in the prefrontal cortex. Lower brain regions (limbic system) take over and begin to stop higher functioning. Van der Kolk 1; Goodyear-Brown, p. 34; Szalavitz.

125. PTSD-sufferers' symptoms are similar: Burgess and Holmstrom; Courtois; Foa and Rothbaum, p. 10; Scheeringa.

125. simple vs. complex trauma: Complex PTSD, now known as the dissociative subtype, is a more severe kind of disorder that often arises from chronic trauma. It features the core symptoms of PTSD but includes impairments in affective, self, and relational functioning. The *DSM-5* also features the preschool subtype, which affects children under 6 who are unable to verbalize their traumatic experiences. See sources in previous note.

125. attachment difficulties following trauma: Buczynski and Lanius, p. 6.

125. personality disorders following trauma: People with PTSD often receive personality disorder diagnoses, too. Some researchers question whether the latter is merely latent, existing before the former. They consider the relationship unclear. Bollinger et al; Schore.

125. traumatic event intrudes like reality: Herman 1, p. 37; Van der Kolk 3, p. 4.

126. hyperawareness and hyperarousal: McClelland 35; National Center for PTSD 1.

126. traumatic nightmares can occur during REM, as well as NREM, stages: Lydiard and Hamner.

127. World War I method of trying to electrically shock and emotionally abuse PTSD out of soldiers: Herman, p. 21; Jones and Wessely, p. 33; Linden.

127. VA funding more than a hundred treatment studies: Ballesteros.

127. more than a quarter of a million Iraq and Afghanistan vets with PTSD: Tanielian et al, p. xxi.

127. methods ranged from giving patients hypertension drugs to mitigate intrusive symptoms: U.S. Department of Veterans Affairs 9; Raskind et al.

127. to quantifying the effectiveness of meditation therapy: U.S. Department of Veterans Affairs 3 and 4; Hölzel et al.

128. trials where people took Ecstasy while talking about trauma to promote more positive associations with the events: Mithoefer et al; Oehen et al.

128. acupuncture as treatment: Kim et al.

128. meditation as treatment: U.S. Department of Veterans Affairs 3 and 4; Hölzel et al.

128. some methods played to the same principle as somatic therapy, namely getting the body to feel safe: Emerson; Korn.

128. eating synthetic pot: Rabinak et al.

128. trials where rats were lightly tortured and then injected with a peptide that stopped enzymes in their brains from being able to form memories of it: Shema, Sacktor, and Dudai.

128. centers dedicated to teaching yoga for traumatized people: Emerson.

128. all of the above had got great results: Mithoefer et al; Oehen et al; Kim et al; Hölzel et al; Shema, Sacktor, and Dudai; Rabinak et al; Raskind et al.

128. reports of vast improvement in cognitive-behavioral-therapy and exposure-therapy patients: Schnurr. Not all practitioners agree that these improvements/desensitizations offer a high enough bar for healing. See Interlandi.

128. much of the treatment community endorsed EMDR, including the VA: U.S. Department of Veterans Affairs 10.

128. some experts believe that EMDR is effective primarily in cases of single-trauma events: Schore; Brunet 3.

128. can't cure PTSD with pills alone: National Collaborating Centre for Mental Health; Van der Kolk 3, p. 15; Brunet 1. According to the aforementioned they should be used as second-line intervention.

129. importance of validation to healing: Brewin, Andrews, and Valentine; Fanflik.

129. TBI difficult to treat on top of PTSD: Schore; Sornborger.

129. Denise didn't think I was ready to handle EMDR: See Herman 1, p. 173 for more on need for stability in exploring memories.

130. first stage of treatment: Buczynski and Lanius, p. 15; Herman 1, p. 155; Ogden, Minton, and Pain, p. 206.

132. Freud's speculation that new trauma is often about old trauma: Freud.

132. researchers' screening cops and soldiers to determine who gets PTSD: Marmar et al; Litz.

132. contemporary studies' identifying risk factors of PTSD: Ozer et al; Brewin, Andrews, and Valentine.

132. risk factors for PTSD: Brewin, Andrews, and Valentine; Mayo Clinic staff; National Institute of Mental Health.

133. group therapy inappropriate during intrusive symptoms: Herman 1, p. 218. Inadequate for recovery: Acierno. Herman 1, pp. 231-232, calls *expertly* run group sessions helpful *in coordination with* individual sessions.

140. *Full House* abuse episode: No. 137, "Silence Is Not Golden."

142. people drive out of their way to avoid neighborhoods in New Orleans, have nervous breakdowns: McClelland 2.

146. my female friends, also eighteen, also knowing nothing: See Caplan-Bricker for research/discussion of how commonly young women shrug off sexual assault.

147. at least 25 percent of Americans have experienced trauma by adulthood and by age 45 almost all have: Norris and Slone.

147. getting divorced, other emotional stressors can lead to PTSD: Lilienfeld and Arkowitz.

147. ditto watching too much terrorist-attack footage: Holman, Garfin, and Silver; Silver et al.

147. long assignments risk factor for journalists: Smith and Newman.

148. other studies found that trauma's character, not person's, mattered most: Brewin, Andrews, and Valentine; King, Vogt, and King.

148. previous trauma risk factor, but not guarantee: Buczynski and Lanius, p. 9.

150. resilience factors: National Institute of Mental Health.

150. "anyone can get PTSD at any age": National Institute of Mental Health.

150. "doctors aren't sure why": Mayo Clinic staff.

151. dissociation in Haiti likely predictor of long-lasting PTSD: Brunet 2; Schore; Brewin, Andrews, and Valentine; DePrince, Chu, and Visvanathan.

151. need to stay on the bench until trauma is healed: See Herman 1, p. 60, for discussion of how extant psychological trauma makes it harder to deal with trauma.

151. incidence of PTSD in soldiers goes up with number of tours and amount of combat: Kline et al; Reger et al; Phillips et al; Smith et al. 2008; Clancy et al; Cozza.
151. repeated exposure to trauma can affect difficulty of recovery: Brunet 3; Sornborger; Emerson.
151. PTSD sufferers move between intrusive and constrictive symptoms: Van der Kolk 3, p. 4; Herman 1, pp. 34-35, 162.
151. trauma turns sneaky: See Herman 1, p. 49; Van der Kolk 3, p. 13.
151. might get misdiagnosed: Herman 1, pp. 118, 122.
152. triggered because of nothing at all: Van der Kolk 3, p. 4.
152. "A secure sense of connection . . .": Herman 1, p. 52.
153. playing Whac-A-Mole: Normal: Herman 1, p. 155. "[P]atients and therapists alike frequently become discouraged when issues that have supposedly been put to rest stubbornly reappear."

CHAPTER TEN

155. seventeenth-century French writer: de Guilleragues.
161. "as the psyche matures . . .": Boulanger, p. 74.
167. no longer knew the person I was supposed to be looking for: Normal. Herman 1, p. 96. "Repeated trauma in adult life erodes the structure of the personality already formed."

CHAPTER ELEVEN

170. not unlike some cutters: Studies show that people cut for many reasons. To feel anything at all, to avoid emotional pain, to avoid doing something else unpleasant, for attention. Nock and Prinstein.
172. work part time to take recovery/falling-apart time: Herman 1, p. 176. "The patient should also expect that she will not be able to function at the highest level of her ability, or even at her usual level, during this time."
173. acute stress inducing shaking in animals: Beerda et al.
173. VA provides Cognitive Processing Therapy (CPT) and Prolonged Exposure (PE) therapy to veterans: National Center for PTSD 2.
173. needs of trauma patients are changing and complex: Herman 1, p. 156.
174. EMDR best for simple trauma: Van der Kolk 2; Brunet 3.

176. between 500 and 600 tons of ordnance are collected and detonated a year; since the French demining department was founded, after World War II, 632 French *démineurs* have been killed: Hannauer.
176. The book in which I'd recently been reading about the leftover ordnance was Hochschild.

CHAPTER TWELVE

185. on the merits of grounding: Goleman; Schawbel.
187. fear that everything will fall apart: Herman 1, p. 188 talks about trauma patients' fear that once they start grieving they won't be able to stop. Page 189, she points to resistance to mourning as "probably the most common cause of stagnation in the second stage of recovery."
187. difference between surrender and submission: Denise and Strozzi-Heckler call it "blending." His book, p. 92.
189. 3,000 repetitions: Strozzi-Heckler 2.
189. 10,000 hours: Ericsson et al; Ericsson interview.
190. changing motor patterns is very difficult: Schmidt.
191. the National Institutes of Health funded Van der Kolk's yoga research: Emerson; Van der Kolk et al. 2014.
191. trauma damaging sensory-processing and self-care parts of brain: Van der Kolk 3, p. 14.
191. Australian soldiers' EEGs showed increased hyperarousal/memory problems/attention-processing problems: Davy et al.
191. limbic system overreacting: Van der Kolk 4.
191. limbic system includes the amygdala, the structure responsible for conditioned fear, emotional memory, and motivation: Davis; Wright.
191. chemical hangover: Dysregulation of stress hormones, such as cortisol. Delaney.
192. trauma-sensitive yoga can teach tolerance of feelings and sensations: *Integral Yoga Magazine*.
192. army giving out millions in grants for "alternative" research: Shachtman.
192. evidence that yoga could change your brain: Emerson; Van der Kolk 3, p. 14.
192. Van der Kolk's yoga/training programs: Emerson.
192. Van der Kolk's chronic-abuse yoga study: Van der Kolk et al. 2014.

196. Haitians protest MINUSTAH presence: Associated Press staff; Doucet; McClelland 10.
196. MINUSTAH and cholera: Quigley; Centers for Disease Control and Prevention.
200. AA says don't date during first year of recovery: Moore and Manville.

CHAPTER THIRTEEN

203. "Navy SEALs are screened carefully for vulnerability to PTSD": *Criminal Minds*, season 7, episode 3 ("Dorado Falls"), about 20 minutes in.
205. 18 veterans a day/one every 80 minutes commit suicide: Kemp and Bossarte.
205. Chris's suicide: KVOA; Gliha and Gilger; interviews author conducted with family.
206. undercover warehouse story: McClelland 34.
207. PTSD can alter physiology indefinitely: Schore; Herman 1, p. 238; Bremner et al.
208. scenes and details from the reported secondary-trauma feature: McClelland 35.
208. VA had a program to pay spouses as caretakers: U.S. Department of Veterans Affairs 8.
209. lots of soldiers coming back with degenerative joint disease: Horton; Robbins; Patzkowski et al.
209. government-funded PTSD service-dog study: U.S. Department of Veterans Affairs 1, 2, and 5.
212. secondary trauma/STSD definition: Frančišković et al.
212. documented in spouses of PTSD veterans from Vietnam: Galovski and Lyons; Lyons.
212. and spouses of Israeli veterans with PTSD: Ben Arzi, Dekel, and Solomon.
212. and spouses of Dutch veterans with PTSD: Dirkzwager et al.
212. 30 percent secondary trauma in wives of Croatian war vets: Koić et al.
212. or 39 percent: Frančišković et al.
212. symptoms in offspring of veterans: Dekel and Goldblatt.
212. one study with 45 percent of kids reporting significant PTSD signs, etc.: Beckham et al.
212. veterans' kids' symptoms similar to Holocaust survivors': Rosenheck and Fontana; Barocas and Barocas; Helen Epstein; Rosenheck 1986.
212. meta-analysis of Holocaust survivors' families: Van IJzendoorn.

213. Jewish groups offer home care, counseling, support groups to Holocaust survivors and families: Pevtzow; Jewish Family Service of North Jersey.

213. another recent study of PTSD combat vets' spouses found up to 15.5 percent STSD but mostly generic psychological distress: Renshaw et al.

213. Twenty-year, 10,000-family study about Iraq and Afghanistan vets under way: Collier; McClelland 35.

213. "in a family system, every member of that system is going to be impacted . . .": Robichaux.

213. psychiatrists and social workers can speak to contagion of trauma: Pfifferling and Gilley.

213. people who work with traumatized people have support groups: Herman 1, p. 153; National Child Resource Center for Organizational Improvement.

217. learn to listen to what my body was saying: Strozzi-Heckler 1, p. 8.

219. veterans with PTSD 69 percent more likely to have marriages fail: Koenen et al.

219. 65 percent of active-duty suicides precipitated by broken relationships: U.S. Department of Defense Task Force on the Prevention of Suicide by Members of the Armed Forces, p. 105.

219. active-duty suicides outpacing combat deaths: Timothy Williams.

221. traumatic brain injury exacerbates problems such as memory, sleep, balance, and irritability issues after PTSD: Hoge et al.

CHAPTER FOURTEEN

223. e-mails about trauma: Used with permission.

225. trigger plans for sex: Haines, p. 157.

229. high proportion of Vietnam veterans in Republic: Hughes.

230. fifth-highest percentage of vets of any county in Washington: U.S. Department of Veterans Affairs 7.

230. Washington a vet-heavy state: U.S. Census Bureau 2.

230. no organization dedicated to vet families: Hughes.

230. nearly all vets in Republic men: Hughes.

230. closest VA hospital 130 miles away: "Spokane VA Medical Center."

231. nearby Indian reservation had 450 vets: Sherri Williams.

231. county of 7,500: U.S. Census Bureau 1.

231. county spread among 2,000 square miles: U.S. Census Bureau 1.

232. a third of medical disability discharges were psychiatric in World War II: Marble; Reister, pp. 13, 43.

233. cultural amnesia Herman talked about: Herman 1, pp. 26, 31.

234. fewer government resources for rape victims than for vets: But there *are* some: Acierno; National Association of Crime Victims Compensation Boards.

234. rate of PTSD for rape survivors 65 percent for men, 45 percent for women: Kessler et al. 1995.

234. rate of PTSD for Vietnam combat veterans 31 percent for men, 27 percent for women: Kulka et al.

234. reports of severe impairments of children from violent backgrounds: Delaney-Black et al; Osofsky; Glass; Mitchell.

234. unresolved early life trauma can lead to host of problems: Buczynski and Lanius.

234. including brain damage: Márquez et al.

234. book about multigenerational post-slavery trauma: DeGruy.

234. field called postcolonial trauma studies: Nikro; Baxter.

234. An estimated 30 percent of children who've suffered sexual abuse develop PTSD: National Institute of Justice.

234. 35 percent of children who are exposed to violent neighborhoods develop PTSD: DeMaso.

234. as many as 2.9 million children are abused and neglected a year: Sedlak et al.

234. 30 percent lower verbal IQ in abused kids with PTSD: Saltzman, Weems, and Carrion.

234. fear centers of brains overdeveloped, self-care, etc. underdeveloped: Child Welfare Information Gateway.

234. movement to get developmental trauma in *DSM*: Wylie 2; Interlandi.

234. 90 percent of "juvenile delinquents" traumatized: Dierkhising et al.

234. large proportion of national prison population traumatized: Wolff and Shi.

234. PTSD rate of 21.6 percent in venomous-snakebite survivors: Williams et al. 2011.

235. VA footing $600 million that year: U.S. Department of Veterans Affairs 6.

235. plus $25 million on funding studies: U.S. Government Accountability Office, p. 13.

235. stress-related health problems: Also Van der Kolk 3, p. 4.

235. estimated 100,000 homeless vets on the street any given night: U.S. Interagency Council on Homelessness.

235. veterans 1 percent of U.S. population but 20 percent of suicides: U.S. Department of Veterans Affairs 7; Kemp and Bossarte.

236. sexually molested girls are more than twice as likely to be sexually assaulted as adults: Black et al.

236. history of dissociation makes future dissociation/immoral behavior easier: Strozzi-Heckler 1, p. 131.

237. PTSD and Fleet Week: McClelland 31.

237. Brannan's blog post: Vines.

CHAPTER FIFTEEN

239. 9/11 survivors who make sense of the tragedy feel better: Park, Riley, and Snyder.

240. some leaders of posttraumatic growth think PTSD is overdiagnosed: Joseph; Karekezi.

240. some studies suggest majority of trauma survivors may experience PTG, maintain long-term positive changes: Linley and Joseph.

240. trauma opportunity for big optimistic life changes: Joseph; Feldman and Kravetz.

240. most 9/11 survivors experiencing some PTG two months later: Peterson and Seligman.

244. "The core experiences of psychological trauma . . .": Herman 1, p. 133.

245. Lakota Indians and PTSD: Manson.

245. Russians sent psychiatrists to the front with Japan: Gabriel.

245. schizophrenics in India: Sousa 1 and 2.

CHAPTER SIXTEEN

247. San Francisco City Hall details: National Park Service.

247. gay couples flocking to City Hall to marry: KPCC staff; Renaud, Lin, and Vara-Orta.

251. vice president of International Society for Traumatic Stress Studies sentiments: Brunet 1.

253. the magic mix of being open and connected but together and prepared: More at Strozzi-Heckler 1, p. 83.

SOURCES

Acierno, Ronald. Professor, National Crime Victims Research and Treatment Center, Medical University of South Carolina; researcher, Ralph H. Johnson, VA Medical Center. E-mail interview. April 28, 2014.

American Civil Liberties Union National Prison Project. "Abandoned & Abused: Orleans Parish Prisoners in the Wake of Hurricane Katrina." August 10, 2006.

American Psychiatric Association. "Trauma- and Stressor-Related Disorders." *Diagnostic and Statistical Manual of Mental Disorders: DSM-5*. Washington, DC: American Psychiatric Association, 2013.

Amnesty International. "Aftershocks: Women Speak Out Against Sexual Violence in the Camps." January 2011.

Amnesty International USA. "Maze of Injustice." April 24, 2007.

Anderson, David. "Dying of Nostalgia: Homesickness in the Union Army during the Civil War." *Civil War History* 56, no. 3 (2010): 247-282.

Animal Legal Defense Fund. "Katrina's Animal Victims: Notes from the Field." September 27, 2005. Accessed May 2014 at *aldf.org*.

Anker, Elisabeth. "Villains, Victims and Heroes: Melodrama, Media, and September 11." *Journal of Communication* 55, no. 1 (2005): 22-37.

Archibold, Randal C. "U.S. Reduces Estimates of Homeless in Haiti Quake." *The New York Times*, May 31, 2011.

Associated Press staff. "Peacekeepers break up anti-UN protest in Haiti." Associated Press, October 15, 2010.

B., Clarice. "New Orleans Voices: Clarice B." *Alternet*, October 28, 2005.

Babbel, Susanne. "Post Traumatic Stress Disorder After 9/11 and Katrina." *psychologytoday.com*, September 12, 2011.

Bachman, Ronet and Dianne Cyr Carmody. "Fighting fire with fire: The effects of victim resistance in intimate versus stranger perpetrated assaults against females." *Journal of Family Violence* 9, no. 4 (1994): 317-331.

Ballesteros, Mark. VA spokesman. Phone and e-mail interviews, November 2012.

Barocas, Harvey A. and Carol B. Barocas. "Manifestations of concentration camp effects on the second generation." *American Journal of Psychiatry* 130, no. 7 (1973): 820-821.

Barrow, Bill. "Area's mental health much worse than before Katrina, experts say." *The Times-Picayune*, September 21, 2009.

Baxter, Katherine Isobel. "Memory and photography: Rethinking postcolonial trauma studies." *Journal of Postcolonial Writing* 47, no. 1 (2011): 18-29.

Beckham, Jean C., Loretta E. Braxton, Harold S. Kudler, Michelle E. Feldman, Barbara L. Lytle, and Scott Palmer. "Minnesota Multiphasic Personality Inventory profile of Vietnam combat veterans with posttraumatic stress disorder and their children." *Journal of Clinical Psychology* 53, no. 8 (1997): 847-852.

Beerda, Bonne, Matthis Schilder, Jan van Hoof, Hans de Vries, and Jan Mol. "Behavioral saliva cortisol and heart rate responses to different types of stimuli in dogs." *Applied Animal Behaviour Science* 58, no. 3-4 (1998): 365-381.

Beliard, Mildrede. Former communications officer, Ministry of Women in Haiti. E-mail interview, November 9, 2010.

Ben Arzi, N., R. Dekel, and Z. Solomon. "Secondary traumatization among wives of PTSD and post-concussion casualties: distress, caregiver burden and psychological separation." *Brain Injury* 14, no. 8 (2000): 725-736.

Benson, Denise. Phone interviews, April 16, 2014, and April 23, 2014. E-mail interview, May 15, 2014. Manuscript review, March-April 2014.

Bentley, Steve. "A Short History of PTSD: From Thermopylae to Hue, Soldiers Have Always Had A Disturbing Reaction To War." *The VVA Veteran*, March/April 2005.

Black, M.C., K.C. Basile, M.J. Breiding, S.G. Smith, M.L. Walters, M.T. Merrick, J. Chen, and M.R. Stevens. "The National Intimate Partner and Sexual Violence Survey (NISVS): 2010 Summary Report." Atlanta, GA:

National Center for Injury Prevention and Control, Centers for Disease Control and Prevention, 2011.

Bloomberg, Michael. "Michael Bloomberg at 9/11 memorial dedication: We saw kindness on a 'colossal scale.'" *New York Daily News*, May 16, 2014.

Blumenson, Martin. *The Patton Papers: 1940-1945*. Boston: Da Capo Press, 1974.

Bollinger, Andreas R., David S. Riggs, Dudley D. Blake, and Josef I. Ruzek. "Prevalence of Personality Disorders Among Veterans with Posttraumatic Stress Disorder." *Journal of Traumatic Stress* 13, no. 2 (2000): 255-270.

Bonanno, George A., Sandro Galea, Angela Bucciarelli, and David Vlahov. "Psychological Resilience After Disaster." *Psychological Science* 17, no. 3 (2006): 181-186.

Boulanger, Ghislaine. *Wounded by Reality: Understanding and Treating Adult Onset Trauma*. New Jersey: The Analytic Press, 2007.

Bovin, Michelle. Clinical psychologist, U.S. Department of Veterans Affairs (VA). E-mail interview. May 23, 2014.

Brackbill, Robert M., James L. Hadler, Laura DiGrande, Christine C. Ekenga, Mark R. Farfel, Stephen Friedman, Sharon E. Perlman, Steven D. Stellman, Deborah J. Walker, David Wu, Shengchao Yu, and Lorna E. Thorpe. "Asthma and Posttraumatic Stress Symptoms 5 to 6 Years Following Exposure to the World Trade Center Terrorist Attack." *The Journal of the American Medical Association* 302, no. 5 (2009): 502-16. doi: 10.1001/jama .2009.1121.

Bremner, J. Douglas, Bernet Elzinga, Christian Schmahl, and Eric Vermetten. "Structural and functional plasticity of the human brain in posttraumatic stress disorder." *Progress in Brain Research* 167 (2008): 171-186.

Breslau, Naomi, Ronald C. Kessler, Howard D. Chilcoat, Lonni R. Schultz, Glenn C. Davis, and Patricia Andreski. "Trauma and posttraumatic stress disorder in the community: The 1996 Detroit area survey of trauma." *Archives of General Psychiatry* 55, no. 7 (1998): 626-632.

Breuer, Josef and Sigmund Freud. *Studies on Hysteria*. Translated and edited by James Strachey and Anna Freud. New York: Basic Books, 1957. Accessed May 2014 from the Universal Library Project.

Brewin, Chris, Bernice Andrews, and John D. Valentine. "Meta-Analysis of Risk Factors for Posttraumatic Stress Disorder in Trauma-Exposed Adults." *Journal of Consulting and Clinical Psychology* 68, no. 5 (2000): 748-766.

Broome, Meredith. Phone interview, March 24, 2014. E-mail interviews, April 22, 2014, and May 4, 2014. Manuscript review, March 2014.

Brunet, Alain. Former vice president, International Society for Traumatic Stress Studies.
  1. Phone interview. August 21, 2012.
  2. E-mail interview. April 7, 2014.
  3. E-mail interview. May 23, 2014.

Buczynski, Ruth and Ruth Lanius. "The Neurobiology of Trauma: How the Brain Experiences Unresolved Trauma." National Institute for the Clinical Application of Behavioral Medicine. Webinar, 2012.

Bulzomi, Michael. "Indian Country and the Tribal Law and Order Act of 2010." *FBI Law Enforcement Bulletin*, May 15, 2012.

Burdeau, Cain. "Leaky New Orleans levee alarms experts." Associated Press, May 22, 2008.

Burgess, Ann Wolbert and Lynda Holmstrom. *Rape, Crisis and Recovery.* Bowie: R.J. Brady Company, 1979.

Bush, George W.
  1. "Remarks on Corporate Responsibility in New York City." Speech, New York City, July 9, 2002. *cnn.com.*
  2. "Address to the Republican National Convention." Speech, New York City, September 2, 2004. Accessed June 2014 at *archives .gov.*

Butler, Katy. "Clashing Memories, Mixed Messages." *Los Angeles Times Magazine*, June 26, 1994.

Campbell, Rebecca, Emily Dworkin, and Giannina Cabral. "An ecological model of the impact of sexual assault on women's mental health." *Trauma, Violence & Abuse* 10, no. 3 (2009): 225-246.

Caplan-Bricker, Nora. "'They Grab You . . . But It's Okay': How Girls Learn That Rape Is Normal." *newrepublic.com.* April 14, 2014.

Cave, Damien (damiencave). "Her sex with a beefy UN man means she slept with 1 who many see as the enemy. Human rights reporter, or hint, geisha to NGO Republic?" July 1, 2011, 10:26 A.M. Tweet.

Center for Economic Policy and Research. "MINUSTAH by the Numbers." December 8, 2011.

Centers for Disease Control and Prevention. "Laboratory Test Results of Cholera Outbreak Strain in Haiti Announced." Press release, November 1, 2010.

Central Intelligence Agency. "Haiti." *The World Factbook*. Accessed May 2014 at *cia.gov*.

Child Welfare Information Gateway. "Understanding the Effects of Maltreatment on Brain Development." Washington, DC: U.S. Department of Health and Human Services, 2009. Accessed May 2014 at *childwelfare.gov*.

Chodron, Pema. *The Places That Scare You: A Guide to Fearlessness in Difficult Times*. Boston: Shambhala Publications Inc., 2001.

Clancy, Carolina P., Anna Graybeal, Whitney P. Tompson, Kourtni S. Badgett, Michelle E. Feldman, Patrick S. Calhoun, Alaattin Erkanli, Michael A. Hertzberg, and Jean C. Beckham. "Lifetime trauma exposure in veterans with military-related posttraumatic stress disorder: Association with current symptomatology." *Journal of Clinical Psychiatry* 67, no. 9 (2006): 1346-1353.

Coffey, Scott F., Berglind Gudmondsdottir, J. Gayle Beck, Sarah A. Palyo, and Luana Miller. "Screening for PTSD in motor vehicle accident survivors using the PSS-SR and IES." *Journal of Traumatic Stress* 19, no. 1 (2006): 119-128.

Collier, Desiree. Assistant to Dr. Charles Marmar. E-mail interview. October 2012.

Courtois, Christine. "PTSD in the *DSM-5*." PowerPoint presentation for the International Society for the Study of Trauma and Dissociation annual conference, November 26, 2013.

Cozza, Stephen. "Combat Exposure and PTSD." *PTSD Research Quarterly* 16, no. 1 (2005): 1-8.

Crocq, Marc-Antoine and Louis Crocq. "From shell shock and war neurosis to posttraumatic stress disorder: a history of psychotraumatology." *Dialogues in Clinical Neuroscience* 2, no. 1 (2000): 47-55.

Danticat, Edwidge. "Edwidge Danticat Speaks on Mac McClelland Essay." *essence.com*, July 10, 2011.

Davis, Michael. "The Role of the Amygdala in Fear and Anxiety." *Annual Review of Neuroscience* 15 (1992): 353-375. doi: 10.1146/annurev.ne.15.030192.002033.

Davy, C., A. Dobson, E. Lawrence-Wood, M. Lorimer, K. Moores, A. Lawrence, K. Horsley, A. Crockett, A. McFarlane. *The Middle East Area of Operations (MEAO) Health Study: Prospective Study Summary Report*. University of Adelaide, Centre for Military and Veterans' Health, Adelaide, Australia, 2012.

de Guilleragues, Gabriel. *Les Lettres Portugaises*. Paris: Claude Barbin, 1669.

DeGruy, Joy. Assistant professor of research, Portland State University; member, international faculty, London's Department of Health. Phone interview. May 23, 2014.

DeJonghe, E.S., G. A. Bogat, A. A. Levendosky, and A. von Eye. "Women survivors of intimate partner violence and post-traumatic stress disorder: Prediction and prevention." *Journal of Postgraduate Medicine* 54, no. 4 (2008): 294-299.

Dekel, R. and H. Goldblatt. "Is There Intergenerational Transmission of Trauma? The Case of Combat Veterans' Children." *American Journal of Orthopsychiatry* 78, no. 3 (2008): 281-289.

Delaney, Eileen. "The Relationship between Traumatic Stress, PTSD and Cortisol." San Diego, CA: Naval Center for Combat & Operational Stress Control (NCCOSC). Accessed May 20, 2014, at *med.navy.mil*.

Delaney-Black, Virginia, Chandice Covington, Steven J. Ondersma, Beth Nordstrom-Klee, Thomas Templin, Joel Ager, James Janisse, and Robert J. Sokol. "Violence exposure trauma and IQ and/or reading deficits among urban children." *Archives of Pediatrics and Adolescent Medicine* 156, no. 3 (2002): 280-285.

Dell, Paul F. and John A. O'Neill. *Dissociation and the Dissociative Disorders: DSM-V and Beyond*. New York: Taylor & Francis Group: Routledge, 2009.

DeMaso, David. "Posttraumatic Stress Disorder (PTSD)." Boston Children's Hospital, 2011. Accessed May 20, 2014, at *childrenshospital.org*.

DePrince, Ann, Ann Chu, and Pallavi Visvanathan. "Dissociation and Posttraumatic Stress." *PTSD Research Quarterly* 17, no. 1 (2006): 1-8.

Desvarieux, Jessica. "Haiti's Latest Problem: Clearing Away the Rubble." *time.com*, June 6, 2010.

Dierkhising, Carly B., Susan J. Ko, Briana Woods-Jaeger, Ernestine C. Briggs, Robert Lee, and Robert S. Pynoos. "Trauma histories among justice-involved youth: findings from the National Child Traumatic Stress Network." *European Journal of Psychotraumatology* 4, 2003. doi: 10.3402/ejpt.v4i0.20274.

Dirkzwager, Anja J. E., Inge Bramsen, Herman Adèr, and Henk M. van der Ploeg. "Secondary traumatization in partners and parents of Dutch peacekeeping soldiers." *Journal of Family Psychology* 19, no. 2 (2005): 217-226. doi: 10.1037/0893-3200.19.2.217.

Disasters Emergency Committee. "Haiti Earthquake Facts and Figures." Accessed May 2014, at *dec.org.uk*.

Doocy, Shannon, Gabrielle Jacquet, Megan Cherewick, and Thomas D. Kirsch. "The injury burden of the 2010 Haiti earthquake: a stratified cluster survey." *Injury* 44, no. 6 (2013): 842-847. doi: 10.1016/j.injury.2013.01.035.

Doucet, Isabeau. "Why desperate Haitians want to kick out UN troops." *theguardian.com*, November 18, 2010.

Dyer, Kevin, Martin J. Dorahy, Geraldine Hamilton, Mary Corry, Maria Shannon, Anne MacSherry, Geordie McRobert, Rhonda Elder, and Bridie McElhill. "Anger, aggression, and self-harm in PTSD and complex PTSD." *Journal of Clinical Psychology* 65, no. 10 (2009): 1099-1114. doi: 10.1002/jclp.20619.

Epstein, Donald. *Healing Myths, Healing Magic: Breaking the Spell of Old Illusions; Reclaiming Our Power to Heal*. San Rafael: Amber-Allen Publishing Inc., 2000.

Epstein, Helen. *Children of the Holocaust: Conversation with Sons and Daughters of Survivors*. New York: Putnam, 1979.

Ericsson, K. Anders. Cognitive faculty, Florida State University Department of Psychology. E-mail Interview. June 9, 2014.

Ericsson, K. Anders, Ralf T. Krampe, and Clemens Tesch-Romer. "The Role of Deliberate Practice in the Acquisition of Expert Performance." *Psychological Review* 100, no. 3 (1993): 363-406.

European Society for Traumatic Stress (ESTSS). "DSM IV PTSD Diagnostic Features." Accessed May 20, 2014, at *estss.org*.

Evans, Benjamin F., Emily Zimmerman, Steven H. Woolf, and Amber D. Haley. "Social Determinants of Health and Crime in Post-Katrina New Orleans Parish." Richmond, VA: Virginia Commonwealth University Center on Human Needs, 2012. Accessed May 20, 2014, at *societyhealth.vcu.edu*.

Fanflik, Patricia. "Victim Responses to Sexual Assault: Counterintuitive or Simply Adaptive?" Alexandria, VA: National District Attorneys Association, August 2007.

Farzaneh, Kayvan. "The Biggest Oil Spills in History." *foreignpolicy.com*, April 30, 2010.

Fenton, Ben. "Pardoned: the 306 soldiers shot at dawn for 'cowardice.'" *Telegraph.co.uk*, August 16, 2006.

Federal Emergency Management Agency (FEMA). *National Urban Search and Rescue (US&R) Response System Field Operations Guide*. Washington, DC, 2003. Accessed May 2014 at *fema.gov*.

Federal On-Scene Coordinators. *On Scene Coordinator Report: Deepwater Horizon Oil Spill*. Submitted to the National Response Team, 2011. Accessed May 2014 at *uscg.mil*.

Feldman, David B. and Lee Daniel Kravetz. *Supersurvivors: The Surprising Link Between Suffering and Success*. New York: HarperWave, 2014.

Felton, Chip. "Project liberty: a public health response to New Yorkers' mental health needs arising from the World Trade Center terrorist attacks." *Journal of Urban Health* 79, no. 3 (2002): 429-433.

Filipovic, Jill. "But Sometimes It Is About You." *Feministe*, July 5, 2011.

Finkelhor, David. "The international epidemiology of child sexual abuse." *Child Abuse and Neglect* 18, no. 5 (1994): 409-417.

Fletcher, Matthew L. M. "Tribal Law and Order Act Details." *Turtle Talk*, Indigenous Law and Policy Center at Michigan State University College of Law blog, July 2010.

Foa, Edna and Barbara Olasov Rothbaum. *Treating the Trauma of Rape: Cognitive Behavioral Therapy for PTSD*. New York: Guilford Press, 1998.

Forsyth, John. Director, Anxiety Disorders Research Program, University at Albany-State University of New York. E-mail interview. May 23, 2014.

Frančišković, Tanja, Aleksandra Stevanović, Ilijana Jelušić, Branka Roganović, Miro Klarić, and Jasna Grković. "Secondary Traumatization of Wives of War Veterans with Posttraumatic Stress Disorder." *Croatian Medical Journal* 48, no. 2 (2007): 177-184.

Freud, Sigmund. "The Aetiology of Hysteria," in *The Assault on Truth: Freud's Suppression of Seduction Theory,* by Jeffrey Moussaieff Masson. Belmont: Untreed Reads, 2012. Kindle edition.

Friedersdorf, Conor. "How to Talk About Haiti's Rape Epidemic." *theatlantic .com*, July 3, 2011.

Friedman, Ann. "I Believe Dylan Farrow: But Whom You Believe Depends on Which Story You Recognize." *nymag.com*, February 5, 2014.

Friedman, Matthew J., Patricia A. Resick, Richard A. Bryant, and Chris R. Brewin. "Considering PTSD for *DSM-5*." *Depression and Anxiety* 28, no. 9 (2011): 750-769.

Frontline. "14 Days: A Timeline." *pbs.org*, November 22, 2005.

Galea, Sandro. Chair of epidemiology, Mailman School of Public Health, Columbia University. E-mail interview. May 12, 2014.

Galea, Sandro, Arijit Nandi, and David Vlahov. "The Epidemiology of Post-

Traumatic Stress Disorder after Disasters." *Epidemiologic Reviews* 27, no. 1 (2005): 78-91. doi: 10.1093/epirev/mxi003.

Galea, Sandro, Jennifer Ahern, Heidi Resnick, Dean Kilpatrick, Michael Bucuvalas, Joel Gold, and David Vlahov. "Psychological Sequelae of the September 11 Terrorist Attacks in New York City." *The New England Journal of Medicine* 346, no. 13 (2002): 982-987. doi: 10.1056/NEJMsa013404.

Gabriel, Richard A. *No More Heroes: Madness and Psychiatry in War.* New York: Macmillan, 1987.

Galliano, Grace, Linda M. Noble, Carol Puehl, and Linda A. Travis. "Victim Reactions During Rape/Sexual Assault: A Preliminary Study of the Immobility Response and Its Correlates." *Journal of Interpersonal Violence* 8, no. 1 (1993): 109-114. doi: 10.1177/088626093008001008.

Galloway, Steven. "Sean Penn's yearlong project turns Haiti golf course into camp for 55,000." *suntimes.com*, January 8, 2011.

Gallup, Gordon G. Associate editor, *Evolutionary Psychology*; professor of psychology, University at Albany-State University of New York. E-mail interview, May 23, 2014.

Galovski, Tara and Judith Lyons. "Psychological sequelae of combat violence: A review of the impact of PTSD on the veteran's family and possible interventions." *Aggression and Violent Behavior* 9, no. 5 (2004): 477-501.

Garcia, Joe. "The Timeless Promise of America: Renewed Hope in Indian Country." National Congress of American Indians, 8th Annual State of Indian Nations Address, February 10, 2009. Accessed May 2014 at *buder .wustl.edu*.

Gay, Roxane. "Still With the Scarlet Letters." *The Rumpus*, July 5, 2011.

Glass, Ira. "474: Back to School." *This American Life.* Podcast audio, September 14, 2012. Accessed May 2014 at *thisamericanlife.org*.

Gliha, Lori Jane and Lauren Gilger. "Christopher Palmer." *abc15.com*, April 16, 2013.

Goleman, Daniel. "On stress." *danielgoleman.info*, May 20, 2011.

Goodman, Amy. "Three Years After Katrina, New Orleans Levee System Still Vulnerable." *Democracy Now*, September 1, 2008.

Goodyear-Brown, Paris. *Handbook of Child Sexual Abuse: Identification, Assessment, and Treatment.* Hoboken: Wiley, 2011. doi: 10.1002/9781118094822.

Graumman, Axel, Tamara Houston, Jay Lawrimore, David Levinson, Neal Lott, Sam McCown, Scott Stephens, and David Wuertz. *Hurricane Katrina:*

A Climatological Perspective. Asheville: NOAA's National Climatic Data Center, 2005. Accessed May 2014 at *ncdc.noaa.gov.*

Haines, Staci. *Healing Sex: A Mind-Body Approach to Healing Sexual Trauma.* San Francisco: Cleis Press Inc., 2007.

Hallett, Stephanie. "To the FBI, Lara Logan Wasn't Raped." *msmagazine .com,* May 1, 2011.

Hannauer, Edouard. Head engineer, Remediation Pyrotechnics; head *démineur,* French Ministry of the Interior. E-mail interview. May 8, 2014.

Harryman, William. "The Body Keeps the Score (part 1)." *Beyond Meds: Alternatives to Psychiatry* blog, December 16, 2013. Accessed May 2014 at *beyondmeds.com.*

Hartocollis, Anemona. "10 Years and a Diagnosis Later, 9/11 Demons Haunt Thousands." *The New York Times,* August 9, 2011.

Hassig, Susan. Professor of clinical epidemiology at the Tulane University School of Public Health. E-mail interview. April 28, 2014.

Herman, Judith Lewis.
    1. *Trauma and Recovery.* New York: Basic Books, 1997.
    2. E-mail interview. April 25, 2014.

Herodotus. *The History.* Translated by George Rawlinson. London: John Murray, 1859. Accessed May 2014 at *classics.mit.edu.*

Hochschild, Adam. *To End All Wars: A Story of Loyalty and Rebellion, 1914-1918.* New York: Houghton Mifflin Harcourt, 2011.

Hoge, Charles W., Dennis McGurk, Jeffrey L. Thomas, Anthony L. Cox, Charles C. Engel, and Carl A. Castro. "Mild Traumatic Brain Injury in U.S. Soldiers Returning from Iraq." *New England Journal of Medicine* 358, no. 5 (2008): 453-463. doi: 10.1056/NEJMoa072972.

Hollander, Jocelyn A. "Does Self-Defense Training Prevent Sexual Violence Against Women?" *Violence Against Women* 20, no. 3 (2014): 252-269. doi: 10.1177/1077801214526046.

Holman, E. Alison, Dana Rose Garfin, and Roxane Cohen Silver. "Media's role in broadcasting acute stress following the Boston Marathon bombings." *Proceedings of the National Academy of Sciences of the United States of America* 111 (2013): 93-98. doi: 10 1073/pnas1316265110.

Hölzel, Britta James Carmody, Mark Vangel, Christina Congleton, Sita M. Yerramsetti, Tim Gard, and Sara W. Lazar. "Mindfulness practice leads to increases in regional brain gray matter density." *Psychiatry Research*

Neuroimaging 181, no. 1 (2010): 36-43. doi: 10.1016/j.pscychresns. 2010.08.006.

Horton, Alex. "Younger vets develop arthritis too." *VAntage Point,* Department of Veterans Affairs blog, September 28, 2011. Accessed May 2014 at *blogs.va.gov.*

Howard, Rachel. *The Lost Night.* New York: Dutton, 2005.

Hughes, Danna. Founder, Vietnam Veteran Wives. Phone interview. May 23, 2014.

Human Rights Watch.
> 1. "Bosco Ntaganda." Accessed May 2014 at *hrw.org.*
> 2. "DR Congo: Arrest Bosco Ntaganda for ICC Trial." April 13, 2012. Accessed May 2014 at *hrw.org.*

Hyams, Kenneth C., F. Stephen Wignall, and Robert Roswell. "War Syndromes and Their Evaluation: From the U.S. Civil War to the Persian Gulf War." *Annals of Internal Medicine* 125, no. 5 (1996): 398-405. doi:10.7326/0003-4819-125-5-199609010-00007.

Integral Yoga Magazine. "Yoga and Post-Traumatic Stress Disorder: An Interview with Bessel Van der Kolk, MD." 2009. Accessed May 2014, at *traumacenter.org.*

Interlandi, Jeneen. "A Revolutionary Approach to Treating PTSD." *The New York Times Magazine.* May 25, 2014.

International Criminal Court. "The Prosecutor v. Bosco Ntaganda." August 22, 2006. Accessed May 2014 at *icc-cpi.int.*

International Federation of Red Cross and Red Crescent Societies. "World Disasters Report 2010: Focus on Urban Risk." Accessed May 2014 at *ifrc.org.*

Janet, Pierre. *Psychological Healing: A Historical and Clinical Study.* Translated by Eden and Cedar Paul. London: G. Allen and Unwin, 1925.

Jewish Family Service of North Jersey. "Support Services for Holocaust Survivors." Accessed May 2014 at *jfsnorthjersey.org.*

Jones, Edgar and Simon Wessely. *Shell Shock to PTSD: Military Psychiatry from 1900 to the Gulf War.* New York: Psychology Press, 2005.

Joseph, Stephen. *What Doesn't Kill Us: The New Psychology of Posttraumatic Growth.* New York: Basic Books, 2011.

Kaelin, Walter. "Human Rights of Internally Displaced Persons in Haiti: Memorandum based on a Working Visit to Port- au-Prince (12-16 October 2010)." United Nations. Accessed May 2014 at *ijdh.org.*

Karekezi, Alice. "How PTSD Took Over America." *Salon*, November 15, 2011.

Kemp, Janet and Robert Bossarte. "Suicide Data Report, 2012." Department of Veterans Affairs. December 2012. Accessed May 2014 at *va.gov*.

KERA public media, North Texas. "Aftershocks in Haiti." *Think*, January 25, 2011.

Kessler, Ronald C., Amanda Sonnega, Evelyn Bromet, Michael Hughes, and Christopher B. Nelson. "Posttraumatic Stress Disorder in the National Comorbidity Survey." *Archives of General Psychiatry* 52, no. 12 (1995): 1048-1060. doi: 10.1001/archpsyc.1995.03950240066012.

Kessler, Ronald C., Sandro Galea, Michael J. Gruber, Nancy A. Sampson, Robert J. Ursano, and Simon Wessely. "Trends in mental illness and suicidality after Hurricane Katrina." *Molecular Psychiatry* 13, no. 4. (2008): 374-384. doi: 10.1038/sj.mp.4002119.

Kilpatrick, Dean. Director, National Crime Victims Research and Treatment Center; professor of psychiatry, Medical University of South Carolina. Phone interview. April 30, 2014.

Kilpatrick, Dean G., Heidi S. Resnick, Melissa E. Milanak, Mark W. Miller, Katherine M. Keyes, and Matthew J. Friedman. "National Estimates of Exposure to Traumatic Events and Prevalence Using DSM-IV and DSM-5 Criteria." *Journal of Traumatic Stress* 26, no. 5 (2013): 537-547. doi: 10.1002/jts.21848.

Kim, Young-Dae, In Heo, Byung-Cheul Shin, Cindy Crawford, Hyung-Won Kang, and Jung-Hwa Lim. "Acupuncture for Posttraumatic Stress Disorder: A Systematic Review of Randomized Controlled Trials and Prospective Clinical Trials." *Evidence-Based Complementary and Alternative Medicine* Vol. 2013 (2013). doi: 10.1155/2013/615857.

King, Daniel W., Dawn S. Vogt, and Lynda A. King. "Chapter 3: Risk and Resilience Factors in the Etiology of Posttraumatic Stress Disorder." *Early Intervention for Trauma and Traumatic Loss*, edited by Brett T. Litz. New York: Guildford Press, 2004.

Kleck, Gary and Jongyeon Tark. "Draft Final Technical Report: Victim Self Protection on Rape Completion and Injury." Tallahassee: U.S. Department of Justice, 2005.

Kline, Anna, Maria Falca-Dodson, Bradley Sussner, Donald Ciccone, Helena Chandler, Lanora Callahan, and Miklos Losonczy. "Effects of Repeated Deployment to Iraq and Afghanistan on New Jersey Army National Guard

Troops: Implications for Military Readiness." *American Journal of Public Health* 100, no. 2 (2010): 276-283. doi: 10.2105/AJPH.2009.162925.

Kluft, Richard P., Sandra Bloom, and John D. Kinzie. "Treating the Traumatized Patient and Victims of Violence." *Psychiatric Aspects of Violence: Issues in Prevention and Treatment,* edited by Carl C. Bell. *New Directions for Mental Health Services* 86 (2000): 79-102. doi: 10.1002/yd.23320008610.

Koenen, Karestan, Steven Stellman, John F. Sommer Jr., and Jeanne Mager Stellman. "Persisting Posttraumatic Stress Disorder Symptoms and their Relationship to Functioning in Vietnam Veterans: A 14-Year Follow-Up." *Journal of Traumatic Stress* 21, no. 1 (2008): 49-57. doi: 10.1002/jts.20304.

Koić, Elvira, Tanja Francišković, Lana Mužinić-Masle, Veljko Đorđević, Snježana Vondraček, and Jasmina Prpić. "Chronic Pain and Secondary Traumatization in Wives of Croatian War Veterans Treated for Post Traumatic Stress Disorder." *Acta Clinica Croatica* 41, no. 4 (2002): 295-306.

Kolbe, Athena R. and Royce A. Hutson. "Human rights abuse and other criminal violations in Port-au-Prince Haiti: a random survey of households." *The Lancet* 368, no. 9538 (2006): 864-873. doi: 10.1016/S0140-6736(06) 69211-8.

Kolbe, Athena R., Royce A. Hutson, Harry Shannon, Eileen Trzcinski, Bart Miles, Naomi Levitz, Marie Puccio, Leah James, Jean Roger Noel, and Robert Muggah. "Mortality crime and access to basic needs before and after the Haiti earthquake: a random survey of Port-au-Prince households." *Medicine, Conflict and Survival* 26, no. 4 (2010): 281-297. doi: 10.1080/13623699.2010.535279.

Korn, Martin L. "Trauma and PTSD: Aftermaths of the WTC Disaster—An Interview With Bessel A. Van der Kolk, MD." *Medscape General Medicine* 3, no. 4 (2001). Accessed May 2014 at *medscape.com.*

KPCC (Southern California Public Radio) staff. "Prop 8 timeline: A look back at same-sex marriage legislation in California." March 25, 2013.

Krumm, Caroline E., Mary M. Conner, N. Thompson Hobbs, Don O. Hunter, and Michael W. Miller. "Mountain lions prey selectively on prion-infected mule deer." *Biology Letters* 6, no. 2 (2010): 209-211. doi: 10.1098 /rsbl.2009.0742.

Kulka, Richard A., William E. Schlenger, John A. Fairbank, Richard L. Hough, Kathleen Jordan, Charles R. Marmar, and Daniel S. Weiss. *Trauma and the Vietnam War Generation: Report of findings from the National Vietnam Veterans Readjustment Study.* New York: Brunner/Mazel, 1990.

KVOA (News 4 Tucson). "Distressed vet was suicide victim." *kvoa.com*, July 28, 2011.

Lachmann, Suzanne. "Matching Therapy to the Culture of the FDNY After 9/11." *psychologytoday.com*, June 20, 2013.

Leri, Andre. *Shell Shock: Commotional and Emotional Aspects*. London: Military Medical Manuals, 1919.

Levine, Peter. *Waking the Tiger: Healing Trauma*. Berkeley: North Atlantic Books, 1997.

Lewin, Veronica. Spokesperson, New York City Department of Mental Health and Hygiene. Phone interview. May 23, 2014.

Lilienfeld, Scott O. and Hal Arkowitz. "Does Post-Traumatic Stress Disorder Require Trauma?" *Scientific American Mind* 23, no. 2 (2012). Accessed May 2014 at *scientificamerican.com*.

Linden, Stefanie C., Edgar Jones, and Andrew J. Lees. "Shell shock at Queen Square: Lewis Yealland 100 years on." *Brain* 136, no. 6 (2013): 1976-1988. doi: 10.1093/brain/aws331.

Linley, P. Alex and Stephen Joseph. "Positive Change Following Trauma and Adversity: A Review." *Journal of Traumatic Stress* 17, no. 1 (2004) 11-21.

Litz, Brett T. "PTSD in Service Members and New Veterans of the Iraq and Afghanistan Wars." *PTSD Research Quarterly* 20, no. 1 (2009): 1-8.

Logistics Cluster. "Haiti Situation Update No 1: Rainstorm in Port-Au-Prince on 24 September 2010, 15:00-15:30H." September 25, 2010. Accessed June 2014 at *logcluster.org*.

Louisiana Department of Health and Hospitals. "Mortality in the Greater New Orleans Area Louisiana—Post Katrina—5/29/2007." November 5, 2007. Accessed May 2014 at *new.dhh.louisiana.gov*.

Lydiard, R. Bruce and Mark H. Hamner. "Clinical Importance of Sleep Disturbance as a Treatment Target in PTSD." *Focus* VII, no. 2 (2009): 176-183.

Lyons, Margaret. "Living with post-traumatic stress disorder: the wives'/female partners' perspective." *Issues and Innovations in Nursing Practice* 34, no. 1 (2001): 69-77.

Manson, Spero. Director, Centers for American Indian and Alaska Native Health, University of Colorado-Denver. Phone interview. April 29, 2014.

Marble, Sanders. Senior historian, Office of Medical History, Office of the Chief of Staff, United States Army Medical Command. E-mail interview, November 13, 2012.

Marmar, Charles R., Shannon E. McCaslin, Thomas J. Metzler, Suzanne Best, Daniel S. Weiss, Jeffery Fagan, Akiva Liberman, Nnamdi Pole, Christian Otte, Rachel Yehuda, David Mohr, and Thomas Neylan. "Predictors of Posttraumatic Stress in Police and Other First Responders." *Annals of the New York Academy of Sciences* 1071 (2006): 1-18. doi: 10.1196/annals.1364.001.

Márquez, C., G. L. Poirier, M. I. Cordero, M. H. Larsen, A. Groner, J. Marquis, P. J. Magistretti, D. Trono, and C. Sandi. "Peripuberty stress leads to abnormal aggression, altered amygdala and orbitofrontal reactivity and increased prefrontal MAOA gene expression." *Translational Psychiatry* 3, e216 (2013). doi: 10.1038/tp.2012.144.

Marx, Brian. Principal investigator, U.S. Department of Veterans Affairs; professor of psychiatry, Boston University School of Medicine. E-mail interview. May 23, 2014.

Marx, Brian P., John P. Forsyth, Tiffany Fusé, and Jennifer M. Lexington. "Tonic Immobility as an Evolved Predator Defense: Implications for Sexual Assault Survivors." *Clinical Psychology Science and Practice* 15, no. 1 (2008): 74-90.

Masson, Jeffrey Moussaieff.
    1. *The Assault on Truth: Freud's Suppression of Seduction Theory*. Untreed Reads, 2012. Kindle edition.
    2. Skype interview, e-mail interviews, May 2014.

Matloff, Judith. "Unspoken." *Columbia Journalism Review*, May/June 2007.

Mayo Clinic staff. "Post-traumatic stress disorder (PTSD)." Accessed May 2014 at *mayoclinic.org*.

McClelland, Mac.
    1. *For Us Surrender Is Out of the Question: A Story From Burma's Never-Ending War*. Berkeley: Soft Skull Press, 2010.
    2. "New Orleans Notebook: Disaster Tourism." *motherjones.com*, May 18, 2010.
    3. " 'It's BP's Oil.' " *motherjones.com*, May 24, 2010.
    4. "La. Police Doing BP's Dirty Work." *motherjones.com*, June 22, 2010.
    5. "Depression, Abuse, Suicide: Fishermen's Wives Face Post-Spill Trauma." *motherjones.com*, June 25, 2010.
    6. "Uniformed Cops on BP's Payroll? Enter the ACLU." *motherjones.com*, June 29, 2010.
    7. "BP Cleanup Workers Gone Wild." *motherjones.com*, July 22, 2010.

8. "Woke up from rape nightmares when the electricity went out, and was too afraid to open my ground-floor windows." September 21, 2010, 5:47 A.M. Tweet.

9. "I'm coming home." E-mail (unpublished) to Alex, September 28, 2010.

10. "UN Peacekeeper to Photographer: Shoot Me and I'll Shoot You." *motherjones.com*, October 21, 2010.

11. "A Fistful of Dollars." *Mother Jones*, November/December 2010.

12. "Aftershocks." *Mother Jones*, January/February 2011.

13. "In Search of Progress in Haiti." *motherjones.com*, January 10, 2011.

14. "Rebuilding Haiti for the Rich." *motherjones.com*, January 11, 2011.

15. "Clinton, Ninjas, and Protests: Snapshots of Haiti." *motherjones. com*, January 12, 2011.

16. "Baby Doc Is Back." *motherjones.com*, January 16, 2011.

17. "Haiti's Orphans, Still Waiting for Homes." *motherjones.com*, January 18, 2011.

18. "Haiti's Rape Crisis: An Update." *motherjones.com*, January 21, 2011.

19. "Hanging With the Robber Barons of Haiti." *motherjones.com*, February 9, 2011.

20. "Tips for Dick-Kicking." *motherjones.com*, February 11, 2011.

21. "What Journalism Might Learn from the Lara Logan Story." *motherjones.com*, February 15, 2011.

22. "More Tips for Kicking Ass Before Yours Gets Grabbed . . . Or Worse." *motherjones.com*, February 25, 2011.

23. "Be a Man of Your Word and Dish Out This Money." *motherjones. com*, March 31, 2011.

24. "Seven Questions About the International Criminal Court Answered." *motherjones.com*, April 8, 2011.

25. "A Nuremberg for Libya?" *motherjones.com*, May 15, 2011.

26. "ICC Prosecutor Seeks Qaddafi Arrest Warrant." *motherjones.com*, May 16, 2011.

27. "I'm Gonna Need You to Fight Me on This: How Violent Sex Helped Ease My PTSD." *good.is*, June 27, 2011.

28. "Farewell, Ohio." *Mother Jones*, July 15, 2011.

29. "To Catch A Warlord." *Mother Jones*, September/October 2011.

30. "Fear and Loathing in Congo." *motherjones.com*, September 29, 2011.

31. "The Blue Angels' Psychological Warfare." *motherjones.com,* October 10, 2011.

32. "Goodbye, Columbus." *Mother Jones,* November/December 2011.

33. "The Love That Dares." *Mother Jones,* January/February 2012.

34. "Shelf Lives." *Mother Jones,* March/April 2012.

35. "Hearts and Minds." *Mother Jones,* January/February 2013.

Mechanic, Michael. "Breaking: Oil Makes Landfall, Cops Blocking Beaches, MoJo on the Scene [Video and Photos]." *motherjones.com*, May 20, 2010.

Mitchell, Ta Lynn. "Trauma-Informed Care Emerging as Proven Treatment for Children, Adults with Behavioral, Mental Health Problems." *Youth Law News* xxxi, no. 3 (2012). Accessed May 2014 at *youthlaw.org.*

Mithoefer, Michael C., Mark T. Wagner, Ann T. Mithoefer, Lisa Jerome, and Rick Doblin. "The safety and efficacy of ±3,4-methylenedioxymethamphetamine-assisted psychotherapy in subjects with chronic, treatment-resistant posttraumatic stress disorder: the first randomized controlled pilot study." *Journal of Psychopharmacology* 25, no. 4 (2011): 439-452.

Moore, David and Bill Manville. "Why does staying sober have to do with being celibate? Struggling with Alcoholics Anonymous and sex." *New York Daily News,* May 4, 2012.

Moore, Lorrie. *Birds of America.* London: Faber and Faber, 2010.

Moving Forward Gulf Coast, Inc. "State of Black Men & Boys in New Orleans, LA." 2011. Accessed May 2014 at *movingforwardgc.org.*

Moye, Dorothy. "Katrina + 5: An X-Code Exhibition." *southernspaces.org*, August 26, 2010.

National Association of Crime Victim Compensation Boards. "Crime Victim Compensation: An Overview." Accessed May 2014 at *nacvcb.org.*

National Center for PTSD.

1. "Symptoms of PTSD." Accessed May 2014 at *ptsd.va.gov.*

2. "Treatment of PTSD." Accessed February 2014 at *ptsd.va.gov.*

National Child Resource Center for Organizational Improvement. "Supporting Child Welfare Workers: An Interview with David Conrad, LCSW." *Child Welfare Matters,* Spring 2006.

National Coalition of Anti-Violence Programs. "Hate Violence Against Lesbian, Gay Bisexual, Transgender, Queer, and HIV-affected Communities in the United States in 2011." Accessed May 2014 at *avp.org.*

National Collaborating Centre for Mental Health (UK). *Post-Traumatic Stress*

Disorder: The Management of PTSD in Adults and Children in Primary and Secondary Care. Leicester (UK): Gaskell, 2005.

National Crime Victim Center. "Rape in America: A Report to the Nation." 1992. Accessed May 2014 at *victimsofcrime.org.*

National Institute of Justice. "Youth Victimization: Prevalence and Implications." Washington, DC: U.S. Department of Justice, 2003.

National Institute of Mental Health. "Post-Traumatic Stress Disorder (PTSD)." Accessed May 2014 at *nimh.nih.gov.*

National Park Service. "Historic American Buildings Survey, City Hall, San Francisco." 1989. Accessed May 2014 at *lcweb2.loc.gov.*

Newman, Elana, Roger Simpson, and David Handschuh. "Trauma Exposure and Post-Traumatic Stress Disorder Among Photojournalists." *Visual Communication Quarterly* 10, no. 1 (2003): 4-13.

New York City Fire Department.
> 1. "Testimony of Fire Commissioner Nicholas Scopetta Before the National Commission on Terrorist Attacks Upon the United States." May 18, 2004. Accessed May 2014 at *govinfo.library.unt.edu.*
> 2. Public affairs, phone interview. May 20, 2014.

NIH Medline Plus, the U.S. National Library of Medicine and the National Institutes of Health. *"PTSD: A Growing Epidemic."* 2009. Accessed May 2014 at *nlm.nih.gov.*

Nikro, Norman Saadi. "Situating Postcolonial Trauma Studies." The University of Pennsylvania Department of English Web site, December 7, 2012.

Nock, Matthew and Mitchell Prinstein. "Contextual Features and Behavioral Functions of Self-Mutilation Among Adolescents." *Journal of Abnormal Psychology* 114, no. 1 (2005): 140-146.

Norris, Fran H. "Epidemiology of trauma frequency and impact of different potentially traumatic events on different demographic groups." *Journal of Consulting Clinical Psychology* 60, no. 3 (1992): 409-418.

Norris, Fran H. and Laurie B. Slone. "Understanding Research on the Epidemiology of Trauma and PTSD." *PTSD Research Quarterly* 24, no. 2-3 (2013): 1-13.

Norris, Fran H., Matthew J. Friedman, Patricia J. Watson, Christopher M. Byrne, Eoilia Diaz, and Krzysztof Kaniasty. "60,000 disaster victims speak: Part I. An empirical review of the empirical literature, 1981-2001." *Psychiatry* 65, no. 3 (2002): 207-239.

O'Connor, Lynn E. "PTSD: The Latest, Hottest, Maybe Most Controversial Diagnosis." *psychologytoday.com*, May 8, 2012.

O'Connor, Maura. "Two Years Later, Haitian Earthquake Toll in Dispute." *Columbia Journalism Review*, January 12, 2012.

The Ochberg Society for Trauma Journalism. *Acts of Witness* 7, "Telling," Summer 2014.

Oehen, Peter, Rafael Traber, Verena Widmer, and Ulrich Schnyder. "A randomized controlled pilot study of MDMA (±3,4-Methylenedioxymethamphetamine)-assisted psychotherapy for treatment of resistant, chronic Post-Traumatic Stress Disorder (PTSD)." *Journal of Psychopharmacology* 27, no. 1 (2013): 40-52. doi: 10.1177/0269881112464827.

Office of the White House Press Secretary. "President Remembers 9/11 Heroes at Medal of Valor Award Ceremony." September 9, 2005.

Ogden, Pat, Kekuni Minton, and Claire Pain. *Trauma and the Body: A Sensorimotor Approach to Psychotherapy*. New York: W.W. Norton & Company Inc., 2006.

Oliphant v. *Suquamish Indian Tribe*, 435 U.S.191 (1978). Accessed May 2014 at *congressional.proquest.com*.

Oliver, Mary. "Wild Geese." *New and Selected Poems, Vol. 1*. Boston: Beacon Press, 1992.

Open Letter. "Female Journalists and Researchers Respond to Haiti PTSD Article." *Jezebel*, July 1, 2011.

Osofsky, Joy D. "The effect of exposure to violence on young children." *American Psychologist* 50, no. 9 (1995): 782-788.

Ozer, Emily J., Suzanne R. Best, Tami L. Lipsey, and Daniel S. Weiss. "Predictors of posttraumatic stress disorder and symptoms in adults: a meta-analysis." *Psychological Bulletin* 129, no. 1 (2003): 52-73.

Park, Crystal L., Kristen E. Riley, and Leslie B. Snyder. "Meaning making coping, making sense, and post-traumatic growth following the 9/11 terrorist attacks." *Journal of Positive Psychology* 7, no. 3 (2012): 198-207.

Park, Rebecca. Head, Oxford Brain-Body Research into Eating Disorders. E-mail interview. April 29, 2014.

Patzkowski, Jeanne C., Johnny G. Owens, Ryan V. Blanck, Kevin L. Kirk, and Joseph R. Hsu. "Management of Posttraumatic Osteoarthritis with an Integrated Orthotic and Rehabilitation Initiative." *Journal of the American Academy of Orthopaedic Surgeons* 20, no. 1 (2012): S48–S53.

Perlstein, Michael. "For tales of life and death, the writing's on the walls." *The Times-Picayune*. September 17, 2005.

Perry, Steven W. "American Indians and Crime: A BJS Statistical Profile, 1992-2002." Washington, DC: Bureau of Justice, 2004.

Peterson, Christopher and Martin E. P. Seligman. "Character Strengths Before and After September 11." *Psychological Science* 14, no. 4 (2003): 381-384.

Pevtzow, Lisa. "Echoes from the Holocaust in Chicago area." *Chicago Tribune*. June 10, 2013.

Pfifferling, John-Henry and Kay Gilley. "Overcoming Compassion Fatigue." *Family Practice Management* 7, no. 4 (2000): 39-44. Accessed May 2014 at *aafp.org*.

Phillips, Christopher J., Cynthia A. LeardMann, Gia R. Gumbs, and Besa Smith. "Risk Factors for Posttraumatic Stress Disorder Among Deployed US Male Marines." *BMC Psychiatry* 10 (2010). doi: 10.1186/1471-244X-10-52.

Plyer, Allison. "Facts for Features: Katrina Impact." The Data Center, August 14, 2013.

Pyevich Caroline M., Elana Newman, and Eric Daleiden. "The relationship among cognitive schemas, job-related traumatic exposure, and post traumatic stress disorder in journalists." *Journal of Traumatic Stress* 16, no. 4 (2005): 325-328.

Quigley, Fran. "Haiti Strikes Back." *foreignaffairs.com*, May 13, 2014.

Rabinak, Christine A., Mike Angstadt, Chandra S. Sripada, James L. Abelson, Israel Leberzon, Mohammed R. Milad, and K. Luan Phan. "Cannabinoid facilitation of fear extinction memory recall in humans." *Neuropharmacology* 64 (2013): 396-402.

Raskind, Murray A., Kris Peterson, Tammy Williams, David J. Hoff, Kimberly Hart, Hollie Holmes, Dallas Homas, Jeffrey Hill, Colin Daniels, Jess Calohan, Steven P. Millard, Kirsten Rohde, James O'Connell, Denise Pritzl, Kevin Feiszli, Eric C. Petrie, Christopher Gross, Cynthia L. Mayer, Michael C. Freed, Charles Engel, and Elaine R. Peskind. "A trial of prazosin for combat trauma PTSD with nightmares in active-duty soldiers returned from Iraq and Afghanistan." *American Journal of Psychiatry* 170, no. 9 (2013): 1003.

Reger, Mark A., Gregory A. Gahm, Robert D. Swanson, Susan J. Duma. "Association between number of deployments to Iraq and mental health screening outcomes in US Army soldiers." *Journal of Clinical Psychiatry* 70, no. 9 (2009): 1266-1272. doi: 10.4088/JCP.08m04361.

Reister, Frank. *Medical Statistics in World War II*. Washington, DC: Office of the Surgeon General, Department of the Army, 1975. Accessed May 2014 at *dtic.mil*.

Renaud, Jean-Paul, Joanna Lin, and Francisco Vara-Orta. "Spike in marriage licenses statewide." *Los Angeles Times*, February 3, 2009.

Renshaw, Keith D., Elizabeth S. Allen, Galena K. Rhoades, Rebecca K. Blais, Howard J. Markman, and Scott M. Stanley. "Distress in Spouses of Service Members with Combat-Related PTSD: Secondary Trauma Stress or General Psychological Distress?" *Journal of Family Psychology* 25, no. 4 (2011): 461-469.

Robbins, Seth. "Rigors of war leave troops battling with arthritis at a young age." *Stars and Stripes*, September 25, 2011.

Robichaux, Rene. Manager, Family Advocacy Program, U.S. Army Medical Command. Phone and e-mail interviews. October-November 2012.

Rosen, Gerald M. and Christopher Frueh. *Clinician's Guide to Posttraumatic Stress Disorder*. Hoboken: John Wiley & Sons, 2010.

Rosenheck, Robert. "Impact of posttraumatic stress disorder of World War II on the next generation." *Journal of Nervous and Mental Disease* 174, no. 6 (1986): 319-327.

Rosenheck, Robert and Alan Fontana. "Transgenerational Effects of Abusive Violence on the Children of Vietnam Combat Veterans." *Journal of Traumatic Stress* 11, no. 4 (1998): 731.

Rothbaum, Barbara. Director, Trauma and Anxiety Recovery Program, Emory University School of Medicine. E-mail interview. May 23, 2014.

Rudowitz, Robin, Diane Rowland, and Adele Shartzer. "Health Care in New Orleans Before and After Hurricane Katrina." *Health Affairs* 25, no. 5 (2006): w393-w406. doi: 10.1377/hlthaff.25.w393.

Saltzman, Kasey, Carl F. Weems, and Victor G. Carrion. "IQ and Posttraumatic Stress Symptoms in Children Exposed to Interpersonal Violence." *Child Psychiatry and Human Development* 36, no. 3 (2006): 261-272.

Sarkar, N. N. and Rina Sarkar. "Sexual assault on woman: Its impact on her life and living in society." *Sexual and Relationship Therapy* 20, no. 4 (2005): 407-419. doi: 10.1080/14681990500249502.

Sarnquist, Clea, Benjamin Omondi, Jake Sinclair, Carolinah Gitau, Lee Paiva, Munyae Mulinge, David Cornfield, and Yvonne Maldonado. "Rape Prevention Through Empowerment of Adolescent Girls." *Pediatrics* 133, no. 5 (2014): X24.

Schawbel, Dan. "Daniel Goleman: Why Professionals Need Focus." *forbes .com*, October 8, 2013.

Schechner, Sam. "CBS Reporter Targeted in Sexual Assault." *wsj.com*, February 15, 2011.

Scheeringa, Michael. "PTSD for Children 6 Years or Younger." National Center for PTSD, January 3, 2014. Accessed May 2014, from *ptsd.va.gov*.

Schlosser, Eric. "A Grief Like No Other." *The Atlantic*, September 1997.

Schmidt, Richard A. Professor emeritus, Cognitive Psychology, University of California-Los Angeles; coauthor of *Motor Learning and Performance: From Principles to Application*. Phone interview. May 22, 2014.

Schore, Allan. Clinical faculty, University of California-Los Angeles Geffen School of Medicine and the university's Center for Culture Brain and Development. Phone interview. April 22, 2014.

Schwartz, Timothy T., Yves-François Pierre, and Eric Calpas. "Building Assessments and Rubble Removal in Quake Affected Neighborhoods in Haiti." Washington, DC: USAID Haiti, BARR Survey Final Report, May 13, 2011.

Sedlak, Andrea J., Jane Mettenburg, Monica Basena, Ian Petta, Karla McPherson, Angela Greene, and Spencer Li. *Fourth National Incidence Study of Child Abuse and Neglect (NIS–4): Report to Congress*. Washington, DC: U.S. Department of Health and Human Services, Administration for Children and Families, 2010. Accessed June 2014 at *acf.hhs.gov*.

Shachtman, Noah. "Army's New PTSD treatments: Yoga, Reiki, 'Bioenergy.'" *wired.com*, March 23, 2008.

Sharp, David. "Shocked, shot, and pardoned." *The Lancet* 368, no. 9540 (2006): 975-976.

Shema, R., T. C. Sacktor, and Y. Dudai. "Rapid erasure of long-term memory associations in the cortex by an inhibitor of PKMzeta." *Science* 317, no. 5840 (2007): 951-953.

Silver, Roxane Cohen, E. Alison Holman, Judith Pizarro Anderson, Michael Poulin, Daniel N. McIntosh, and Virginia Gil-Rivas. "Mental- and Physical-Health Effects of Acute Exposure to Media Images of the September 11, 2001, Attacks and the Iraq War." *Psychological Science* 24, no. 9 (2013): 1623-1634. doi: 10.1177/0956797612460406.

Smith, River and Elana Newman. "Covering Trauma: Impact on Journalists." Dart Center for Journalism and Trauma, January 1, 2009. Accessed May 2014 at *dartcenter.org*.

Smith, Tyler C., Margaret A. K. Ryan, Deborah L. Wingard, Donald J. Slymen, James F. Sallis, and Donna Kritz-Silverstein. "New onset and persistent symptoms of post-traumatic stress disorder self reported after deployment and combat exposures: prospective population based US military cohort study." *British Medical Journal* 336, no. 7640 (2008): 366-371.

Solomon, Roger. Board member, EMDR Institute. E-mail interview. May 14, 2014.

Sornborger, Jo. Director, Operation MEND-Focus Family Resilience Program, University of California-Los Angeles. Phone interview. May 23, 2014.

Sousa, Amy. Cultural anthropologist.
    1. "Pragmatic ethics, sensible care: Psychiatry and schizophrenia in north India." Ph.D. dissertation, University of Chicago, 2011.
    2. Phone interview. May 23, 2014.

Spiegel, Alix. "Hurricane Katrina Victims' Mental Health Worsens." *npr.org*, November 1, 2007.

"Spokane VA Medical Center." Google Maps. *maps.google.com*. Accessed May 2014.

Strozzi-Heckler, Richard.
    1. *The Anatomy of Change: A Way to Move Through Life's Transitions.* Berkeley: North Atlantic Books, 1993.
    2. E-mail interview. May 20, 2014.

Szalavitz, Maia. "How Terror Hijacks the Brain." *time.com*, April 16, 2013.

Tanielian, Terri, Lisa H. Jaycox, David M. Adamson, M. Audrey Burnam, Rachel M. Burns, Leah B. Caldarone, Robert A. Cox, Elizabeth D'Amico, Claudia Diaz, Christine Eibner, Gail Fisher, Todd C. Helmus, Benjamin R. Karney, Beau Kilmer, Grant N. Marshall, Laurie T. Martin, Lisa S. Meredith, Karen N. Metscher, Karen Chan Osilla, Rosalie Liccardo Pacula, Rajeev Ramchand, Jeanne S. Ringel, Terry L. Schell, Jerry M. Sollinger, Mary E. Vaiana, Kayla M. Williams, and Michael R. Yochelson. *Invisible Wounds of War: Psychological and Cognitive Injuries, Their Consequences, and Services to Assist Recovery.* Santa Monica, CA: RAND Corporation, 2008.

The Petionville Club. "Home." *thepetionvilleclub.com*, May 2014.

Trauma Center at Justice Resource Institute. "Trauma Center Brochure 2011." Accessed May 2014 at *traumacenter.org*.

Ullman, Sarah and Raymond Knight. "Fighting Back: Women's Resistance to Rape." *Journal of Interpersonal Violence* 7, no. 1 (1992): 31-33. doi: 10.1177/088626092007001003.

United Nations.

    1. "Secretary-General Ban regrets death of UN peacekeeper in eastern DR Congo clashes." United Nations News Center, July 6, 2012.

    2. "Resolution 1927 (2010)." United Nations Security Council, June 4, 2010.

United Nations Environment Programme. "Haiti Earthquake." Accessed December 2013 at *unep.org*.

U.S. Agency for International Development (USAID). "Haiti Shelter and Housing." February 10, 2014. Accessed May 2014 at *usaid.gov*.

U.S. Census Bureau.

    1. "Ferry County, Washington." State and County Quickfacts. Accessed May 2014 at *quickfacts.census.gov*.

    2. 2012 American Community Survey 1-Year Estimates. "Percent of the Civilian Population 18 and Over Who are Veterans." Using American FactFinder, accessed May 2014 at *factfinder2.census.gov*.

U.S. Department of Defense Task Force on the Prevention of Suicide by Members of the Armed Forces. "The Challenge and the Promise: Strengthening the Force, Preventing Suicide and Saving Lives." Washington, DC: Department of Defense, 2010. Accessed May 2014 at *health.mil*.

U.S. Department of Health and Human Services, Administration for Children and Families, Administration on Children, Youth, and Families, Children's Bureau. *Child Maltreatment 2012*. Washington, DC: U.S. Department of Health and Human Services, 2013. Accessed May 2014 at *acf.hhs.gov*.

U.S. Department of Homeland Security. *A Performance Review of FEMA's Disaster Management Activities in Response to Hurricane Katrina*. Washington, DC: Department of Homeland Security, 2006. Accessed May 2014 at *oig.dhs.gov*.

U.S. Department of State. "State Dept. Fact Sheet on Shelter and Housing in Haiti." Office of the Haiti Special Coordinator. October 22, 2012. Accessed May 2014 at *iipdigital.usembassy.gov*.

U.S. Department of Veterans Affairs (VA).

    1. "A Study of Dog Adoption in Veterans With Posttraumatic Stress Disorder." *clinicaltrials.gov*. Bethesda (MD): National Library of Medicine (US), April 2014. NLM Identifier: NCT01729026.

    2. "Can Service Dogs Improve Activity and Quality of Life in Veterans with PTSD?" *clinicaltrials.gov*. Bethesda (MD): National Li-

brary of Medicine (US), January 2014. NLM Identifier: NCT02039843.

3. "Effects of Mindfulness-Based Cognitive-Behavioral Conjoint Therapy (MB-CBCT) on Post-Traumatic Stress Disorder (PTSD) and Relationship Function." *clinicaltrials.gov*. Bethesda (MD): National Library of Medicine (US), January 2014. NLM Identifier: NCT01035788.

4. "Meditation Interventions for Treatment of PTSD in Veterans (VMP)." *clinicaltrials.gov*. Bethesda (MD): National Library of Medicine (US), January 2014. NLM Identifier: NCT01548742.

5. "Service Dogs for Veterans With PTSD." *clinicaltrials.gov*. Bethesda (MD): National Library of Medicine (US), January 2014. NLM Identifier: NCT01329341.

6. "FY 2013 Funding and FY 2014 Advance Appropriations Request." Vol. II: Medical Programs & Information Technology Programs.

7. "Population Tables—Counties." National Center for Veterans Analysis and Statistics. Accessed May 20, 2014, at *va.gov*.

8. "VA to take applications for new family caregiver program." Press release, May 3, 2011. Accessed May 2014 at *va.gov*.

9. "Prazosin Treatment for Combat Trauma PTSD (Post-traumatic Stress Disorder) Nightmares and Sleep Disturbance." *clinicaltrials.gov*. Bethesda (MD): National Library of Medicine (US), May 2007. NLM Identifier: NCT00108420.

10. *VA/DoD Clinical Practice Guideline for the Management of Posttraumatic Stress*. Washington, DC: Department of Veterans Affairs/Department of Defense, May 2002. Accessed May 2014 at *healthquality.va.gov*.

U.S. Geological Survey. "Magnitude 7.0 HAITI REGION January 12, 2010." Significant Earthquake Archive, 2010. Accessed May 2014 at *earthquake.usgs.gov*.

U.S. Government Accountability Office (GAO). "VA Spends Millions on Post-Traumatic Stress Disorder Research and Incorporates Research Outcomes into Guidelines and Policy." Washington, DC, 2011. Accessed May 2014 at *gao.gov*.

U.S. Interagency Council on Homelessness. "Opening Doors: Federal Strategic Plan to Prevent and End Homelessness." Washington, DC: U.S. Interagency Council on Homelessness, 2010. Accessed May 2014 at *usich.gov*.

Valbrun, Marjorie. "Mac McClelland: What's Happening in Haiti Is Not About You." *Slate*, June 30, 2011.

Van der Kolk, Bessel.

1. "Clinical Implications of Neuroscience Research in PTSD." *Annals of the New York Academy of Sciences* 1071 (2006): 277-293. doi: 10.1196/annals.1364.022.
2. Phone interview. February 20, 2014.
3. Interview by Ruth Buczynski. "What Neuroscience Teaches Us About the Treatment of Trauma." The National Institute for the Clinical Application of Behavioral Medicine. Webinar, June 2012.
4. "Mt. Sinai Adolescent Health Center Resilience in the Face of Trauma." April 3, 2003. Presentation transcript PDF. Accessed May 2014 at *mountsinai.org*.

Van der Kolk, Bessel A., Laura Stone, Jennifer West, Alison Rhodes, David Emerson, Michael Suvak, and Joseph Spinazzola. "Yoga as an Adjunctive Treatment for Posttraumatic Stress Disorder: A Randomized Controlled Trial." *Journal of Clinical Psychiatry* 75 (2014).

Van IJzendoorn, Marius H., Marian J Bakermans-Kranenburg, and Abraham Sagi-Schwartz. "Are Children of Holocaust Survivors Less Well-Adapted? A Meta-Analytic Investigation of Secondary Traumatization." *Journal of Traumatic Stress* 15, no. 5 (2003): 459–469.

Vines, Brannan. "Dancing in the Laundry Room . . . Finding Romance Even in Life After Combat." *familyofavet.com*, March 12, 2012.

Wagner, Amanda. Program director, IMPACT Bay Area. E-mail interview, May 9, 2014.

Weathers, Frank W., Dudley P. Blake, Paula P. Schnurr, Brian P. Marx, and Terence M. Keane. "Clinician-Administered PTSD Scale for DSM-5 CAPS-5." National Center for PTSD, May 2, 2014. Accessed May 2014 at *ptsd.va.gov*.

West End Animal Hospital. "New Orleans—10/07/05." New Orleans Katrina blog, October 7, 2005. Accessed May 2014 at *westendanimal.net*.

Wilensky, Ann E., Glenn E. Schafe, Morten P. Kristensen, and Joseph E. LeDoux. "Rethinking the Fear Circuit: The Central Nucleus of the Amygdala Is Required for the Acquisition, Consolidation, and Expression of Pavlovian Fear Conditioning." *The Journal of Neuroscience* 26, no. 48 (2006): 12387–12396. doi: 10.1523/JNEUROSCI.4316-06.2006.

Williams, Mary Elizabeth. "What Not to Say About Lara Logan." *Salon,* February 15, 2011.

Williams, Shehan S., Chamara A. Wijesinghe, Shaluka F. Jayamanne, Nicholas A. Buckley, Andrew H. Dawson, David G. Lalloo, and H. Janaka de Silva. "Delayed Psychological Morbidity Associated with Snakebite Envenoming." *PLoS Neglected Tropical Diseases* 5, no. 8 (2011): e1255. doi: 10.1371/journal.pntd.0001255.

Williams, Sherri. "Soldiers Before Citizens." *News21*, Syracuse University, August 1, 2010.

Williams, Timothy. "Suicides Outpacing War Deaths for Troops." *The New York Times.* June 8, 2012.

Wolff, Nancy and Jing Shi. "Childhood and Adult Trauma Experiences of Incarcerated Persons and Their Relationship to Adult Behavioral Health Problems and Treatment." *International Journal of Environmental Research and Public Health* 9, no. 5 (2012): 1908–1926. doi: 10.3390/ijerph9051908.

Wooley, Charles F. *The Irritable Heart of Soldiers and the origins of Anglo-American Cardiology: the US Civil War (1861) to World War I (1918).* Aldershot/Burlington: Ashgate, 2002.

Wright, Anthony. "Chapter 6: Limbic System: Amygdala." *Neuroscience Online.* Accessed May 2014.

Wylie, Mary Sykes.
1. "The Limits of Talk: Bessel van der Kolk wants to transform the treatment of trauma." *Psychotherapy Networker*, October 19, 2010.
2. "The Puzzle of Trauma: Redefining PTSD in the *DSM.*" *Psychotherapy Networker*, Clinical Report.

ACKNOWLEDGMENTS

Some of the most significant recognition for this book belongs to people who couldn't be named in it. I hope I've made it clear to those sources and survivors in private correspondence who they are. My deepest gratitude to them, and to those who can be listed: Brannan and Caleb Vines, Kateri and James Peterson, Danna Hughes, Steve and Charlene Payton Holt, Montana Mike, Shannon Gramley, Erin and Anthony Rodriguez, Jack Bauer, Jessica Wanderlust, the loved ones of Sergeant Chris Palmer, and the amazing men and women at Burma Action. They have trusted me with and helped me tell their stories, as have others over the years, including Annette Keys, Houston Herczog, Marilyn Herczog, and other members of my family, who have endless patience and endurance for fact-checking, regardless of tough times or tough questions. Thanks especially to Aunt Luci, Aunt Paula, and my mother-in-law. And to my parents, of course, who've always done their utmost to make me feel loved and supported. This book was my father's idea, suggested to me as a purpose in a time I direly needed one, and was made possible by a love and legacy of lyricism given to me by my mother. Also of invaluable support have been Andy Wright, Tana Ganeva, Lauren Rice, Elizabeth Gettelman, Leigh Ferrara (the best yoga instructor living), Julia Scott, Katie J. M. Baker, Stella and Leon Alesi, John Hazlett, Vanessa Mobley, whose encouragement meant more than she could know, and various staff and board members of *Mother Jones*, including David Corn and Adam Hochschild. Clara Jeffrey and Monika Bauerlein always put their full faith and financial backing behind whatever inkling of a story idea I had, and I was privileged to have Clara's amazing editing, too, behind me.

On this book, I'm fortunate to have worked with Colin Dickerman, who enthusiastically believed in it the moment he saw it, and Gail Ross, who thankfully never broke up with me. Both of them are brilliant and kind. Bob Ickes is my personal copyediting hero, and he gave the manuscript incredible care.

Most of this book was written at the San Francisco Writer's Grotto, and thanks to all the supportive geniuses who work there, particularly Caroline Paul, for that unparalleled environment. Residencies at the Mesa Refuge were invaluable in writing both of my books. I'm also much obliged for the hospitality of Ken Fulk and his Durham Ranch, Don Hazen, and Jon Pult of the inimitable Sugar Shack.

A final and repeated thanks to the experts and sources, listed in the bibliography, whom Sydney Brownstone and I harangued over months and in some cases years while trying to get the details right.

And another to my magnificent husband, who is my joy and my universe.

I am lucky in countless ways, but one of them is to have been able to go through the process I did—and to share it. So thank you.